Entertaining Tucson
Across The Decades

Volume I: 1950s through 1985

❧

An *Entertainment Magazine/Newsreal*
Time Capsule Compilation

Compiled by Robert E. Zucker

BZB Publishing, Inc. Tucson, Arizona

Entertaining Tucson Across The Decades
Volume I: 1950s through 1985
An Entertainment Magazine/Newsreal Time Capsule Compilation
Compiled by Robert Edward Zucker
With selections from the *Newsreal*

ISBN-13: 978-1939050069
ISBN-10: 1939050065

First Edition: 2014, April 12th; May 1.

Published by
BZB Publishing, Inc.
P.O. Box 91317
Tucson, Arizona 85752-1317

Email: publisher@emol.org

Web: http://emol.org/entertaintucson/

Printed in the United States of America by CreateSpace, an Amazon.com company.
Available for sale through Amazon.com and other outlets in print and digital formats.
See back page for more available titles.

Entertaining Tucson
Across The Decades

Volume I:
The Years Between
1950s through 1985

Entertaining Tucson Across the Decades

If you enjoyed Tucson's local entertainment anytime between the 1950s through the early 2000s, then you probably will be familiar with many of these people and places. Step back into time and live, or relive, Tucson's local culture, music and entertainment scene – evolving and revolving– over five decades.

Volume One: Entertaining Tucson from 1950s through 1985

The local entertainment scene in Tucson, Arizona during the 1950s through 1985 was vibrant– from the '50s rock and roll of the **Dearly Beloved** to the '80s with the **Pills**, **Giant Sandworms** and everything in between– classic rock, disco, jazz, alternative, punk, hard core, reggae, country, western, swing and Big Band– thousands of entertainers over three decades.

Within these pages are the memories and the experiences of those people and places. These are the original articles and interviews published in several local newspapers which covered the Tucson entertainment scene. Follow their stories through the years. Read about the big breaks, record releases, hot performances and duds, break ups, tragedies, personal insights and struggles.

This book is in recognition to all of the Tucsonans who kept us entertained over those decades and to those reporters, staff and photographers who contributed their time to keep Tucson informed.

Volume II carries on the entertainment from 1986 through the early 2000s.

Presented by

The Entertainment Magazine

Entertainment Magazine

Newsreal

& Newsreal

(Top Left to Right) **Nadine & the MoPhonics** (from 1986); **Statesboro Blues Band** (1984); **Dean Armstrong** (from 1991); **Los Lasers** (1985); **Jonny Sevin** (1981) Photo credits on inside pages.

"Entertaining Tucson Across the Decades" web site:
EMOL.org/entertaintucson/

Entertaining Tucson Across the Decades
Contents

Volume 1: 1950s through 1985

1980: Technology becomes personal 93

1981: Evolving Music Trends 103

1982: Revolving musicians 109

1983: Alternative Music Scene Emerges 123

Tucson, Arizona performers, band names and venues are in bold face type, first occurrence, to emphasize the local focus. Advertisements are for historical purposes only and not paid placements.

The Compilation

B etween 1974 and 1994 several local tabloid newspapers reported on the Tucson, Arizona entertainment scene. Although these papers are no longer published, their archives have been preserved and collected into a compilation of articles and images that historically record Tucson's culture.

This content is compiled from selected images and articles previously published in:

- *Youth Alternatives*
- *Youth Awareness Press*
- *Tucson Teen*
- *The Magazine*
- *Entertainment Magazine*
- *EMOL.org*
- *Newsreal*

This first volume spans between the 1950s until the end of 1985. The second volume features 1986 through the early 2000s.

Since these articles and advertisements were published at least 30 years ago, the schedules, addresses and events are no longer current.

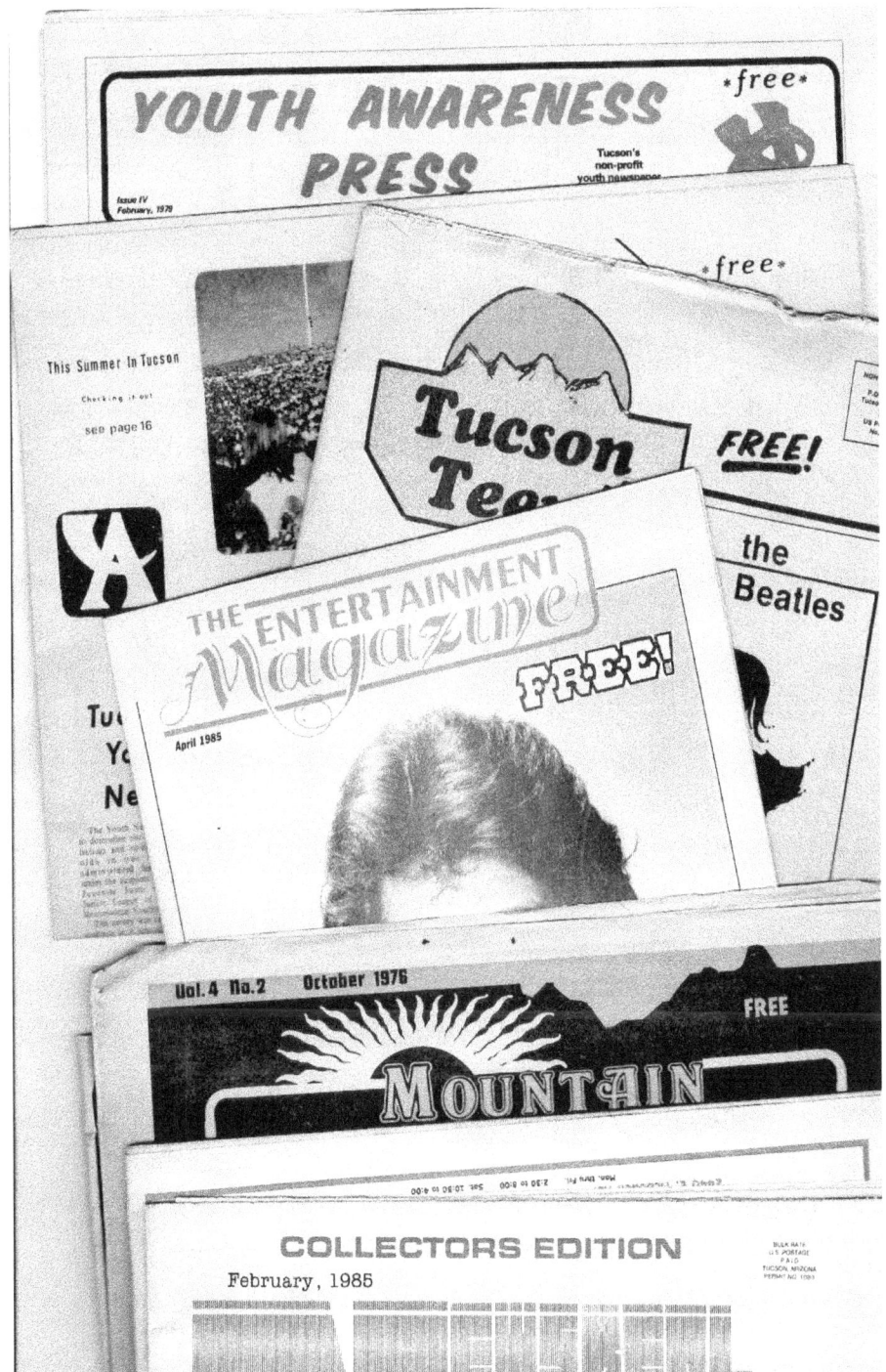

Covers of the *Youth Awareness Press, Tucson Teen, Youth Alternatives, Entertainment Magazine* and *Newsreal* newspapers.

Mountain Newsreal & Newsreal

The *Mountain Newsreal* started in 1974 as a monthly alternative culture tabloid by **Jonathan L** and evolved into the popular music magazine, *Newsreal.*

Jonathan L is an American radio presenter, programmer, and international entertainment media publisher.

His radio career began in Tucson, Arizona in 1982 at **KLPX**-FM with a show "**Virgin Vinyl**" which predates Alternative radio. He left Tucson in 1986 to start up alternative radio station KEYX-FM.

Jonathan L organized his first large music festival for alternative station KUKQ in Phoenix, Arizona in 1989, years before the launch of festivals like Lollapalooza and the KROQ Weenie Roasts. For this reason, he is often called the "Father of all radio festivals."

In 2005, he returned form Los Angeles to create "Lopsided World of L" which ran on Saturday mornings and Sunday evenings on KUPD-FM until he moved to Germany in 2010. The "Lopsided World of L" is now produced and presented internationally every week by Jonathan L from his flat in Berlin, Germany.

Lopsided World of Jonathan L Web Site: http://www.jlradio.com/

Photos: First edition of Mountain Newsreal, 1974 and last edition of Newsreal, October 1985.

Youth Alternatives, Youth Awareness, Tucson Teen, Entertainment Magazine

The first newspaper published for youth in Tucson was the **Youth Alternatives** (summer and fall 1979). An experimental project funded by grants later became titled **Youth Awareness Press** (December 1979 through December 1980). The newspapers provided Tucson youth an opportunity to gain journalism skills and learn how to publish a newspaper.

The **Tucson Teen** newspaper continued the concept of a youth newspaper beginning in June 1981 through September 1990. **The Magazine** published from September 1982 when it became titled **Entertainment Magazine** in April 1985.

In January 1995, the *Entertainment Magazine* became one of the first Arizona newspapers to go online as **EMOL.org (Entertainment Magazine On Line)**. More than a quarter-million visitors a month, from around the world, browse the EMOL web site.

The monthly tabloids were published through the **Tucson YWCA** until 1981 when **Southwest Alternatives Institute, Inc.,** a non-profit organization, became the publication sponsor. **BZB Publishing Inc.** acquired rights in 2006.

Robert Zucker, the author, was the founder and publisher of all of the publications. Zucker spent over a decade teaching at the **University of Arizona** (1992-2005), taught at **Pima Community College** (1998-2005) and was advisor of *Aztec Press* for several years.

Entertainment Magazine Web Site: http://emol.org

First editions of Youth Alternatives, Youth Awareness Press, Tucson Teen, Magazine, Entertainment Magazine.

1950s: Rockin' & Cruisin'

Tucson's musical memories of the '50s

By Michael Hamilton [1]

Hey *Daddy-O*! Let's hearken back once again to when today's baby boomers– those born between 1946 and 1964– were assembling their first mini-crystal sets and searching for their first station with "rock and roll" rhythms. It was a chance to dig the world of cars, cliques and class, with this new mod music in the background. This was the 1950s in Tucson, Arizona.

The newest fad– customizing cars in California– set the pace for a few local car clubs. Tucson's **"Banshees"** beamed proudly with vehicles sporting fender skirts, flipper hubcaps and continental kits. The twin aerials brought in radio signals from a society of high fidelity, both fraternal and familial. Yah, man, Ike smiled, Khrushchev rattled his rockets, but all else was well!

From '53 to '63, the nation cruised as smooth as a finely tuned engine. Life was lived for the daily fun of it like an adventure rather than a venture as it is today. Young lads had fun pegging the five local stations on their brother's car radio before he went on the "big date" that evening. She looked neat with his class ring hung on a chain around her neck, as they smooched (in front of people). He looked cagey in his flashy car club jacket as they roared down the lane with the open pipes purring.

Kids sure wanted to be 16 in a hurry to cruise about– even in an Edsel! Vroom! But, kids just rode their bikes and settled for a "transistor" sister radio hanging from the handlebars listening to **KTKT-990 AM** [2] – Tucson's top rock and roll radio station. This reporter reminisces each time he sees a '50s logo, be it cars, soda pop, or petrol! *Like wow man!*

Pop art Americana comes to Tucson in the '50s. The sweet, colorful echoes of heartfelt "Fabulous Fifties" music sprung to life in the form of the **Sonic Drive-in** restaurant, on West Grant Road east of the Interstate. Baby boomers, who once cruised the four **Johnnie's Drive-In's**, then **Ritchie's** on 22nd Street, with great pride, will reminisce with much fervor once again here, as the spontaneity of youthful life whiles on and idles by ...

This classy red arid white striped burger eatery by day becomes a "Sea of Neon," Jewel of Illumination," "In the

Jeri Denslow

Dick Anklam

Henrietta Martz

and Ann Hall

at

GRABE'S

RECORD CENTER

26 E. Congress St.

Grabe's Record Center, from 1951 *Tucsonian*, Tucson Senior High School yearbook.

---

[1] **Michael Hamilton** is a long time Tucson musician who performed with the Vibrations, a popular local rock and roll band of the 1960s.

[2] **KTKT**, Tucson's fifth radio station, went on the air in 1946. Popular disc jockey, Frank Kalil, was hired in the mid-50s to play the new "rock and roll" music format. Tucson's first FM station was KTKT-FM (99.5). Source: "Remembering Tucson Radio...From the Beginning! By Russ Jackson.

Still of the Night" and under "A Thousand Stars in the Sky." Golden oldies ooze through the atmosphere from radios of a line of parked cars nosed into nostalgia. One needs merely to push the menu button and order from the past... Elvis, Fabian, Dionne, Bobby Rydell. Sadly, there are no skating carhops.

Lighthearted frolic has given way to liability, Still "Only You" can watch the sprightly lasses disperse the fast food, as they display their darling derring-do, while the drive-thru lane "rumbles" on with "busyness." Even today's teens and preteens will 'dig' the "bob-shoobob" tunes of yesteryear, in this super Sonic place of fun. Look for the classic car out front.

As the "Nifty Fifties" came to a close, lazy contemplative weekends in our amiable, affable town were celebrated by folks in myriad ways. Some viewers watched "**Dean Armstrong**'s Country Music Store" on **KOPO-TV**, Channel 13.

Dean occasionally featured the perennial national craze for square dancing. Dancers also promenaded at **Old Tucson** each Sunday, or at nearby ranches. There were a dozen colorful clubs and even more callers. **KTKT**, the Old Pueblo's mainstay station, highlighted its "Swinging Seven" rock and roll DJs. One recalls **Jerry Stowgram** and **Dave Nelson** 'swinging through,' among others.

Yes, we even had fun high-jinx crafted by mobile transmitter announcers at shopping centers then, too!

Radio 99 (KTKT) also sanctioned The **Miss Tucson Trailer Court** contest in the late '50s.

Then, they really revved things up by sponsoring the **Speed Sport** dragster at the **Tucson Strip**. This was located on what is now Golf Links Rd. on the Davis-Monthan Air Force Base. City folk also reveled in **PhD Richardson's** radio-editorials. Noted, too, were daily ditties, such as "Sleep well tonight, your Air National Guard is awake."

Ah, Tucson in the '50s...

Photo of a brand new 1953 Chevy, by Bertram Zucker, 1953.

This story was compiled from articles published in the March 1989 edition of Entertainment Magazine, page 5;
June 1989 Entertainment Magazine, page 23; and April 1989 Entertainment Magazine. Page 13.

Sons of the Pioneers: Rooted in Tucson's history

By Nick Nicholas [3]
December 1990 – Entertainment Magazine. Page 5

Sons of the Pioneers, the legendary group, founded by **Roy Rogers** along with former Tucsonan, **Bob Nolan** and **Tim Spencer** as the **Pioneer Trio** in 1933, is well into its fifty-seventh year (as of 1990) entertaining millions with a great musical tradition.

The Sons of Pioneers has included such past notable members as **Hugh** and **Karl Farr, Pat Brady, Lloyd Perryman, Ken Curtis, Shug Fisher, Tommy Doss, Roy Lanham** and present trail boss **Dale Warren**.

This world famous group, whose popularity is greater today than ever has been making Tucson its winter headquarters since their 50th anniversary year in 1983 appearing at the **Triple C Chuckwagon**, serving up western-style entertainment five nights a week, Tuesdays through Saturdays.

Trail boss, **Dale Warren**, in his 39th year (as of 1990) with the Sons of the Pioneers possesses a superb singing voice. He began his musical career in his home state of Kentucky. As a young boy, he would be standing on a box to play the bass fiddle and singing into the microphone with his parents famous group, **Uncle Henry's Original Kentucky Mountaineers**.

In 1953, he was recommended as a replacement for **Ken Curtis** (Festus of "Gunsmoke" TV series) who himself had replaced original Pioneer member Tim Spencer. Warren, well aware of both past and present feelings among Western music fans wherever the Pioneers perform, has managed to preserve the traditional classic western musical style of the group while adding new instruments with a touch of big band sound designed to please fans of all age groups.

---

[3] **Nick Nicholas**, a Tucson musician, had his own radio program, "Western Music Caravan," on KXCI-FM 91.7 Community Radio each Sunday afternoon from 2:00PM to 3:00PM. The show featured all time western music artists.

As part of their stage performance the Pioneers also include salutes to the silver screen cowboys and their sidekicks and especially, to the godfather of the group, Roy Rogers and former Pioneers who have been a part of the group across the years by means of a multi-media slide show. Known as "The Aristocrats of the Range," Sons of the Pioneers are on the Advisory Board of the **Western Music Association**. Members of both the Country and Western Music Hall of Fame and have been acclaimed as an American Institution by the Smithsonian Institution. Their class recording of "Cool Water" is in the Grammy Hall of Fame.

The Sons of the Pioneers have preserved the western musical heritage from their summer home in Branson, Missouri and their winter home in Tucson through their relentless efforts while creating innovations in western swing music that brings thousands to their feet.

The Sons of the Pioneers photos, *Entertainment Magazine* archives.

Rex Allen: The legend of "Mr. Cowboy"

Rex Allen [4] is one of only a handful of silver screen cowboys who actually came from a cattle ranching background. Rex hailed from Willcox, Arizona– about 80 miles east of Tucson. He learned to ride almost as soon as he could walk, and helped with the livestock and ranch chores before and after school.

From early childhood, music filled the Allen house. His dad played fiddle and Rex learned to play a Sears Roebuck mail-order guitar to accompany him at dances. Wherever and whenever possible, he would sing. At age 12, he had a fine bass voice that spanned three octaves.

For awhile, young Allen considered competing professionally in rodeos, but found riding a two thousand pound bull was quite a different story from the steers he'd conquered locally. Music was undoubtedly more rewarding and definitely a lot safer. But he never lost his love for the rodeo and its bronco and bull riders, many of whom became good friends.

Rex left Willcox in the early '40s and worked various jobs in the east while waiting for his big break. The break came in 1945, when WLS in Chicago gave him a job on the National Barn Dance. During that time, Mercury Records signed him and released his first hit "Take It Back and Change It For A Boy."

In 1949, Republic Pictures in Hollywood gave him a screen test. Allen negotiated his own contract, something unheard of at the time, and after almost six months of watching from behind the scenes, made his first Republic picture, "The Arizona Cowboy." And Rex Allen became forevermore known as "The Arizona Cowboy."

A second film, "The Hills of Oklahoma," saw the introduction of "Koko the Wonder Horse," the stallion who would carry him in 18 westerns and accompany him on almost a million miles of personal appearance tours across the country.

At the height of his movie popularity, Dell Comic Books published 30 Rex Allen comics and his picture appeared on cigarette cards, Dixie Cup lids and dozens of other promotional items. But for many people, he is most familiar as the narrator of over one hundred Walt Disney TV shows and movies. Literally thousands of TV and radio commercials throughout the country featured that distinctive, deep voice pitching everything from fertilizer to trucks, and racetracks to cowboy boots.

In 1989, the Rex Allen Arizona Cowboy Museum opened in Willcox, as a tribute to the man who never forgot his roots. The town also hosts the annual **Rex Allen Days** in October that features a golf tournament, PRCA rodeo, musical concerts and events for the whole family. It began back in 1951, and he's never missed appearing there. There is a Rex Allen star on the Hollywood Walk of Fame. Other cherished honors include being elected the Rodeo Man of the Year, the first recipient of the Golden Boot Award and being inducted into the Cowboy Hall of Fame.

Photo of Koko the Wonder Horse, courtesy of Rex Allen. *Entertainment Magazine* archives.

[4] **Rex Allen** passed away on December 17, 1999. He was born on December 31, 1920. Allen was 70 years old at the time of this interview.

Talking with Rex Allen

By Nick Nicholas and Michelle M. Sundin
September 1991 – Entertainment Magazine. Page 15

Just before the dedication of a bronze statue of famed Western singer and actor Rex Allen on July 20, 1991, this reporter visited with Rex at this ranch near Sonoita to spend an enjoyable afternoon talking with him about his life and show business career. The following are highlights of that conversation.

Rex, you were born and raised here in Arizona and you had a real cattle and horse background. Tell us a little about those early days.
I was born in my grandmother's house in Willcox and shipped back to the homestead a week later and didn't get back to town until I was five or six years old when my older brother, Wayne, was bit by a rattlesnake. We lost him because there was no medical care within 40 miles so there wasn't much that could be done.

You also had a couple of famous cousins in show business, didn't you?
Yeah, Glenn Strange who made a ton of westerns and was more familiar as the bartender in Kitty's "Long Branch Saloon" in "Gunsmoke." Did you know that he was also the first Frankenstein in the movies? It was a non-speaking role in which he just lumbered through the picture. This was way before Boris Karloff.

I believe you first met Roy Rogers through your other cousin, Cactus Mac Peters, who had the first band Roy performed with.
The O Bar O Cowboys– they came through Willcox during their first barnstorming trip where Mac called it quits. But Roy and Tim Spencer and the rest of the guys went on to New Mexico and Texas. It was during this trip that Roy met his first wife in Roswell.

When did you first begin singing and performing?
I can't really remember. But, I used to go down to the barbershop in Willcox down on Main Street and I thought that was the biggest audience in the world. I had a hat turned upside down in which the men would throw nickels. Some days I'd make thirty cents, usually, on Saturdays.

You've received numerous compliments through the years for both your excellent guitar playing and more so, as an outstanding yodeler.
My kids liked it. Can't yodel much anymore, unless I rear way back and just let go. Take a deep breath and I can do it.

You were a rodeo performer, especially locally. Did you make any money at it?
No, but I rodeo'd just long enough to realize that I was no Jim Shoulder or Casey Tibbs, even though I was pretty good as I rodeo'd in Willcox ridin' old milk cows and steers. When I entered the Tucson rodeo, I found out then that Rodeo was something else after I rode my first Brahma bull. I never knew why such a monster existed. After one trip on one of those, I decided to move to something safer like playing guitar.

When did you first leave home after deciding to try a singing career?
Well, I went to Phoenix first. I worked in construction during the summer and had a little radio show on KOY on Saturday afternoons for 15 minutes. From there I went to New Jersey, then Philadelphia where I did more radio. Then, on to Chicago and the National Barn Dance. There, the whole world seemed to open up for me. I was on about 12 radio shows during the week ... for $12 a week!

This was around 1945 and I was saving money! You see, at that time, WLS and the "Barn Dance" was a Mecca for all country music. This was long before the Grand Ole Opry in Nashville that at that time was just a small town local show.

In fact, many of today's big country stars were calling me and asking how they could get on WLS and the National Barn Dance. In fact, the "Opry" performers at that time were getting $14. But, we in Chicago had a stronger union and were getting $30 a performance. And, we had national sponsors like Alka Seltzer and Phillip's Petroleum and we got nationwide exposure.

Was it about this time when you cut your first record and what was it called?
Some people from Mercury Records called me to cut a record called "Won't You Take It Back And Change It For A Boy." Two weeks after it was released it was a smash hit. Number one on all the charts. It sort of opened up the world for me.

How long did your recording career last?
It started a 30-year span for me. You know, Nick, it's much different today, as you know. It happens instantaneously today and recording artists don't stay on top very long. The only way they can go is down. There are no artists today with the talent of a Frank Sinatra, for example. Frank's had a 50-year career and he's still going! Rock stars today are lucky if they last two years.

When did you record your first western or cowboy song?
All I really wanted to be was a Western singer, but I kind of interspersed them as I went along. I recorded songs I wrote that people never heard of and songs, other people wrote which were not too well known. So, I was singin' 'em right along with the others.

What's the best pop record you ever recorded?
Well, the best selling pop record I ever recorded– which has been real good to me– was "Crying in the Chapel." It was both number one pop and number one country at the same time. Somehow, both pop and country disc jockeys

started playing it and it stayed up there on the charts for 19 weeks and longer than that on the country charts. I sold over three million. Ten years after I cut it, Elvis Presley cut one, at which time RCA released mine once again. So we both did well with it.

Who's your favorite songwriter?
Without question– Bob Nolan– he's my favorite. After that, Billy Hill, Cole Porter, Irving Berlin, and you know, these last three were Tin Pan Alley writers who had never been west. They wrote some of the greatest western songs and they've lasted.

What about female songwriters?
Cindy Walker and Jenny Lou Carson. You know, Cindy Walker once showed me a song she's written and I told her that it was too "pop" for me. She said it wasn't and should be done country and told me that if I didn't do it, she'd take it to Eddy Arnold. Well, I didn't and Eddy recorded it. It was called, "I Really Don't Want To Know." Yeah, this "dum, dum" turned it down.

How did your movie career come about?
I think I sort of lucked into it. Roy Rogers was leaving the studio (Republic) to go into which was becoming a force to be reckoned with. The people at Republic still believed that the "B" Western wasn't through. They wanted me to go ahead with a few more and remembering that they discovered Gene Autry at the National Barn Dance in Chicago 25 years earlier. I felt it could happen again with me. They just came in and offered me a contract and I grabbed it. We did 19 Westerns in 11 years for Republic.

Let's talk about your museum (Rex Allen Museum) in Willcox. When did it open?
The museum opened about a year and a half ago (1989)... right across the park. That was the realization of a longtime project that we're proud of.

And the big day is July 20, 1991 when your big, beautiful bronze by Buck McCain will be unveiled and dedicated in your honor across from the museum. What about that?
Well, Buck flattered me pretty well. I gave him $5 an inch to cut down my waist and a dollar an inch to make me real handsome.

What is you favorite Rex Allen movie?
I watch some of the from time to time. There's one I made called "The Last Musketeer" which I think had the most believable story. Slim Pickens is in it. And I have to say that was my favorite. I also looked better in this one than I did in the others...

I see you in town occasionally where you drop in to record a modern commercial or two in a local studio. Are you doing much of this sort of thing these days?

I come to Tucson and record a few. I had been going to Orlando, Florida to film "Church Street Station" but don't

do that anymore. I do an occasional guest shot on the Nashville network. But, you know, I've been in this business 50 years and there comes a time to quit. You know, retire, and do what you want to do. I'm retired! Oh, I still get involved in lots of things here in Arizona, mostly charity things. It's a food way to live the rest of my life. And, it's fun. But, I'd rather just sit and take it easy and the world goes by.

Recently, a book on your remarkable life was published in both hard and soft cover and is presently available both in bookstores and at the Rex Allen Museum in Willcox. Its title is "The Arizona Cowboy, Rex Allen, My Life Sunrise to Sunset." Can we talk about it?
The funny part about doing the book was after they typed it all up and sent the galley back to me. I saw how bad my grammar was. So, I said, "For God's sake, fix my grammar because it was terrible." Well, they fixed it and corrected it. But some wanted to leave in some of the bad stuff and call it "casual conversation." There weren't many bad experiences to put in. The fun things are what you want to remember. The longer you live, the more you remember the good and pay less attention to the things that were not very pleasant. You forget those.

What would you still like to do?
Live to the year 2000, drink a toast to the new century and then check out...seriously. (Note: Rex lived until the year 1999).

At a combination birthday and New Year's bash held in Willcox on December 31, 1989, Rex, as usual, was a hit. He entered the banquet room and his presence lit up the room. Friends all got a smile, a handshake or a hug. The fans found out his patience and attention was genuine. Requests for autographs and photos were never turned down.

When he stepped up to the microphone, the applause was deafening. The audience's love glowed in their eyes. The magic was still there. The power of his million selling record, "Streets of Loredom," is still able to move the crowd.

Talking with Rex Allen was one of the greatest experiences and pleasures of this reporter's life. There was never a nasty word said about anyone. His friends circle the globe and cover all walks of life. His fan mail fills two tables, still, and he's embarrassed that he takes so long to get it all answered. He loves the good things about his life and remembers the fun most of all.

A mutual friend describes him best ... he's a born entertainer and performer. A gentleman, and a gentle man.

© 1990 portions by Michelle Sundin, also printed in "Wrangler's Roast," Bristol, England and "Cowboy" in the U.S. Rex Allen photos, biography and autograph, courtesy of Rex Allen, 1990. *Entertainment Magazine* archives.

1950s-1960s: Tucson radio's misty memories

By Michael Hamilton
September 1989 – Entertainment Magazine. Page 19

B rushing aside the glossy gossamers off one's memory, one recalls rising for high school to the radio alarm clock and the **Guy Williams** program of the city's flagship rocker station **KTKT**. Williams' shifty mercurial shenanigans were so symbolic of the late 1950s to early '60s era.

The "wild one" of the **Swingin' Seven** played a variety of tunes typical of the times. Listeners sometimes cringed as groups cut songs like "Did Your Chewing Gum Lose It's Flavor On the Bedpost Over Night" and "Itsy Bits' Teeny Weeny, Yellow Polka Dot Bikini" and the like! Thank your lucky airwaves that these melodies we interspersed among better ballads like "The Battle of New Orleans" or "Big John" by Jimmy Dean. "El Paso" with Marl Robbins' eerie alto wail was on the Top 40 for 14 months.

There were several crossover country songs back then. **KMOP** and **KHOS** were favorite footpattin' frequencies of those days. This reporter walked to school and played sax in a "before classes" combo that belted "big band" sounds like "In the Mood," etc. Understandably, it was not too popular with the student rockers of the day.

One thing, though, almost any student could make music during voluntary study halls. Ample students were allowed to leave the campus, head for burgervilles, thinking that was just neat, choice, and boss ... !

Lil' John's Café menu, 401 North 6th Avenue, Tucson, New Year's Eve, 1952.

From Lil' John's Café Menu:

Hamburger and Fries .... .50¢
Top Sirloin Steak......................... $3.00
Filet Mignon with Mushrooms $3.25
Lobster Out of Shell on Dinner...... $4.75

Pizza (Tomato Sauce, Cheese, Olive Oil)   Small .75   Large $1.00
Pizza a la Johnny Special (Italian Sausage, Salami, Cheese, Mushrooms, Bell Peppers, Onions, Tomato Sauce, Olive Oil)
          Small $2.25   Large $3.00

Special Dinner for $1.35:
Home Made Soup, Salad, Choice of Spaghetti and Meat Balls or Ravioli, Spaghetti and Meatballs, Vanilla Ice Cream, Coffee.

Shopping Tucson Downtown

Downtown was *the* "shopping center" in Tucson during the 1950s. Most businesses stretched along a few blocks between Congress, Alameda and Pennington Streets. Congress Street was also the hub for the major four indoor movie theaters, including a Spanish movie house.

The 1,300-seat **Fox Theatre,**[5] 17 W. Congress, opened on April 11, 1930 with the showing of "Chasing Rainbows." The Fox closed in 1974 because of economic conditions and competition from TV, outdoor drive-ins and new multiplex movie theaters. The Fox has been refurbished and reopened December 31, 2005.

The **Rialto Theatre,**[6] 318 E. Congress Street, opened in 1920 and was closed in 1984 after a gas explosion and has since reopened for performing arts and concerts.

Early 1953. On Congress Street. Looking south at The State Theatre on (right), next to the Letty Shop. On the marquee: "Two Fast Adventures: 'Decision Before Dawn,' (December 1951) also Dale Robertson in 'Return of the Texan.' " (December 1952)

The Curio Box, a jewelry, store is sandwiched between State Theatre and The Letty Shop. Payless Drug Store is to the far left.

The **State Theatre,**[7] 51 E. Congress, originally opened in 1897 as the Tucson Opera House. The 1,000-seat movie house closed on September 22, 1953.

The **Letty Shop** next door, 47 E. Congress, carried "ladies' ready-to-wear" apparel from New York and Los Angeles. The shop, owned by Mr. and Mrs. **Jules Abelow**, originally opened at 34 E. Congress on June 24, 1944 in a building formerly occupied by **Sayer's Linen Shop**. The store moved across the street some years later and closed about 1956. The Letty Shop was named for the Abelow's daughter, **Letty**, who later opened her own mid-town clothing stores, **simply Samples** and **Career Threads** in the 1980s.

The main downtown department store was **Steinfeld's** at the corner of Stone Avenue and Pennington Street. The two-story building with a mezzanine carried everything from glassware to neckwear, shoes to lamps and a "Tucsonian Shop." Nearby, at 26 E. Congress, was the popular **Grabe's Record Center** where 45 RPMs filled the record containers. Other department stores included, **Jacomes**, **J.C. Penny**, **Sears** and **Levy's**.

---

[5] Fox Theatre, http://www.foxtheatre.org/
[6] Rialto Theatre, http://www.rialtotheatre.com/
[7] The State Theatre, http://cinematreasures.com/

Tucson's culture in fried chicken

The **Polar Bar** [8] was a popular carhop hot spot of the early 1950s, located on the north side of Speedway Blvd. between Country Club and Alvernon. On weekend nights, the parking lot was filled with hungry cruisers and gazers.

The Polar Bar served the Zombie– the "World's Largest Sundae." For $1.00, a patron would get approximately one quart of ice cream, five kinds of fresh fruit, crushed nuts and "anything else that's handy." The Sissy Zombie was "twice as little for half as much." The Wildcat Deluxe Sundae, topped with strawberries, marshmallows and nuts, was only 30 cents. Take home a quart of hand packed ice cream for only 70 cents.

The Zombie Burger, for 40 cents, had all the trimmings. For five cents more, add grilled ham.

The inside of the menu is hand stamped: "All price are our O.P.S. ceiling prices or lower. A list showing our ceiling price for each item is available for your inspection."

Derald Fulton [9] and **Paul E. Shaar** owned the Tucson Polar Bar. **Don Morris** was the manager. Fulton moved to Phoenix in 1948 where he started the first Polar Bar. The second location came to Tucson a few years later.

Fulton opened the Tucson's first fast food restaurant, **Lucky Wishbone** at 4872 South Sixth Avenue, in July 1953. Hundreds of hungry Tucsonans waited to get a taste of its trademark fried chicken. Three Tucson employees, **Don Morris**, **Clyde Buzzard** and **John Kinder**, became managing partners. There are now seven locations in Tucson and the Wishbone still endures as a living Tucson tradition.

—POLAR BAR FEATURES—

GOLDEN BROWN CHICKEN
Served with crisp fries, garlic buttered roll and choice of soup or mixed salad bowl.

JUNIOR—TWO pieces chicken....	.80
MOM—THREE pieces chicken	1.05
POP—FIVE pieces chicken	1.35
Giblets — Generous Order	1.05

JUMBO SHRIMP – With our delicious Sauce
Served with crisp fries, garlic buttered roll and choice of soup or salad.

JUNIOR — FOUR SHRIMP	.80
MOM — SEVEN SHRIMP	1.05
POP — ELEVEN SHRIMP	1.35

HALF AND HALF 1.05
TWO PIECES CHICKEN —— THREE SHRIMP —
With crisp fries, garlic buttered roll and choice of soup or salad bowl.

STEAKS

TOP SIRLOIN — 8 oz. Top Quality Steak 1.85
with French Fries, Buttered Roll and Choice of soup or salad bowl.

HAM STEAK 1.30
Generous portion of center cut ham grilled to a turn, with Apple Sauce, crisp fries, cottage cheese and pineapple salad, garlic buttered roll.

APPETIZERS

TOMATO COCKTAIL	.15
ORANGE JUICE	.15
SHRIMP COCKTAIL	.50

SALADS

MIXED SALAD BOWL	.25
LETTUCE AND TOMATO	.25
CRISP HEAD LETTUCE	.20
COTTAGE CHEESE & TOMATO	.30
SHRIMP SALAD	.75
CHICKEN or TUNA SALAD with TOMATOES	.65

SOUPS

HOME MADE SOUP	.20
CAMPBELL'S TOMATO VEGETABLE MUSHROOM	.25
CHILI WITH BEANS	.30

DRINKS

COFFEE	.10
TEA	.10
BUTTERMILK	.10
MILK	.10
CHOCOLATE MILK	.15
HOT CHOCOLATE	.15

DESSERTS

SMALL SUNDAE	.15	PIE	.15
ICE CREAM (2 Dips)	.15	PIE A la mode	.20
STRAWBERRY SHORT CAKE WITH DIP OF CUSTARD	.35

ICE CREAM

The Polar Bar's signature Golden Brown Chicken (see menu above) served with fries, garlic buttered roll and a choice of soup or mixed salad bowl became the main menu (less soup or salad) for the new Lucky Wishbone. The chicken is still sold under the Junior, Mom and Pop names, but the price has gone up a bit.

"In Paris it's the Riza Bar –
In New York it's the Astor Bar
In Phoenix and in Tucson, it's the Polar Bar. [10]

Polar Bar menu, page 3, circa 1952-1953.

---

[8] **The Polar Bar** was located at 3440 East Speedway Blvd
[9] **Derald Fulton** passed away in October 2011. Source: luckywishbone.com
[10] Quote from the Polar Bar menu, circa 1952-1953.

1960s:
Rock Evolves
& Standards Endure

The 1960s: A look back on Tucson's past

By Michael Hamilton
January 1989 – Entertainment Magazine. Page 18 and
September 1989 – Entertainment Magazine. Page 19

As we enter the new decade with high aspirations, let's think back once again to the time when pop music played such an important part in the lives of baby boomers, when they first became teenagers. In Tucson, the local scene was taking hold.

This reporter played tenor sax for The **Vibrations**. Our lead guitar struck rapid-fire notes, like traces of flamenco .... Buddy Holly had a tremendous influence upon our style of playing in this '61 through '65 era. In Sierra Vista, we once played off an early remote desert generator ... our volume covered its noisemaking! Now that's entertainment!

Cruising Speedway (let's make that speeding Cruiseway) was just as popular then as nowadays. We had our car radios pegged to **KTKT-99 AM** and **KFIF-1550 AM**, rocking all the way. The gang made the big circuitous route around town which included: **Frank Kalil's Teen Town** on the north side, the **HIHO Club** on the east, and **Sunset Rollerama** on the south central side, near the **Cactus Drive-In Theatre**. They were all non-alcoholic clubs for teens back then.

We were proud of our "cool cars" then, too! We noted that many of the singing groups were automotive namesakes: The Larks, The Edsels, The Continentals, Little Anthony and the Imperials... We cruised the four **Johnnie's Burger Shoppes** and, when inside, pumped nickels in the mini-table jukeboxes.

We dug the barbershop harmony of the rock group Pendletones, who later became the Beach Boys. Rock chords and rhythms were somewhat simplistic compared to today's tunes, but we had just as much fun. Brushing aside the glossy gossamers off mind's memory, one recalls rising for high school to the radio alarm clock and the **Guy Williams** program of the city flagship rocker station **KTKT**.

Car photo by Byron McClure, August 1979, *Youth Awareness Press*.

A run-in with Tucson's Drive-In's

By Michael Hamilton
June 1988 – Entertainment Magazine. Page 17

Tucson is known in some cinema circles as quite a movie-going town. Indeed, the price of admission makes one think that local cinema fans have paid for part of those giant new letters in H.O.L.L.Y.W.O.O.D.! As searchlights rove outside the indoor theatres, let's pay tribute to several of Tucson's Drive-In's– some gone, some refurbished, and some still the same (editor's note: the last Tucson Drive-In, the DeAnza, closed in 2009).

Condominiums now rise over the ground where the **Prince Drive-In** [11] gave us "Tammy" and "PT 109." Northbound cars on Campbell Avenue would often stop to view the showings until landscaping was installed. Gusts of wind felled one screen, yielding a strange sight, like that of white dominoes, lying scattered on the ground ...

The **Biltmore Drive-In** [12] (the defunct **Miracle**) on Oracle Road gave us "Charades" and "The Day the Earth Stood Still." Films here were projected after kids vacated the amusement rides below the tall screen at twilight. Now, only the tumbleweeds are threatened by encroaching apartment complexes.

The **Apache Drive-In** [13] added two screen years ago and was famed for the $3 a carload entry ticket (others were trunkload). Once a single plane-and-truss sculpture in the deserted desert, the threes screens are now surrounded by a gathering of Tucson's new industrial growth.

But the most fun of all lay just beyond the mid-60s marquee of the **Midway Drive-In** [14] that has since yielded to commerce. The white uniformed attendants took our dollars and my date and I chose a space on a special terraced row between two monaural speakers, known to be working. No doubt it was humorous to watch this scramble for favorite spots in the last row.

Thinking about those good old days brings back memories of lip-reading back-row patrons, lightly pompous Universal Newsreels, and "squelching Cupids," attendants with red-nibbed flashlights whose job it was to interrupt any activity which did not involve directing your whole attention at the screen.

The July 4th holiday evening was about 80 degrees (my friends in the east couldn't believe that our drive-ins were also open in the winter). I'd tell them we had two feet of sunshine on the ground. Some jazz music started playing discovered our first "Pink Panther" cartoon complimented by our homegrown "Roadrunner" caricature (Beep! Beep!) Yep, truly the funniest one-word vocabulary around!

The screen dimmed. Floodlights flooded. My date waited loyally in the car while I went to the snack bar for some sarsaparilla and "red hots." Curiously, all Drive-In eateries seem to be grubby on purpose. Here was an example of a 1949 "adobe abode," laced with hard cement which had oozed out of the brick joints. Inside? Instant California prices! The precursor of today's inflation, but few foresaw it.

A look around noted a line of teens, bikers, cowboys and standard Americans. So, back to my car I strolled with

---

[11] The **Prince Drive-In Theater** was located at 2015 E. Prince on the Northeast corner of the intersection of Prince Road and Campbell Avenue. It opened in 1953 and closed around 1979. Two workmen were killed when a 57-foot movie screen collapsed during construction ("*Arizona Daily Star*," January 11, 1953).
[12] The **Biltmore Drive-In**, located at 600 W. Glenn at Miracle Mile, opened in the early 1950s. Its named was changed to the Miracle Mile Drive-In in 1963 and closed in 1978. (driveinmemories.com)
[13] The **Apache Drive-In**, located at 1600 E. Benson Highway opened in May 1955 and closed in 1994. (driveinmemories.com)
[14] The **Midway Drive-In**, 4500 E. Speedway, was built in 1948 and closed in 1979. (cinematreasures.org)

my unbalanced divided box of beverages and goodies, even as the rolling topography beneath me was uneven. Tilt! Whew! Almost. … I located my wheels amid the usual sprinkling of '57 Chevies, Corvettes and a few "T" bucket roadsters. Getting into my car while avoiding the speaker wire cause me to chip the car paint on the post … damned "doorknick city."

My date said her classmate just had her friend call at the theatre so she could have her name paged over the speakers. Oh, those nocturnal shenanigans ...

When it was over, the grove of cars exiting the theatre formed a flotilla waiting to exchange the Midway for the Speedway thoroughfare. We joined the late-night traffic in cruising our favorite "burgerville," while radio **KOMA**'s deejay's dazzled more of the nation's teen world from Oklahoma City at night.

Those truly were the days-the "sizzling sixties." Many drive-ins have been driven out, but the soul or "The Last Picture Show" remains... [15]

A. V. Humphrys and Gail LaBeau

ordering at

Pinky's

Drive-Inn

Famous for its Fat Boys

and Chicken in the Rough

3424 East Speedway

Pinky's Drive-Inn, 3424 E. Speedway, advertisement from the 1951 *Tucsonian*, Tucson Senior High School yearbook. Pictured: A.V. Humphrys and Gail LaBeau.

---

[15] At one time, Tucson had 10 different Drive-In theaters. All are now closed. The **DeAnza,** located just south of 22nd Street at 1401 N. Alvernon, opened in 1977 and was the last to close on October 3, 2009. (Source: driveinmemories.com)

The Tucson Rodeo Parade

The Tucson Rodeo Parade in Downtown Tucson, February 1963. Photo by Bertram J. Zucker. *Entertainment Magazine* archive.

The **Tucson Rodeo Parade** is the longest non-motorized parade in the nation. This Tucson tradition– started in 1925– brings the vibrant history and colors of the Southwest to life each February in conjunction with **La Fiesta de los Vaqueros**, the Tucson Rodeo.

Over 150,000 spectators line Tucson streets each year in anticipation of this historic event. The Rodeo Parade is traditionally broadcast live on **KOLD**-TV channel 13 and **Public Access TV**.

The starting point of the Annual Tucson Rodeo Parade is Ajo and Park Avenues – restoring the traditional 2.5-mile parade route. The Parade begins at 9:00AM and proceeds south on Park Avenue to Irvington Road, then west past the grandstand viewing area to South Sixth Avenue and north to the Rodeo Grounds. The parade is FREE to spectators along most of its route. Included in the procession are local and national dignitaries, Native American royalty and performers, historical wagons and colorful floats, marching bands and mariachis, royalty from five rodeos and working cowboys. The League of Mexican-American Women and Mormon Battalion are entries that have been in the parade greater than 30 consecutive years.

History of the Tucson Rodeo Parade

The Rodeo parade was conceived in 1924, when **Frederick Leighton Kramer**, President of the **Arizona Polo Association**, and later recognized as the Founder of the Tucson Rodeo and Rodeo Parade, gathered a group of local business men to discuss the possibility of having a Rodeo. This was the inspiration and moving force that made it possible for the Tucson Rodeo and Tucson Rodeo Parade to take place on February 21, 1925.

The first rodeo and parade brought out the best in Tucson nightlife. Cecil B. DeMille's "The Golden Bed" was playing at the **Rialto Theatre** and at the **Opera House**, Thomas Meigan starred in "Tongues of Flame." The rodeo dance at the **Santa Rita Hotel** the night before was well attended by tourists, cowboys, cowgirls and local society members. Sleeping accommodations were scarce, and pleas went out to hotels and private homes to spare a bedroom. Taxi rides from downtown to the rodeo grounds were set at $.25 for a party of four.

Source: Entertainment Magazine On Line (EMOL.org/tucsonrodeo) and Tucson Rodeo Parade Committee.

1960s: KTKT's Battle of the Bands

By Michael Hamilton
October 1990 – Entertainment Magazine. Page 14

Truly, the greatest night on the town for baby boomers in mid-1960s Tucson was the annual **Battle of the Bands**, sponsored by **KTKT** rock and roll radio station at the **Ramada Inn Hotel**, downtown Tucson.

The evening was personified by about a dozen elite rock instrumental bands that performed the absolute best of the perfected electric pickin' of that era. Indeed, a capacity crowd of over a thousand young people gathered to listen intently or dance with dash below the decorated stage. There were smiles everywhere.

Each local high school (**Palo Verde** was the latest one) and some premiere Southern Arizona bands entered and entertained in short 15-minute super sessions; full of all the guitar gusto the groups could muster! The battlin' bands cranked creative chord work at a dizzying and dazzling pace throughout the night.

The electricity carried from one combo to another, as groups set up their drums and angled the Fender amps swiftly behind the curtain, ready for the next rippin' trip toward the 'trophy of twang!'

As the nocturnal strident strumming raved on, fans voted for their favorite band. There was a subtle rivalry among different schools as their followings each roared their approval, devotedly. It was shear fun to watch and admire all of the nattily attired groups at their stellar best. Cheers abounded as 1st, 2nd and 3rd awards were given in a brief ceremony. There was a final applause for all the grand bands, The **Viscounts**, The…, et al.

Then, the multitude of teens, with their ears still ringing, fled to their custom cars to cruise the streets of Tucson … one more time!

The Vibrations: rockin' into the night

By Michael Hamilton [16]

While enjoying listening to the "soundtrack of life" on the "golden oldies" station, I'm reminded of the showmanship and chicanery of the local **Vibrations** in the early 1960s.

There was great fun and gratification in creating solid, more simple, rock sounds than those of today with a lead, rhythm and bass guitar, a colossal set of drums and a tenor sax, wailed on "with vigor," as was the order of the day. Well-heeled combos had electric pianos and organs; brass horns were considered "out" (years later, Disneyland's miraculous Mustangs disproved that outlook!).

Tucson's own Vibrations took pride in always finding a "fragile-fingered" lead that could strike rapid-fire notes. The best compliment a band could receive was, "It sounded just like the record. Really realistic, man!" The melodies then seemed more decipherable since many old standard songs were placed over driving rhythms.

The most requested melody was one of music's prettiest songs with the perfidious title "Slaughter on Tenth Avenue." Indeed, "Perfidia" was another. Hard rock was developing on the sidelines with raunchy recordings by John Lee Hooker. Still, there were crystal-clear chords in mid-range rock like "Poison Ivy." The Vibrations played many Tucson high school cafeterias and, after challenging students with "rocket rock," the band would slow the pace with the auditory entrapment of soothing songs like "Summer Time," "Harlem Nocturne" and "Moon Over Monakura." Most bands did casually swaying steps, in beat to the music until the mega-jungle drum solo ignited, leaving dancers to admire in awe.

Tucson's consummate dozen rock bands, in the mid-60s, stoked high expectations, whether they played school dances, drive-in openings, clubs or carnivals. Times brought both tragedy and serendipity ... The **Vibrations** ignited their first set with "Last Nite" by The Marquees. As the convivial dancers kept cruising, the groovin' group revved the pace with, naturally, "You Can't Sit Down!" Frolic continued as ragin' **Ron Dunn** struck articulated, double-pickin' lead melody. Bassist **Chuck Haas** gunned glissandos with gusto in "Drivin' Guitars," a powerful instrumental of the era.

Chuck took pride in his handcrafted solid wood guitar and rejuvenated junk jukebox amp, fabric and grille-cloth included. It appeared and sounded factory-made. His torquing technique of playing melody with the lead guitar was a cool, dual effect! Unfortunately, that once blew both speaker cones; he hence played gingerly through the same amp as **Mike Walker**, rhythmic and leader.

Audiences rarely knew musical miscues like this actually occurred, since they were casually covered by **Reggie Miller**, the deft, dynamic drummer. Reg delivered a wail of a drum solo, from mini-bongo through tom-tom. Overt exuberance once snapped a drumhead; the evening's pay frittered away! (bandsmen divvied in). (This reporter fluttered in a riff of rock or silky sax, where appropriate. There was vast contrast between the loads of locomotion and silence between the sets. No soothing cassettes mellowed intermissions; just red dot amp lights guarded the guitars ...). By closing set, The Vibrations really rocked, with guitar necks weaving in sync! Moreover, it was gratifying to notice the exhausted, exuberant fans staying until the final note of the night. When the gig was gone, the group loaded the gear into a classic '56 Ford pickup, then jaunted to **Johnnie's Drive-In**, [17] creating more later memories.

Published in July 19, Entertainment Magazine, page 4; and November 1990 Entertainment Magazine, page 9.

---

[16] **Michael Hamilton** played tenor sax for the Vibrations.
[17] One **Johnnie's Drive-In** Restaurant was located at 2545 E. Speedway, just east of Tucson Blvd. A shopping strip now occupies that spot.

Dearly Beloved: The faces of the 60s

HIGHLIGHTS OF TUCSON MUSIC

In June of 1964 five young gentlemen, all with a great deal of musical ability, formed a pop group in Tucson, Arizona. Their name .... "Intruders." They weren't much to see at first, in fact, they weren't much to hear but as time rolled on the "Intruders" became the most popular attraction in the Southwest.
Photo of Dearly Beloved, *Newsreal* Magazine, February 1985, cover.

By Lee Joseph
February 8-March 18, 1985 – Newsreal. Page 6

During the early to mid '60s, Tucson consisted of an Air Force Base, which greatly contributed to the city's existence, a college, and a population not too far from 25,000. This writer has many memories of Tucson, Arizona as a small, but busy town. I can even visualize the 22nd St. and Swan Road area, when it was nothing more than a four-lane road with no divided median!

Tucson also had a great deal of rock and roll. Besides the usual healthy dose of local, national, and British rock exposed on TV in the '60s, and two rock radio stations, Tucson also had over 15 rock groups and numerous places to play around town.

In the words of those who played in bands during that era, "there was so much happening because people were truly interested in music." At one time, bands were one of the only outlets for high school and college kids. Groups were a symbol of something kids needed and wanted in their lives. When audiences came to a gig, they knew the band was playing for them.

Gigs sprung up everywhere! There were bands playing at lumber yard sales, hamburger stands, and just about anywhere else an amp could be plugged in. At one time, there were about four successful local teen clubs. They were national trends at the time.

For fifty cents you could spend an afternoon or evening dancing to the sounds of a live group. There was no alcohol, just guys, girls and groups. Every third week or so a name act showed. Bars also existed, however, with a drinking age of 21. There was a definite local sound, though groups didn't sound exactly alike. Band members were always going to each other's shows, and really paying attention. From '64 to '68 there was a great scene here in Tucson that directly links to the '60s Punk phenomenon. In most every U.S. city, young people formed groups.

They put out their own records, or records were put out by small-time entrepreneurs and local DJ's. These (now) highly sought-after discs are turning up on many compilation LPs. The raw edge and honest adolescent energy of many '60s local records, appeal to those who are fed up with the 'plastic' contemporary sounds heard on radio today.

The Dearly Beloved make the Tucson scene

Out of many local Tucson bands, including: the **Five Of Us**, the **Grodes**, the **Occasionals**, the **Bassmen**, the **Sot Weed Factor**, the **Lewallen Brothers**, and more, the **Dearly Beloved** were definitely the most popular of all.

They had seven 45s, two of which were on Columbia, and the group played in Tucson and cities in and out of Arizona with groups like Paul Revere and the Raiders, The Seeds, The Mammas and The Papas, The Buffalo Springfield, The Leaves, and many others. The Dearly's also had a massive local following.

When the group began in 1963, they called themselves The **Intruders**. They played surf music (influenced by the Ventures) at roller skating rinks for $10 a night. When the Beatles became popular, The Intruders hired localist **Larry Cox**. About a year into the group's existence, they won a local **Battle of the Bands**; the prize– a recording session in a 'real' studio, which turned out to be some guy's living room. One take was ruined by the engineer's mom flushing the toilet! This became their first 45 "Every Time It's You."

At this time, the group consisted of Larry Cox on vocals, **Tom Walker** on guitar and vocals, **Terry Lee** on guitar and vocals, **Pete Schuyler** on drums, and a bassist. Soon after, **Shep Cooke** joined. Shep had been playing folk music at local 'beatnik' clubs. However, when Shep saw girls charging after the group while they were opening for the Tucson premier of "A Hard Days Night," at a local drive-in, he decided he wanted a piece of the action!

At first, Shep was going to play keyboards, but when the bass player quit, the job was handed to him. Although he had never played bass, he learned quickly.

The first three Intruders' 45s represent the group learning to play in a studio. "These records didn't reflect our live sound," said Tom Walker. The cuts do have their moments, especially on "Every Time It's You," a wild Beatleish punker, and the B-side of their third 45 called "Why Me." This song has some ripping fuzz guitar played by Tom, who had just bought a new Maestro fuzz box. During the session, the engineer said, "This is the most awful guitar sound I've ever heard in my life," which made Tom quite happy!

Undated photo of the Dearly Beloved, from *Newsreal*, February 8-March 18, 1985. Page 6.

The success of a black group from Detroit also called the Intruders, prompted the group to change their name. They choose the name The **Quinstrels**. Although a 45 was released under this name, the group never used it on stage.

The next record was released by their manager, **Dan Peters**, on his **Moxie** label. Their manager had put out all the early Intruders records except "Every Time." The Moxie label also had two releases by The **Breakers** and **Five More**, two Tucson groups no one seems to know anything about. The "I've Got a Girl" record (released by the **Quinstrels** in 1965) displayed a new sound for the group. The song began with a 1950s a-cappella intro leading into a ripper, killer, '60s love song with a wild lead for four part harmonies.

For the first time, the group (in their own words) "really let loose in the studio." The fact that everyone in the group could sing, gave them a tight and unique vocal sound. The "I've Got a Girl" single was recorded at Audio Sound Recorders in Phoenix, and was the group's first outing in a 'professional' 8-track studio, The version of "I've Got a Girl" that appears on (this) the Voxx Dearly Beloved LP, is not the 45 version, but an alternate version from 1966. However, the original version would be reissued in the near future.

Enter **Dan Gates**, a disc jockey from the local radio station **KTKT**. Dan had a rich history in radio and was involved in many recording sessions in California in the early '60s. During the time Gates became involved, the band's name was changed to the Dearly Beloved. The name was perfect for media hype, "for they were no longer Intruders because now they are Dearly Beloved," as stated in their press release of late '65.

One evening, Dan came to a Dearly Beloved practice with a tape of a song called "Peep Peep Pop Pop." The tape consisted of a real primitive recording of some Black teens pounding on a piano singing, "Peep, Peep, Pop, Pop," in real high voices. Dan had this tape since the early '60s when he recorded it in California, and always had high hopes for the song. However, the Dearly's refused to touch it because they thought the song sounded stupid, silly, and several other derogatory descriptions. Gates was persistent and finally coaxed the group into recording the song. Dan took the Dearly's back to Audio Recorders for the sessions. A deal was set up with the Boyd label of New Mexico, to release the record. (Note: the Boyd release of "Peep, Peep..." b/w "It Is Better" had the artist's name listed as The **Beloved Ones**. No, the group didn't change their name again. It was purely a mistake on the label's part.)

WEEK ENDING SEPTEMBER 2, 1966

THIS WEEK	TITLE	ARTIST	LAST WEEK
1	PEEP PEEP POP POP	Dearly Beloved, Columbia	2
2	Sunshine Superman	Donavan, Columbia	4
3	Summer in the City	Lovin' Spoonful, Kama Sutra	1
4	They're Coming to Take Me Away	Napolean XIV, W. B.	3
5	Walk Away Renee	Left Bank, Smash	9
6	Yellow Submarine/Eleanor Rigby	Beatles, Capitol	10
7	Sweet Pea	Tommy Roe, ABC	5
8	See You In September	Happenings, B. T. Puppy	6
9	Wipe Out	Surfaris, Dot	14
10	Mothers Little Helper/Lady Jane	Rolling Stones, London	11
11	Sunny	Bobby Hebb, Phillips	12
12	Hungry	Paul Revere & Raiders, Columbia	8
13	Look At Me Girl	Playboys of Edinburg, Columbia	13
14	Guantanamera	Sandpipers, A & M	19
15	Summertime	Billy Stewart, Chess	17
16	Born A Woman	Sandy Posey, MGM	39
17	Lil' Red Riding Hood	Sam The Sham, MGM	7
18	Alfie	Cher, Imperial	18
19	This Door Swings Both Ways	Herman's Hermits, MGM	16
20	Psychotic Reaction	Count Five, Double Shot	28
21	God Only Knows/Wouldn't It Be Nice	Beach Boys, Capitol	24
22	You Make Me Feel So Good	McCoys, Bang	29
23	Somewhere My Love	Ray Conniff, Columbia	15
24	Bus Stop	Hollies, Imperial	30
25	Workin' in the Coal Mine	Lee Dorsey, Amy	31
26	Over Under Sideways & Down	Yardbirds, Epic	25
27	I Want You	Bob Dylan, Columbia	22
28	Turn Down Day	Cyrkle, Columbia	Debut
29	Searchin' For My Love	Bobby Moore, Checker	20
30	Warm & Tender Love	Percy Sledge, Atlantic	37
31	Blowin' In The Wind	Stevie Wonder, Tamla	21
32	Strangers in the Night	Frank Sinatra, Reprise	23
33	Hanky Panky	Tommy James, Roulette	27
34	My Heart's Symphony	Gary & Playboys, Liberty	35
35	I'm Normal	The Emperor, Current	32
36	Make Me Belong to You	Barbara Lewis, Atlantic	Debut
37	You Don't Have to Say You Love Me	Dusty Springfield, Phillips	34
38	With A Girl Like You	Troggs, Fontana	Debut
39	Couldn't Live Without Your Love	Petula Clark, W. B.	Debut
40	The Joker Went Wild	Brian Hyland, Phillips	Debut

COLOR CHANNEL
99

ALBUM SOUND OF THE DAY

MON	OLDIES BUT GOODIES
TUE	THE ORIGINAL HITS VOL. II
WED	OLDIES BUT GOODIES VOL. II
THU	THE ORIGINAL HITS VOL. III
FRI	OLDIES BUT GOODIES VOL. V

KTKT playbill, ranking "Peep Peep Pop Pop" by the Dearly Beloved as Number 1 for the week ending September 2, 1966. From *Newsreal*, February 8-March 18, 1985. Page 6.

"Peep Peep..." became very popular in Tucson, Phoenix and many other Southwestern cities. The record held a No. 1 position on KTKT's Top 40 chart for several weeks and reached the No.1 spot of 1966 in Tucson. **Bobby Boyd** convinced Columbia to sign the group on the strength of reported sales of 250,000 copies of "Peep Peep..." The record entered the bottom of Billboard's Top 100.

"Peep Peep" played on many national radio stations and made it to American Bandstand's "Rate-A-Record" where it was chosen over the Count Fives' "Psychotic Reaction." Unfortunately, when Columbia picked up the record, Boyd label copies were still in stores in several western states. Columbia didn't print many copies because of this, so the record faded into obscurity due to unavailability.

During 1966, The Dearly Beloved played outside Arizona quite often. The group frequented clubs like Gazzaris and the Hullabaloo on Sunset Strip in Hollywood, and also played teen fairs around the country.

The Dearly Beloved had lots of things going for them. The band was tight and powerful in the studio, as well as live. They were superb musicians, vocalists, and had great times traveling, meeting other bands, and just being in the middle of what is now referred to as '60s youth culture." During their peak, the Dearly's played for as many as 14,000 people as an opening act at concerts.

In mid-1966, the group went to L.A. to cut an LP for Columbia, in the Columbia Studios. On the lighter side of things, the group was recording at the same time that Paul Revere and the Raiders were cutting tapes for a 45. The Dearly's rubbed shoulders with the Raiders and enjoyed the spill-off of Raiders groupies. The group rehearsed in the ballroom of the Knickerbocker Hotel in Hollywood, then they would go to the studio and record. In the evening, the group chased girls on the Strip.

On the darker side, though, the group was rushed recording approximately 20 songs in 3 half-day sessions– the same time the Raiders' were allotted to record one single. Although the sessions were rushed, there were a number of great songs recovered from the Voxx LP. Two cuts from the sessions, "Wait Till The Morning," (written by **Tom Walker**), and "You Ain't Gonna Do What You Did To Him To Me" (written by **Grodes** leader, **Manny Freiser**), were released as a 45 and almost made it to Billboard's Hot 100.

Unfortunately, the deal with Columbia didn't go too well. Besides rushed sessions, Columbia never released an LP or even promoted the group. In those days, major labels were always signing groups and just letting them 'hang' due to indecisions as far as which groups should really be pushed, and tax write-offs. So, in the summer of '67, the Dearly's sued Columbia to get out of the contract. The Dearly Beloved became an "available" group.

During this time, drummer **Pete Schuyler** was replaced with Grodes member **Rick Mellenger**. A two-day span during another L.A. trip reads like a soap opera and changed things for the group. The Dearly's were playing a club in Tarzana with the Leaves. Representatives of the White Whale label were present. The label was interested, had an amount of money in mind, and promised to do all the things that Columbia didn't, so contracts were signed.

The band was rehearsing all day and playing that night. They had a new contract, money, and were convinced that things were going straight up. Larry Cox needed to get to Tucson the next day because he was going to get married. They waited for the other groups to tear down, then tore down their equipment and left L.A. at 3:00AM.

Larry Cox killed in crash

Everybody took turns, each driving about 100 miles. The group was exhausted and had all fallen asleep including the driver. The group crashed outside Yuma, Arizona. Larry Cox was killed instantly and the rest of the group suffered injuries. When Larry died, it voided the White Whale contract because of a clause stating the band would have to stay intact.

The Dearly Beloved tried to keep the band going and succeeded for a little while. They rehearsed as a four-piece but didn't feel comfortable without a lead singer. They worked with other singers who were good, but didn't get the same feel.

Another record was released on Tucson's **Splitsound** label, which was owned by **Dan Peters** and **Dan Gates**. Quite a few 45s came out on Splitsound in the '60s. The A-side of the last Dearly's 45, "Merry Go Round," was a haunting tune that Larry Cox had written. It's ironic that "Merry-Go-Round" was a song about death that Larry Cox wrote shortly before the tragedy of his own. The A-side didn't go over too well, but the B-side, "Flight 13" became a regional hit. The song is another punky ripper with a fantastic bass line. **Bo St. Runners'** vocalist **Jim Perry** sang on "Merry-Go-Round," and **Terry Lee** sang on "Flight 13."

Turning point for the Dearly Beloved

The final days of the Dearly Beloved went like this. **Linda Ronstadt** was in L.A. when "Different Drum" was released. The **Stone Poneys** bassist had just quit and Linda Ronstadt kept getting in touch with **Shep Cooke**, asking him to join the group. Shep insisted the Dearly's were too good to quit, but said, "If

Different Drum" goes Top 10, I'll do it." Well, the song went to No. 11 and Shep went for it.

The Dearly's got another bass player. Shep went on tour across the country with the Stone Poneys but ended up coming back to Tucson and rejoined the Dearly Beloved. To top it all off, Shep got into a motorcycle accident and couldn't play for six weeks. At that point, the Dearly Beloved hung it up, leaving an incredible history and era behind them.

Since the group's breakup, only **Tom Walker** and Shep Cooke continue to play music as a profession. Tom joined **Butterscotch** (which includes **Westwood Recording Studio** owner, **Fred Porter**), who later became **Jon Sorrow** and cut a tune for a soundtrack LP for "Hells Angels '69."

However, the Tower record label changed **Jon Sorrow's** name to The **Stream of Consciousness** without ever telling the group. Shep started the **Floating House Band** in 1970, and also played on LP's with Jackson Browne, Linda Ronstadt, Tom Waits, as well as releasing two solo LP's. Walker also played on many records and composed songs used on **Chuck Wagon and the Wheels** LP's.

Tom and Shep also played together off and on between 1974 and 1983 at many Tucson bars and restaurants. Shep and Tom had a very large repertoire with Tom supplying the rock and roll roots and Shep the blues and folk influences. Today, Shep is always on the road with the **Seekers**.

As far as other former members of the Dearly Beloved's post group activities, **Pete Schuyler** joined the Marines and is now working in electronics, **Rick Mellenger** is an inhalation therapist, and **Terry Lee** is a successful architect in Tucson. Other Dearly Beloved 'alumni' (who were in the group but weren't on any records) include, **Lenny Lopez** on drums, **Val Valentino** on bass, and **Rom Ripley** on vocals.

1960s Jon Sorrow advertisements, reprinted from *Newsreal*, February 8-March 18, 1985. Page 10.

Linda Ronstadt: Tucson's "Girl Singer"

By Sharon S. Magee
September 1990 – Entertainment Magazine

Linda Ronstadt [18] is coming home, and in more ways than one. She will appear in concert at the **Tucson Convention Center** on September 27th (1990) with Aaron Neville, her singing partner on four cuts of her new hit album, "Cry Like A Rainstorm, Howl Like the Wind." Besides this physical homecoming, the critics are hailing this new album as her musical homecoming, a return to what she does best, pop rock.

After forays into swing ("What's New," "Lush Life," and "For Sentimental Reasons" with the late arranger-conductor Nelson Riddle), country ("Trio" with long-time buddies, Dolly Parton and Emmylou Harris), mariachi ("Canciones de Mi Padre" with master arranger, Ruben Fuentes), and light opera (Joseph Papp's productions of "La Boheme" and "Pirates of Penzance,") this return seems to be welcomed by critics and fans alike. As Ralph Novak succinctly states in his review in the October 23, 1989 *People Magazine*, " ... it never seems like a retreat: it seems instead like a homecoming."

LINDA RONSTADT

With rave reviews swirling around her, it should indeed be a triumphant homecoming for this "girl singer" (her words), born in Tucson in 1946 to **Gilbert** and **Ruthmary Ronstadt**. Growing up in the age of rock and roll with brothers **Mike** and **Pete** and sister **Suzi**, she was surrounded by music. But rather than rock and roll it was country, and to an even greater extent, the music of her father's Mexican heritage. Lola Beltran, the queen of mariachi, became her idol.

She recalls with fondness singing Mexican songs with her father and being allowed to stay up late into the night listening to the sweet melodies from the frequent informal family songfests. In fact, as late as 1967 when she was well on her way to rock stardom, her Mexican roots tugged and she proclaimed that she aspired to nothing less than being the world's greatest Mexican singer.

As she reached her teen years, rock and roll still did not figure in her plans. Determined to be a folk singer in the vein of Joan Baez or Mary Travers, at age 14 she began to sing folk music on Tucson TV with the **New Union**

---

[18] **Linda Ronstadt** was inducted into the Rock and Roll Hall of Fame on April 10, 2014. She is the first Tucson native to receive the honor.

Ramblers trio comprised of Linda and siblings Pete and Suzi. It wasn't until she heard the Byrds and realized their harmonies were simply bluegrass put to a "groovy beat" that she decided to try rock and roll.

At 18 she left Tucson at the urging of her friend, **Bob Kimmel**, to try her luck in Los Angeles, and the rest is history. Hit has followed upon hit.

That family is important to her may explain why she has experimented with different singing styles. While some critics blame her seemingly dartboard choice of style on ego or immaturity, a lot of it apparently goes back to family.

Her Mexican-born grandfather staged "The Pirates of Penzance" in 1896 in his **Tucson Club Filharmonico**. Her show business aunt, **Luisa (Ronstadt) Espinel**, produced a book of songs in 1946 called "Canciones de Mi Padre" and toured with the show very much as Linda did with her "Canciones" tour. Her early rock and roll she chalks up simply to defiance but the songs with Nelson Riddle she says are based on her mother's Dutch personality, straightforward with no artifice.

Whatever the reason, it must be assumed that it took a lot of courage, or maybe self-confidence, for a successful rock singer to go against the advice of her advisers and strike out on these musical side trips. Or maybe it was just Linda wanting to do something she truly enjoyed.

Case in point, her "Trio" album with Dolly Parton and Emmylou Harris. While these three friends have from time to time performed backup on each others albums, their desire to do an album together took a long time a-birthin' but was a labor of love. Linda says this is the one album she can listen to without being embarrassed or bothered as she is when listening to her other albums. In a recent interview she said about "Trio," "I just love it. I'm real proud of it. It's the one I can listen to without getting real uncomfortable, even a little bit, you know? I just go, 'Wow, I'm on that record, and I'm so glad."

For those of us that remember the "pre-Riddle" Ronstadt, we can only hope that when she performs in Tucson, that in addition to the wonderful soaring songs from "Cry Like A Rainstorm, Howl Like the Wind," we'll get to hear some of the "oldies-but-goodies" such as her emotion-packed renditions of "Blue Bayou" and "I Can't Help It If I'm still In Love With You."

Welcome home, Linda.

1st: Linda Ronstadt photo by Aaron Rapoport, 1982, Asylum Records.
2nd: Linda Ronstadt and Daniel Valdez. Photo by Bob Blakeman, 1987, Asylum Records.

Dean Armstrong: A Tucson legend

By Nick Nicholas
January 1991 – Entertainment Magazine

What more can be said which has already been said many times over for so many years about a well known and loved Tucson performer with a warm and generous personality as well as a graceful magnificent voice?

Well, for starters, just ask the countless thousands whom **Dean Armstrong** [19] and his now legendary **Arizona Dance Hands** have entertained with their brand of Country Western and good time music for well over forty years now and which many think has been just short of forever.

Born in Illinois, and after having served in the army during World War II, Armstrong came to Tucson for a brief visit in 1946. He immediately fell in love with the area's Western mystique, its people and, most of all, the beautiful music of the West and the cowboy.

In 1948, Armstrong formed his first group– a house band for the **Open Door Night Club**, a popular dance hall and nightclub on the Benson Highway. Soon after, he began a radio show from the club. This led to a weekly show on **KOLD-TV** that continued for more than twenty years.

Armstrong also worked for KOLD-TV, Channel 13, as an advertising executive for many years and continues in that capacity. He switched in recent years to **KGVY** radio where he sells radio advertising in addition to his musical appearances.

In 1963, Dean and his Arizona Dance Hands, by now sounding as polished and professional as any of the day's best Western bands, were hired as the house band for the world famous **Lil Abner's Steak House** where they performed every Friday and Saturday night at 8500 N. Silverbell Road. However, much of Dean Armstrong's

---

[19] **Dean Armstrong** passed away on March 6, 2011.

unselfish efforts these days are devoted to singing and playing for residents of Tucson's health care centers, crippled children's homes and patients at the Veteran's Hospital.

Billy Burkes, the beloved steel guitarist joined Armstrong's outfit in 1955 and along with fiddler **Ed Smith** formed both a professional and personal friendship among the three of them that lasted until Burkes' death two years ago (1989).

Burkes made a name for himself a good twenty years prior to joining up with Armstrong recording with the legendary Jimmie Rodgers where he made more records with "The Father of Country Music" than anyone else. Billy Burkes' beautiful steel guitar sounds coupled with his joyful glance and happy grin brought much musical happiness into the lives of those who listened and danced to his sounds.

Some of Dean Armstrong's "personally rewarding" credits over the years include performing for 31 years at the **Tucson Rodeo Breakfast**, 32 years at the **Old Time Fiddler's Contest**, playing for the Grand Opening of the **Tucson Community Center** in 1973 and its expansion in 1989 and benefits for worthy organizations such as the **Arizona Kidney Foundation** and the **Tucson Girls Ranch**.

He has been recently honored with a listing in the 1989-1990 22nd edition of "Who's Who in the West," which limits honors to individuals who have demonstrated outstanding achievement in their own fields of endeavor and who have contributed significantly to the betterment of contemporary society. Dean Armstrong and The Arizona Dance Hands are professional members of the **Western Music Association**. They have performed on the "Today Show" on NBC, "Nashville Now" on the Nashville Network and will appear in the soon-to-be-released movie, "Kid."

In talking to this classy Western gentleman whose voice remains undiminished by time, it's easy to see how his satisfying smile and charming western personality brings an immediate happy response from audiences everywhere who enjoy his brand of good-time music. It is these and other great qualities which account for the fact that Armstrong has built one of Tucson's longest-running and most popular entertainment careers which continues to endure be it on radio or television, at a dance, fair, barbecue, hayride or festival. His brand of Western music blends into the Tucson scene like mesquite, adobe, a silver and turquoise belt, or faded jeans.

It's been a great forty years or so for both Tucson and Dean Armstrong and the Arizona Dance Hands. It's been a happy trail for the legion of fans that have hummed, sung, whistled and danced to their music for all those years. It was wonderful then, and by cracky, it still is. Western music veterans Dean Armstrong and Billy Burkes perform with the Arizona Dance Hands at the upcoming (1991) downtown event, **Tucson Meet Yourself**.

(1st photo) Dean Armstrong; (2nd photo) Armstrong with Billy Burkes. Photos by Bill Doyle. October 9, 1992. *Entertainment Magazine* archives.

Lewallen Brothers: A blast from Tucson's Past

The Lewallen Brothers, June 1989,
Entertainment Magazine. Page 23

By Dan Starr
June 1989 – Entertainment Magazine. Page 23

I waited 18 years to see The **Lewallen Brothers**. At first, I was too young to get into the clubs during their reign as Tucson's most famous band back there in the late '60s. Then, when the drinking age was lowered, I found myself too wrapped up in college when one of the brothers had died and the group was disbanded.

For new Tucsonans, let me fill you in. The Lewallen Brothers actually are all brothers, with the exception of father, **Cal Lewallen**, founder and bassist. They are all Tucson natives. Their band played all over the city from the late 1950s to 1980, quite a feat for any band!

They were in their heyday in the late 1960s and moved into "the big time" with national tours and major dates playing with Paul Revere & The Raiders, The Turtles, The Yardbirds, The Lovin' Spoonful, and Chuck Berry himself.

In 1968, they placed second in a nationwide "Battle of the Bands" produced by Dick Clark, and then appeared in Dick's Television Special "Happenin' '68." They also recorded on the same label as Ritchie Valens and The Bobby Fuller Four. After the death of their brother in 1981, the family stepped away from the spotlight. Their name faded in the memories of old-timers like me, and it's a safe bet that the majority of live music fans in this transient city have never heard of them.

The Lewallen Brothers are back, this time as a trio, and considering the wave of interest in '50s and '60s music now sweeping the Old Pueblo, they're probably headed right back to the top. The group is father **Cal** on bass guitar, brother **Tim** on drums and brother **Keith** on lead guitar.

The Lewallen Brothers appearance is an attempt to cash in on the success of the '50s and '60s music craze. But, the Lewallen Brothers are not a nostalgia band. They are the real-thing. They are playing music they learned when it first appeared on the Top 40. They lived the era, not re-lived it. This gives them a grip on how that music is delivered that is simply impossible to obtain in any other way. They played the tunes on the equipment those tunes were written for, sang the lyrics with three part harmony that is a trademark of that age of music.

Frank Ace: An Ace up his sleeve

By Robert Zucker
June 1990 – Entertainment Magazine. Page 4

Frank Ace lived the music of the 1960s. For years, Tucsonans have flocked to see the **Frank Ace Combo** during the mid-60s at some of Tucson's popular nightclubs. And now, Frank Ace is back in town.

When the **Club La Jolla** was rocking just south of 6th Avenue and Stone Avenue during the mid-60s, Frank and his Combo would be the highlight. He was often featured on **Frank Kalil's** show on rock and roll station **KTKT**. Kalil was Tucson's top local radio personality in the 1960s.

Frank lived a good part of his life in the Tucson and Phoenix area. He grew up in Eloy. In 1962, after he moved to Tucson, he recorded his record "Kirk" (pronounced "cook") and "Lady Margaret." James Brown used the instrumentation of "Kirk" to begin his big hit, "Bring It Up."

Frank says he had a "poor man's copyright" on the song, but never received any royalties or recognition for his effort. To this date, he still reminds Brown of his part. "Originally, "Kirk" was a 'break' song," Ace reminisces. "We would play it just before we took a break. But we got so many requests to finish it that we decided to complete the song. We then used "Lady Margaret" as our break song. Then we got requests as well."

Soon, the two songs were released on vinyl with the efforts of Club La Jolla owner **Verlon Musgrove**, who helped produce the record. "Kirk" was recorded locally in 1962 by **Copper State Recording**, which pressed 500 45s. Frank has one of the few copies still around. The record brought Frank and his Combo a strong following. Frank would have become a boot maker if his father had not given him that guitar.

"I didn't know of any black artists back then," he says about living in Texas. "Country songs were the first ones I learned to play." Chet Atkins was among his idols. "I spent 30 years of drug-free working. No alcohol or drugs. Music is my drug." He recalls he would often wear dark sunglasses and talk slow so people would think he was stoned and leave him alone.

He performed in Kansas with the **Frank Ace Trio** for a decade. In 1984, he wrote *The Working Musician's Guide*, a handy booklet for up and coming musicians. After moving to Phoenix, he became the bandleader for Small Paul and Beat Street and appeared at the 1988 **Tucson Mardi Gras,** sponsored by the *Entertainment Magazine* and KUPD-FM.

Even though returning to Arizona meant leaving the trio, Frank felt his conviction was enough. He says he "saw the light" one winter while on the road. "When our van hit the ice at 60 miles per hour (in Kansas), I decided to go south (back to Arizona)," he remarked. Frank is booked for a special engagement at the **Westward Look** this month where he performs Tuesdays through Thursdays from 7:00PM to11:00PM in the lounge.

Frank Ace graphic by Manuel Abril, June 1990. *Entertainment Magazine* archives.

Up on Bourbon Street

By Katherine Van Holzer
May 1991 - Entertainment Magazine. Page 16

The seed that gave birth to, what is now known as the **Bourbon Street Jazz Band,** was planted about 1963 when the **Tin Ear Cocktail Lounge** opened at 2420 N. 1st Avenue. The Tin Ear featured Ragtime and Honky-tonk music, except on Sunday nights, when **Jack Cavan's Riverboat Six** played Dixieland Jazz.

Some of the musicians that played at the Tin Ear, and other local musicians interested in Dixieland music, got together on Sunday afternoons at **Bob Springate's** home to "jam" and eat barbeque. Sharing the leadership was **Al Saunders**, who played accordion, and then, after some "woodsheding," returned to the banjo. Other "jammers" included **Red Sather, Jim Schultz, Jim Hockings, Fritz Glover, Joe Walsh, Bill Williams, Rudy Stiebrs** and **Art Pepin**. When Cavan's job terminated at the Tin Ear, he joined the group for a short time.

Al was ready to form a Dixieland Band, and in 1964, he went to see **Manny Treumann**, who had retired from the Air Force and was opening a **Dairy Queen**, at 12th Avenue and Ajo Road. Manny was very interested in being a part of the band. Al said, "So, I got the guys together, and we went out to **Ballyhoo Manny's** grand opening. We played a couple of hours and drew quite a crowd."

The **Old Pueblo Jazz Band** (OPJB) emerged with **Al Saunders**, as leader on banjo; **Bob Springate**, drums, **Rudy Stiebrs**, bass; with **Manny Treumann**, cornet; **Red Sather**, clarinet; and **Jim Hockings** on trombone, on the frontline.

After weeks of rehearsing, their first "big" job was in June 1964, playing for the grand opening of the newly refurbished **Schieffelin Hall** in Tombstone, Arizona. The band played about a half-hour concert in front of the Hall at 10:00AM then marched inside, leading the assembled audience, and played another half-hour or so. At noon, they played for a barbeque at the **OK Corral** for a couple of hours. About halfway through the gig, Manny told Al, "Man, my chops are gone." Al told Manny to take a break, get a drink, and relax. Al then put the piano player, **Wally Neal**, on trumpet and invited **Violet Lux**, a piano player from Bisbee, to sit in. After about six choruses of "Indiana," Al said, "Manny came back to join the group, and blew up a storm the rest of the night."

That same year, the OPJB followed the Phoenix based, **Desert City Six** into **Quick Draws** in Casa Grande, Arizona, for an extended engagement with **Pete Daily**, on trombone, and **Joe Marco**, piano. Since Manny had trouble remembering the bridge to "Do You Know What It Means To Miss New Orleans," Pete wrote it out for him on a Christmas card; and Manny carried the card in his cornet case.

According to Al (he tells very interesting stories), "When the front line stood up for the opening ensemble, Manny placed the card on Red's stool. At the end of the chorus, everyone sat down except Manny, who had the first solo. As he approached the bridge, he looked frantically at Red's stool, now occupied by Red. Pete caught the action and said, 'stand up Red,' to which Red replied, 'Hell, it ain't my chorus.' "

Also in 1964, the OPJB did the late, late show at the **Tropical Inn** that used to be on Speedway. They went "on" about 1:00AM, after a trio had finished their gig, and played until 4:00AM. From the TI, Al booked the band for a two-week gig at the **Wooden Nickel** on Country Club. Al said, "The band bombed. The crowd wanted country western music."

In 1965, **Jim Hockings** was back on trombone, with **Jim Berry** on clarinet, when the OPJB was booked for a 13-week engagement at The **Dunes** on Speedway. Al and Jim did a short stint with **Jack Cavan's Riverboat Six** at The **Beachcomber** on 22nd Street, and then the OPJB returned to The **Dunes** for another 13-week gig.

The OPJM was on hand to welcome members of the Arizona Congressional delegation, for the dedication of the first self-service post office in Tucson. Believe it or not, the facility was located in the north parking of the **El Con Mall**. That was September 17,1966.

Shortly after this, **Jim Berry** was replaced by **Jack Hollis** (**Red Sather** and **Al Boyd** had gone to work for Boeing Aircraft in Seattle, WA), **Bob Springate** left town, and was replaced by **John Harrison**. Manny went to Europe (to play golf), and was replaced by Al Smith, who now has The **High Sierra Jazz Band**, in Three Rivers, California. **Rudy Stiebrs** quit and was replaced by **Bob McDonald** on piano and was replaced by **Rupe McCanon** (bass).

After a two-month bout with the flu in 1967, Al left the band. Red returned from Seattle, and reorganized the group as The **High Society Five** with Manny on cornet, as leader in 1969, had **Red Sather**, clarinet, **Jim Hockings**, trombone, with **Al Boyd**, drums and **Clarence "Clare" Svendsen** on piano. One of the many places the newly formed group played, was the **Jester's Court** on Tanque Verde, where two live black panthers were housed across the back of the stage.

It was 1973 when the name of the band changed again. They were billed as the **Bourbon Street Five** when **Eddie Lain** booked the band at **Gus & Andy's Steakhouse**,[20] and became the trombonist, and leader, for the group. Manny took over the band again in 1974, added **Len Ferrone** on bass and billed the group as the Bourbon Street Jazz Band, with Jim Hockings back in the trombone slot.

When the **Bourbon Street Jazz Band** was invited to perform at the Sacramento Dixieland Jubilee International Festival in 1976, the frontline consisted of Manny on cornet, Red Sather on clarinet, Jim Hockings on trombone, Len Ferrone on bass, Al Boyd as drummer, and **Neil Spaulding** on the piano. Neil had been the accompanist for **Phil Harris** for 11 years, and during one of their performances, Phil Harris surprised everyone when he went on stage and gave Neil a big hug.

From 1979-1987, the BSJB played at Gus & Andy's. The front line stated the same, and **Tom Lemmol**, drums, and Clarence Svendsen, piano, joined Len in the rhythm section. **Mary Jane** joined the band in 1981, when Clarence retired, and **Ed Ross** became drummer when Tom left. **Bill Eagle**, trumpet, took Manny's place in 1983. Manny passed away in April 1984.

By popular demand, the Bourbon Street Jazz Band returned to Gus & Andy's the 4th of January 1991. During the three-year intern, **Ed Ross** retired, and **Pete Swan** is the current drummer.

The Bourbon Street Jazz Band, as it is known today, consists of **Len Ferrone**, bass, is in charge of all band instrument repairs for the **Tucson Unified School District**, and has traveled extensively throughout Europe and Australia, playing Tuba, as a member of Beaver's Concert Band.

Mary Jane, piano, is accredited as a professional in the book, "Jazz Women At The Keyboard," and she has played for President Dwight D. Eisenhower, at his request. She has played professionally since age 15. **Pete Swan**, drums, is a full-time musician. He is the Director of the **Pima College Jazz Band**, and the Band Director at **Salpointe High School**.

Jim Hockings, trombone, is a local architect. Prior to opening his own private practice, he designed the original College of Medicine, now known as the **University Medical Center** (UMC), while employed with the large architectural firm of Friedman & Jobusch. **Red Sather**, clarinet, is a retired hair designer, enjoying his retirement, and trying to "perfect his clarinet playing." Red traveled around the Midwest with various road bands, and said, "I was headed for the Big Time, when Uncle Sam sent me an invitation to join his WWII group instead." Bill Eagle, trumpet, is a retired State Accountant and teaches trumpet at **Marana High School**, in addition to being a Literacy Volunteer with the Job Corps.

---

[20] **Gus & Andy's Steakhouse**, located at 2000 N. Oracle Road, south of Grant, is closed.

Mickey Greco swings

By Peggy Rose
August 1989 – Entertainment Magazine. Page 19

Mickey Greco, of the **Mickey Greco Quartet**, is a well known Tucson musician. Well known because he does the job as the public likes it. He is also very versatile and besides his own jazz swing group, he backs up celebrity singers and shows on piano, works as a singer and teaches. Mickey's band is known as the little band with the big band sound.

Mickey Greco photo, August 1989,
Reprinted from *Entertainment Magazine*. Page 19.

Greco moved to Tucson from Pittsburg, Pennsylvania in 1963 and became a regular performer at the **Saddle and Sirloin**. He also played at the **Hilton Hotel** , **Redwood Gay '90s**, The **Doubletree**, **Gaslight Theatre** and **Jester's Court** among others.

Greco owned his own nightclub here in Tucson, known as The **Tender Trap**, a favorite place for Tucsonan's for many years. He is surrounded by long time associates and very competent musicians **Ray Vidal**, on drums, and **Jesse Tovar,** on saxophone and clarinet.

Jesse plays big band a lot and has his own music store called Jesse's Music World on Twelfth Avenue. Ray will also feed you very well where he manages the restaurant **Cora's Café,** comer of Sixth and Irvington.

Then, there is **Glenn Olsen**. He gets around. You have probably noted that he has already been in a couple of the swing articles because as a musician who only plays music, he gets the opportunity to work for a lot of people.

Recently, the quartet added a vocalist– yours truly, **Peggy Rose**.

Carl Guy: Guitarist turns actor

By Peggy Rose
December 1989 – Entertainment Magazine. Page 19

Old musicians never die they just thespian, or at least one of them does. We're talking about guitarist **Carl Guy**. [21]

If you're one of those people who are always wondering out loud, "I wonder whatever happened to that guy (pardon the pun)." I am about to tell you how one very fine musician who is embarking on a whole new career, based on talents long available but just sort of lying in wait for that propitious moment in time.

Harking back to the past just a wee bit, Carl Guy is a talented performer, whose music delighted audiences for twenty years in New York City and other East Coast areas. From 1945 to 1965, he was booked extensively by the Lou Ross Agency, appearing throughout New York City, Long Island and New Jersey. During the season he was a regular performer at the Atlantic City boardwalk hotels and at The American Room in the very exclusive Asbury Park, New Jersey.

He was a regular at Tavern On The Green and was represented in New York by MCA and Spotlight Attractions, both top booking He recorded his music under the Abbey Records Label. In May of 1950, Carl Guy appeared as a contestant on the popular Arthur Godfrey Talent Scout Show, winning top honors and as one might expect an offer for a daily appearance on the CBS TV show.

Since arriving in Tucson, sometime ago, Carl has played the usual myriad of casuals, and met and played with most of the working musicians around. He was a State Farm Insurance agent for many years, but music was his passion.

In most cases when you think about someone you have worked with or watched perform but haven't seen for many years, you wonder if they are still around. If they're not retired and there are no health problems, most of us keep on doing whatever it is we love to do best. Sometimes, if fortunate enough to have diverse talents, one can find a whole new direction and career.

Apparently Mr. Carl Guy has carried this extra depth of talent around with him all his life and even actually used it on occasion, but music was his passion at that time. After experiencing most of the highs and lows in the music business, he is going on to a new dimension and developing the use of his ability to do dialects. He would like to utilize this versatility in doing commercials or voice-overs for TV, radio or films. He still plays a little bit of music when it feels right. For the most part, he is reaching for a new star to hang his hat on.

Photo: Carl Guy, December 1989. Reprinted from *Entertainment Magazine*. Page 19.

---

[21] **Carl (Guy) Giacomazza** passed away on April 28, 2004.

The acoustic ballad of Shep Cooke

By John Thompson
July 1991 – Entertainment Magazine. Page 15

Shep Cooke has seen it all. After working for over 25 years in the music business, Cooke has seen the proverbial "big breaks" come and go. On a recent Saturday morning, Cooke was in his den watching NASCAR races on television. Cooke looks a little dangerous, with long hair, beard, tattoo and a skull-and-crossbones earring. This makes for an interesting contrast, as Cooke plays what is probably the prettiest and the most technically correct acoustic music in Tucson.

His guitar work is impeccable, with a light touch and ringing tones. His voice is smooth and pleasant, complementing his guitar work perfectly.

As Cooke and I talked about his career, the race on the TV hummed along in the background. Cooke's story seemed to parallel the events on the screen: sudden bursts of speed, long straight runs followed by tight curves, and the ever-present threat of wiping out.

Shep Cooke began his tale: "In the early sixties, I started singing folk music around Tucson. I did a couple radio shows with **Linda Ronstadt** when we were still in school."

In 1965, Cooke was recruited to play bass guitar with the **Dearly Beloved**, a local band. Those were the days when local bands could still get airplay on Tucson commercial radio stations, and the Dearly Beloved had two local hit songs.

"We had a Columbia record contract with the Dearly Beloved, and we went to Los Angeles to do some promotional gigs. Our lead singer, **Larry Cox**, decided he wanted to get married, and on the drive back from Tucson I rolled the car about 53 miles this side of Yuma, and Larry was killed. That was pretty much the end of that band, because he was the star, he was a blue-eyed soul singer and a hell of a showman. The heart went out of the band when he was killed.

"So that's when I went off and joined **Linda Ronstadt** in LA for the Stone Poney tour. She went to LA, put a band together, got a Capitol recording contract and made the first Stone Poneys album. Then the second one carne out, the one with "Different Drum" on it, and that got to be a hit. Linda called and said she wanted me to come join the band In fact, she wrote me a letter. I wish I still had it!"

Cooke's first taste of the big time as guitarist for the Stone Poneys was not to last. "The management saw that Linda was the obvious star of the band, was going to go places, and nobody else in the band was, at least in that formation." Before breaking up, the Stone Poneys went on tour, appeared on the "Johnny Carson Show," and opened concerts for the Doors and the Yardbirds before playing their last concert at **Rincon High School** back in Tucson. Cooke briefly rejoined the Dearly Beloved for bar gigs around Tucson, but quit after a motorcycle accident. He soon started working on folk music again, playing solo gigs in Tucson and LA. He eventually joined an acoustic trio called the Floating House Band which cut a record for John Fahey's Takoma label. After that band broke up Cooke began working on a solo album, but that fell through. Cooke retrieved the tapes that later served as the basis for his first solo album release, "Shep Cooke," in 1976. Cooke played in various other bands, with varying measures of success, and at one point found himself providing guitar and vocal parts for Tom Waits' first album, "Closing Time." He then went back to solo work until 1984, when he joined a revamped version of the New Seekers.

"This was a bogus band. None of the real New Seekers were in the band. A production company in LA bought the name and the songs and then put a band together." The band only held together for about six months. "We did 64 shows in 90 days, with 200 or 300 miles between shows and not enough roadies. I was getting too old for that kind of stuff."

Cooke returned to Tucson and solo gigs. He performed with **Anne English** for a year, and has recently gone back to being a part-time bass player in the rock group **General Delivery**. "So now I'm doing both," he says. "I get to play bass in a good rock and roll band, and 1 get to play solo at the **Bambi Lounge** [22] two nights a week."

Cooke describes his solo repertoire as "Country, Folk, Light Rock, Ballads, Oldies and Originals." Cooke's musical talents allow him to duplicate the sound of any song he covers, though he usually adds some creative arranging. As if he knows that his versions are almost too perfect, threatening to drift into the background. He specializes in customizing the lyrics of well-known songs to add a regional touch (lots of songs take place in Eloy) or a slightly off-color twist. Cooke is an accomplished songwriter as well, and is starting to put his original tunes into his show.

Shep Cooke plays at the Bambi Lounge every Monday and Thursday night from 8:00PM to 12:00AM. Cooke's second album, "Concert Tour Of Mars, " is available at his shows or at **Workshop Music Store**.

Shep Cooke song list, from 1991. *Entertainment Magazine* archives.

Shep Cooke photo, July 1991, *Entertainment Magazine*. Page 15.

---

[22] The **Bambi Lounge**, at 5050 E. Speedway at Rosemont Blvd. is still operating.

Jimmy Greenspoon: Leading a Three Dog Life

By Jodi Rigberg
June 1991 - Entertainment Magazine. Page 15

P art-time Tucsonan **Jimmy Greenspoon**, the original keyboardist for **Three Dog Night**, is a member of one of the biggest rock and roll bands the 1960s. He also makes time to manage rock groups and runs his **Entertainment Travel Business**, located here in Tucson. [23]

JIMMY GREENSPOON

Known best for his participation in Three Dog Night, a group that has been around since the 1960s, he helped bring "Joy to the World" with their music. Fourteen gold albums, twenty-two singles and numerous other awards, Three Dog Night is still as strong as ever.

"The band is like a drug- addictive," said Jimmy when asked why he continues to play and tour with the group. He also quickly added that he can't change direction when they have a "hit" formula.

Their devoted fans play a tremendous part in the bands' continued success. The 1960s generation of die hard rock fans who raised their children to the music of Three Dog Night leaves no room for a generation gap.

Greenspoon also spreads his talent managing rock and roll bands, **Bad Habit**, a local group and About Face, a San Francisco band are two groups fortunate enough to have **Jimmy Greenspoon** and his talent on their side.

Greenspoon says he enjoys managing bands because they create a challenge for him. "I can see a lot of myself in the guys," added Jimmy.

The keyboardist of Three Dog Night recently appeared on the television talk show "Geraldo." Although the issue covered the '60s era, Jimmy was able to touch on his most current accomplishment, his autobiography.

His book titled "One is the Loneliest Number," is co-authored by **Mark Bego** and uses material from Jimmy's diary. His autobiography takes place in Los Angeles in the mid-60s and early '70s from Jimmy's early upbringing in Beverly Hills to his 25 years of drug addiction straight through his stardom with Three Dog Night are some of the books' highlights.

"It was the time to be," remarked Jimmy as he described his novel. "You can never re-create the scene."

He made it quite clear that his motivation behind the book wasn't money but to teach kids a lesson, said if his autobiography could help at least one child get it together, it would be worth it.

"It's an inspiration for somebody, a message for someone who looks up to someone like me," concluded Jimmy.

"One is the Loneliest Number" will be in the bookstores this September (1991).

---

[23] **Jimmy Greenspoon** opened his Tucson, Arizona entertainment management business in 1991.

1970s:
Rock goes
mainstream,
disco flickers

Tucson music in the 1970s

1970s standout was the Bob Meighan Band with members (r-l): Bob Meighan, Rodney Bryce, Richard Howard, Milt Miller and Dick Furlow. On "The Dancer" was Meighan's first release, recorded at Lee Furr's Studio. Chuck Graham even contributed handclaps and tap dancing. February 8, 1985, *Newsreal.*

By Caylah Eddleblute
February 8-March 18, 1985 – Newsreal.
Page 20

I remember it as if the entire decade unfolded just a moment ago, like a crisp snapshot just taken. The '70s, perhaps so memorable because I was finally what every kid dreams of… out on my own. When you're 17, everything is vivid.

"Doc," owner of the Night Train. *Newsreal* photo, February 1985.

The summer nights sweated excitement, especially in 1973. **Fourth Avenue** buzzed with anticipation. **Choo Choo's** had come into its own months earlier, at that time under the guide of **Jon Miller**. Destined for fame as rock and roll's cathedral, Choo Choo's would later become the **Night Train**, where Doc (**Michael Zucker** [24]) and **Shag** created a legend that made music and dreams of the times, larger than life. **Ray and Red's** [25] stood crookedly on the corner of 4th and 6th Street, a beacon to transient heaven. A crumbling bar, it still had a quality that tempted one's curiosity to sit ... and watch.

And **Merlin's** (what many of us probably remember as the **Backstage**) was what would now be called a "preppie" bar, filled with warm light and cherubic faces, drinking pitchers of suds, while a band would play an occasional gig. Of course, down the street, at 4th Avenue and 9th Street, The **Shanty** now thrives in yuppieness. But in those days, no one kicked around 9th Street. Not unless you wanted to take a walk down Heroin Avenue.

Down on **Miracle Mile** there was **Jeckle & Hyde's**, the other rock club and dealers' bar. The Strip brashly displayed all of its wonderfully trashy hotels too, where all the out-of-town musicians stayed in those days.

And after Jeckle's changed its clientele, The **Pawnbroker** became the most crucial of venues for musicians during the mid to late '70s. Just ask **Bob Meighan**. Someone happened to watch him perform there. That someone was Veronique, famous European singing star and (at the time) wife of Steven Stills. She watched Bob's band perform and hired them the same night to play as her backup group for two treks to Europe. Meighan's band was undoubtedly one of the most popular. With three LP's to his credit (two on Capitol, produced by himself and Jerry Biopene) he had a following that, for the most part, monopolized the Pawnbroker.

---

[24] **Michael "Doc" Zucker** has a thriving optometric practice, started in 1991, on Tucson's Northwest side.
[25] **Ray & Red's** eventually became **Café Sweetwater** and refined its taste. It's now known as **Plush**.

So, the 1970s was a decade that claimed the popularity of country-rock. **Chuck Wagon and the Wheels**, released five, count 'em, five albums that gained them some national attention as well. Bluegrass was cool too, and **Summerdog** was its pet.

And there were countless bar bands. The decade began with the **Dusty Chaps**, **Firehouse** and **Stinky Felix**. Other names run through my mind ... **Weasel**, **Cash McCall**, **Husky Baby**, **Larkspur**, **Rooty Kazootie** and the **Bendover Band**. Somewhere in the beginning was **Ethyl**, whose original drummer was **David Bromberg**, and **Gamera**, with **Bill Cashman** on synthesizers. **Marx Loeb** was in that one too. He called the band an artistic triumph, otherwise a failure.

Then the Eastside era was upon us. Seems it was around that time pianist **Jeff Daniels** split. **Sam Burkes** and **Steve Itule** played the **Solarium** (on Tanque Verde). And various forms of the breathable stuff were performing.

There was, of course, **Central Air and the Air Brothers**. Meanwhile **Frank and Woody** were causing a raucous at the **Oxbow**. Then somewhere along the line, **Greg White** and **Richie Cavanaugh** formed **Rock Doktor**. The **Dusty Chaps** finally hung up their spurs in 1978. But it wasn't so long after that the spark of **Los Lasers** was ignited.

So came the end of a decade, and with it a change on the horizon. A new generation of minds was stirring, coming with a razor's edge and spirit not really felt since the '60s. Yet in the '70s, the skill and musicianship of a number of talented people was cultivated, as was an appreciation by those of us who listened.

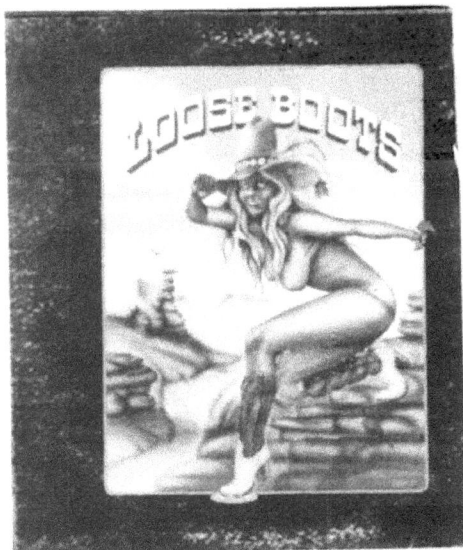

Special thanks to Fred Porter, Roger King, Marx Loeb, Jeff Rudrug, Tom Itule, Richie Cavanaugh, Ernie Rigole, Bob Meighan, and especially, Doc Zucker and Shag.

Album covers of Dusty Chaps, Bob Meighan Band and Loose Boots. February 8, 1985, *Newsreal.*

Choo Choo's

I *walked around these wooden floors before.*
I danced a tune around these tables.
I drank the wine and guzzled the beer.
I stumbled home when I was able.

And I called out for another beer.
It used to rob my guts away.
When I was stoned, they carried me home
To rest up for another day.

With a bottle of beer and cigarettes,
I was the man of the thousand dances.
Wasting my time, drinking cheap wine.
Watching my life dreaming fancy.

Jukebox music brings fond memories
Of those wooden floors and raunchy tables.
And the ladies in waiting, wearing cheap perfume,
They'll still dazzle the sober away.
Some have passed on. Some are gone
To other towns with other names.
And this was home for those few
Who danced every night at Choo Choo's.

By Robert E. Zucker. Poem #411 January 7, 1974. From "Traveling Show," p. 79.
Inspired by "Mr. Bojangles," performed by Nitty Gritty Dirt Band, 1970.

Choo Choo's nightclub wall light fixture, 1973.

Tucson country music bands in the '70s

By Charley Yates [26]
October 1990 – Entertainment Magazine. Page 5

The first entertainer to bring the Las Vegas style country variety show to Tucson was **Roy Clayborne** in 1971. He talked to the crowd. When he walked right off the stage, the crowd went wild. He would do a full show with a follow spotlight, costumes, and a real good band. Roy drew large crowds with his magnetic personality. This dynamic entertainer used comedy, impressive impersonations of many well-known country music stars and motion picture stars, and even stars from the old time rock and roll era. He could really motivate an audience into a frenzy.

As the highest paid entertainer to do a long-term show in Tucson, he made quite an impression that shall be remembered for years to come. However, other bands said that there is no sense in doing a show because no one will pay attention any way. Others followed, such as **Frank and Woody**, **Jean Chastain**, **Kelly Koplin**, The **Original Jacks** and The **Lewallen Brothers**.

But, **Billy Templeton** drew larger crowds than any local entertainer in a 20-year period. He did it with his Elvis snow. So far, no other entertainer has broken his record. Billy drew over 20,000 people into the **Corona De Tucson** Race Track. People jammed the bleachers and aisles and overflowed onto the grounds. Wherever a person could stand or sit, they could see the show in the center of the track.

One of Tucson's local highlights was one hot June in 1972 at **Copper State Recording Company** during the mix downs for the first "Country Sounds of Tucson" album. This is the same studio where **Linda Ronstadt** made her first demo. **Larry Allen**, **Gary Allen** and this reporter arrived at the studio early that morning. **Johnny Leonard**, **Kenny Durrell**, **Gary Skinner**, **Rick Skinner** and **Mike Ramsey** were waiting at the **Sambo's Restaurant** across the street, having breakfast and coffee. **Rocky West** came in to find out who was going to put the guitar parts on his songs. Everyone pointed a finger at **Charley Yates** (me!). Other musicians started filtering in, **Leo Dominguez**, **Mike Atar**, **JoAnna Leroy,** just to mention a few, who wanted to witness this historic event.

The *Mountain Newsreal* makes it's debut

The *Mountain Newsreal*, Tucson's monthly newspaper of popular culture, was first published in May 1974 by **Jon (Jonathan L)** and **Joan Rosen**. The tabloid later became known as the *Newsreal* and focused on music– both local and national. The *Newsreal* continued to publish through October 1985.

---

[26] **Charley Yates** is a local country entertainer who has performed in Tucson since 1967.

Chuck Wagon & the Wheels:
Keepin' those wheels spinnin'

By Tim Martin
November 1990 – Entertainment Magazine

Chuck Wagon & the Wheels are a premier country/western band, but every fan knows they can knock out some pretty mean rock and roll, too. Formed in 1977, Chuck Wagon & the Wheels became familiar to Tucsonans in the late '70s and early '80s for their satirical music when they called the **Stumble Inn** [27] their home.

Chuck Wagon & the Wheels, Wagon Track Records. November 1990, *Entertainment Magazine*.

Best known for their "Country Swings Disco Sucks," these guys hit #1 on the "Dr. Demento Show's Funny 5 Countdown" in 1980, closely followed by "The Gas Song (Let's Drop the Neutron)."

Unfortunately, this was released during the Iranian hostage crisis, and wasn't looked upon as funny. Maybe the time has come now to get some airplay.

After 13 years, five albums, six singles, international airplay, domestic and European tours, and a few changes in the lineup, this

---

[27] The **Stumble Inn** was later called **Mudbugg's** nightclub. It is now called The **Rock** at 136 N. Park Avenue at 9th Street.

band can still get a crowd rowdy, whistling and screaming the names of favorites such as "My Girl Passed Out in Her Food," and "We Ran Out of Gas on the Road to Love."

Popular in California and Colorado, they have opened for such names as Jerry Jeff Walker and have been compared to Asleep at the Wheel.

Performing on a small, low stage spanning the back wall of **Tiny's Saloon**, [28] it seemed to this reporter, like walking into a roadhouse. The only thing missing was the chicken wire in the front of the stage. But as it turned out, this was not the case. It is a nice comfortable place to meet friends.

The band plays music from such divergent groups as Ted Nugent, the Rolling Stones, and does a great impression of Willy Nelson with Chuck reverently holding his nose to achieve just the right nasal quality.

Chuck "Wagon" Maultsby, a Tucsonan since the mid-60s, began his career in various rock bands, and landed a contract from Capitol Records in 1969. He changed format in the mid-70s and got into country/western. He is founder, singer, songwriter, and producer owning **Wagon Tracks Records**. His favorite song is "Carolinda," but it was never a big seller. Chuck has won one music award for "Sales over 100." It is a disc of bubble gum music.

Chuck is married to a raven-haired beauty named **Sharon**, and has two sons from a previous marriage. Chuck and Sharon are both professional leatherworkers. Chuck's goal is "to have just one Top 40 hit before I die. I'd be happy with #39."

Backing Chuck on the steel pedal guitar is **Neil Harry**, a member since 1978, when he left the **Dusty Chaps** band. He played on two albums produced by Capitol Records for them. Neil is a steel guitar instructor and recording session performer.

Bass player and vocalist, **Randy Cochran**, is from Tulsa, Oklahoma. Once a staff musician for Leon Russell's Shelter Recording Studios, he came to Tucson as a member of the Grain of Salt band from Denver. He now works as a civilian at Davis Monthan Air Force Base.

On lead guitar, native Tucsonan **Jay Quiros** has become a "second to none picker and harmony singer," says Chuck. Jay is also a songwriter, and has helped with the **KWFM** radio compilation album.

Doug Parmenter is on drums. As a graduate of the Musician's Institute of L.A., is highly successful studio musician, and has played with many country and rock bands.

This version of the band has been together for a little more than three years.

Kristi Bird, of the *Flagstaff Lumberjack* has described this band perhaps better than anyone. She says, "The music of Chuck Wagon and the Wheels is more humorous than crude, creating a party atmosphere for dancers, drinkers and 'hell-raisers'."

She certainly is right, some of the songs she must be alluding to include "Red Hot Women Ice Cold Beer," "How Can I Love You If You Won't Lay Down!" and "One Less Jogger on the Road."

There is good news for fans of Chuck Wagon and the Wheels. There is going to be a new album. "The Best and Worst of Chuck Wagon and the Wheels" will be released near the middle of November (1990).

---

[28] **Tiny's Saloon**, 4900 W. Ajo Highway.

John Hawk: The Hawk of the desert

By Dan Starr [29]
December 1985 – Entertainment Magazine. Page 18

He describes himself as a velvet voiced Son of the Sonoran Desert, a picker and a singer who covers Hank Williams to Randy Travis, and who can get an audience stomping their feet or leave them laid back and ready for some romance. He's **John Hawk** (his real name) and he's been entertaining in Tucson since 1973, playing with some of the best. He's also a nice guy in general and someone I felt deserved some further recognition.

EM: How would you describe your act?
John: It's traditional to contemporary Country & Western, music of the Sonoran Desert. Right now I'm doing a single, just my voice and my guitar, no drum machines, etc., so it's real authentic, real basic.

EM: What do you consider your strong points?
John: Well, the velvet voice, that's what people have said to me, my ballad voice. It's been called natural, kind of laid back– great for lovers. However, I don't want to give the idea here that it's a laid-back kind of situation only. I guess you could say that I'm a single you can dance to. If people are eating or talking quietly, I'll give them some mood stuff. If they're looking at me expectantly, I get them up and get them rowdy ... My playing is real heavy on the backbeat so it is danceable, especially on the wooden stage I've been playing on lately at The **Gates Pass Inn**.

EM: When did you get started as a performer?
John: I started at 18 and did my apprenticeship playing with **Roy Clayborne & The Alamo** for five years. After that, I continued to seek out the best local guitarists to work with, people like **Mike Sullivan**, **John Chastain**, and **Kevin Thomas**. I've done all sorts of bands and singles.

EM: I understand that you're a full-time musician and that you also run a FREE musicians' referral service. Tell me about that.
John: It's straightforward. If someone needs players for their band or wants to connect with people in the Tucson music scene, I can help. I've been around and know a lot of folks. Musicians call me up and I keep their specifics, type of music, instruments played, etc., in my computer so I can make referrals. It costs nothing to list. I'm interested in increasing the camaraderie in the music scene, in anything that improves the communication. Every now and then I can also get somebody a gig and a few bucks cross my desk and I don't object!

EM: So what does the future hold?
John: I'm working on recording some of my Sonoran music, plus playing, of course, both in public and for private engagements. I'm available, in other words, and I hope you will include that!

As readers of *EM* know, I'm not a friend of musical hype and terminal hippness. I found John Hawk to be an authentic, long-term Tucson entertainer who does just what he says he does and is humble about it in the process.

John Hawk photo, 1991, *Entertainment Magazine* archives.

---

[29] **Dan Starr** is a local musician with the duo **LifeForce!** and a co-founder of Music Instructor's Collective.

Cass Preston keeps on swinging

By Peggy Rose
July 1989 – Entertainment
Magazine.
Page 18

(r-l) Cass Preston, Pete Sevan, Pat McCauley and Glenn Olsen, *Entertainment Magazine*. Photo by Peggy Rose.

Once again in our search for the swinging beat in Tucson, we are glad to report that it is indeed swinging again on a Monday night at The **Baron's Restaurant**, 240 S. Wilmot Rd. Who might you ask is doing the swinging? None other than Tucson's own– **Cass Preston and Ensemble**.

For quite a few months now, the cadre of Preston fans have been wondering where and when they might once again have the privilege and pleasure of hearing Preston locally. Actually, Preston has been playing locally at **Lowe's Ventana Canyon** on Friday and Saturday nights but he is playing and singing in that group as a sideman, so lots of his fans were not aware that he was there. Preston is back as leader of his own group on Monday nights at The Baron's, where it is a perfect atmosphere for Preston's style of music.

Castromo "Cass" Preston was born in Tucson and played trumpet for the **Tucson High School** band. Preston has been playing and singing for Tucsonan's for many years. The **Music Box Lounge**, The **Hilton Hotel** , The **Executive Inn**, The **Tender Trap** are just some of the places he has performed. He has only been at The **Baron's** for several weeks and the stampede has already started.

Preston also serves as a full time physical education teacher but one doesn't have to watch and listen to him very long to know that music is the love of his life. Preston has a loyal group of fans (including me) that have followed him through the years and as a relative newcomer to Tucson, I'm surprised there isn't a Cass Preston fan club– or is there? Preston seems to inspire avid devotion and why not? He soothes you with a touch of Nat King Cole type Ballads, lifts you with a touch of Joe Williams and Lou Rawls type blues, throws in a little calypso, plays a few jazz riffs or melodic lines on his trumpet and *SWINGS*.

The Preston group is ably assisted by **Pat McCauley**, master musician, excellent guitarist, wonderful teacher and a walking musical songbook, if he doesn't know it, just hum a few bars. Pat is married to a lovely songstress, **Lainey**, and they often perform as a duo known as **Nice 'n Easy**.

Another exceptional string player in the group is the bassist, **Glenn Olsen**. Glenn is comfortable with jazz, swing, rock, country and music in general, but the freedom that comes to create and improvise in the jazz idiom as I believe his favorite. Keeping time with flair is **Pete Swan**. His dynamics are terrific. He not only plays well, he listens well, always seems to know the right lick at the right moment and like the song sez "It's alright with me."

John Denman swings with his quartet

By Peggy Rose
June 1989 – Entertainment Magazine. Page 20

In most every major city across the nation and in smaller townships too, Swing is kept alive. Tucson is no exception to the rule. The great Musical, Jazz, Swing, and Ballad standards of the '40s live on. It is surprising how few people realize how much Swing is available "out there."

The **John Denman Quintet** brings Swing and a touch of Jazz and a little Dixie flavor to the well-known **Gus & Andy's Steakhouse Restaurant**, 2000 N. Oracle Road, in Tucson.

You won't want to miss our local swinging Englishman, who also graces a chair in the **Tucson Symphony Orchestra**, plays a mean round of golf and is fortunate enough to be married to a lovely talented pianist, **Paula Fan**.

John Denman performing at Gus & Andy's. June 1989. *Entertainment Magazine*. Page 20.

John Denman [30] is well received in Tucson. His sense of humor, his warm outgoing personality mixed with just a tinge of shyness and his prodigious musical talent are very appealing and the general public responds by showing up in full force wherever he performs.

Denman, born in London, England, immigrated to the United States in 1976 and joined the University of Arizona School of Music faculty. He taught until 1984 where he met **Jeff Haskell**, director of jazz studies and pianist Fan. The Denman-Fan duo toured the US, England, Australia and the Far East.

Walt St. Pierrex, John's swinging partner, doesn't have to take a backseat to anyone when it comes to trumpet playing. The unexpected addition of his unique vocals and humorous approach to music are just one more enjoyable facet to this local musician.

The bassist and balladeer of the group, **Len Ferrone** is so obviously in love with singing, he is a pleasure to watch and to listen to as attested to by his many fans.

Paul Marchek is the newest and youngest member of the group. Paul is just recently out of music school and is playing his first professional job.

---

[30] **John Denman** passed away November 6, 2001 at his home in Tucson, at age 68, after a battle with cancer.

Paul informs us that it is a great pleasure to be in the company of such proficient professionals. Heading up the quartet and turning it into a quintet of well-rounded musical choices, with a repertoire that just about has something for everyone is wry humored, charming and talented English import, **John Denman**.

The **John Denman Quintet** often attracts many other talented Tucson Musicians of note who wander in from time to time and "sit in." A musician's term, meaning they join in and play with the regular band. Even an occasional vocalist is allowed, one of which is "yours truly," **Peggy Rose**, an honor she dearly loves to acknowledge. The John Denman quintet plays on Friday and Saturdays starting at 8:30PM at **Gus & Andy's**.

Peggy Rose &: Company:
A refresher course for "Swingers!"

By Dan Starr
August 1989 – Entertainment Magazine.
Page 19

A few issues ago (June 1989, *Entertainment Magazine*), I suggested that all you swing fans take yourselves down the road a piece to Green Valley, to a little club where a trio of real professionals were raising the roof with authentic swing.

I chose the word "authentic" carefully, because it best describes this group of musicians who have lived (and are living) the swing era, rather than re-living it on some "nostalgia music" kick. It's always seemed time that music is a mirror of the times, and that it only reaches its full flower when played by people who have lived in those times and have the gut feel of them.

It's now my happy duty to inform you that long drives are over and that you can now experience this group right here in town. The trio, **Peggy Rose & Company,** have been booked into an extended engagement for Thursdays, Fridays and Saturdays at **Fay Anne's Memory Lane**, 51 S. Pantano Road. I caught the group's show last Saturday and cornered spokes-lady Peggy Rose on a break for this interview.

"There's our lead instrumentalist, **Johnny Bozec**, on "The Box" (amplified accordion) and male vocals, our bassist, **Glenn "The Spiderman" Olsen**, and myself, Peggy Rose, on female vocals and cocktail drum. Oh, yes, Glenn also solos on pocket trumpet," Peggy remarked.

Peggy Rose & Co. (l-r) Glenn Olsen, Johnny Bozec and Peggy Rose. *Entertainment Magazine* archives.

Billy Templeton: the Elvis shtick

By Robert Zucker

'70s rock and roller, **Billy Templeton** moved to Tucson, Arizona in 1970 from Chattanooga, Tennessee. From his base in Tucson, Templeton began to perform professionally all around the Southwest for any event he could. He is best known for doing an incredible "Tribute to Elvis Vegas Show."

Templeton and his band's talents are not limited there however, as he has gained a wide respect for his guitar playing in the tradition of James Burton, Albert Lee, Roy Buchanan and the likes of these talented musicians.

Billy Templeton

The **Billy Templeton Band** has worked with many other groups and individuals since he arrived here. In 1972, Templeton won the Tucson **Battle of the Bands** as a guitarist and bandleader.

From 1973-1976, he performed with the **Larry Allen Trio** as singer and guitarist. He also did stunt work with **Old Tucson Gunfighters** in 1974 and made a television appearance for the "Country Sounds of Tucson" in 1975. His first 45-RPM single was recorded in 1976. A year later, Billy recorded "A Tribute to Elvis Album," as an Elvis impersonator.

The Billy Templeton Band consists of four players for the most part– guitar, piano, bass, drums. Templeton likes to incorporate showmanship along with the music to form a better entertainment package. The music they play is "high energy" for rock and roll, Blues and Top 40. The Country music they play has a list that contains more than 600 songs. He has performed in many of Tucson's top spots, including **Manny's**, **Music Box Lounge**, **Panama Pete's**, **Boot Hill**, the **Hilton Hotel**, and the **Sheraton Hotel Resort**, among others.

In the 1980s, Templeton expanded his Elvis shtick and worked on his own show called "A Tribute to Elvis As Elvis" and broke a ten-year record attendance at Tucson's **Corona de Tucson Race Track** for his "A Tribute to Elvis Show." A year later, he took his tour across Arizona. He won the 1984 Battle of the Bands competition for performing "A Tribute to Elvis" and was named "Most Professional Act" and "Best Show."

From there, Templeton went to perform in Las Vegas Hotels as an Elvis Presley act. He returned to Tucson in 1985 to do "A Tribute to Elvis Show" at the **Tucson Community Center**. From 1986-88, Templeton worked in various bands for musicians such as Crystal Gale, Freddie Weller and Johnny Rodriguez.

Will the real Billy Templeton please stand up!

By Peggy Rose
January 1989 – Entertainment Magazine

At least, for *Entertainment Magazine* readers, let's set the record straight. **Billy Templeton** is not accused of any crime and was not on the Most Wanted list. The *Tucson Citizen* newspaper featured a front-page story, February 22, 1989, declaring Billy Templeton not to be the same Templeton on the Most Wanted. Unfortunately for Billy, the Templeton they were looking for was a close relative, his brother to be exact.

Nevertheless, please try to remember that his brother has been located and that Billy would like to get on with pursuing his musical career.

With a little help from the **Red Oak Review,** and his own wide range of musical diversity, there is no reason Billy Templeton shouldn't be able to please a lot of people, most of the time.

Not being an Elvis fan, but still a friend of Billy, I went to see the show as good friends do and discovered to my own amazement that Billy was good at what he did. He does seem to have that extra something that makes people respond.

Billy is now appearing on Fridays and Saturdays at the **South Forty**, on Kinney and Bopp Roads on Tucson's far west side, and it didn't take the public too long to find out he was there. His audience is increasing each weekend by leaps and bounds. College kids, yuppies and mature audiences alike are enjoying his wide range of appeal.

Billy told me he feels the time is right to commit to excellence, possibly do some recording and take another step up the ladder to national, even international recognition.

Billy has the experienced musical backup of five professional musicians, several of whom have been with Billy on and off since his early days. They are known as The Red Oak Review and do a lot of communicating with the audiences on their own as they prepare the way for Billy's entrance.

Charley Yates handles lead guitar and **Larry Allen** is a whiz on the bass guitar and vocals. **Darrell Goodwin** plays rhythm guitar and vocalizes while **Ben Garcia** gives the group the solid and strong support needed from a knowledgeable drummer. **Craig Turner** rounds things out playing keyboard with style and the drive that's important in any band. Most of the band members have written and recorded. Charlie, Darrell, and Larry provide additional harmony. Billy often joins the band and plays lead guitar along with Charlie and sings along over and above his tribute to Elvis.

(1ˢᵗ photo) Billy Templeton signature.
(2ⁿᵈ photo) Billy Templeton photo and biography, courtesy of Billy Templeton, 1989.
(3ʳᵈ photo) Billy Templeton in performance, courtesy of Dee Stowe. *Entertainment Magazine* archives.

Where have all the Big Bands gone?
Ask Cliff Juergens!

By Peggy Rose
December 1989 – Entertainment Magazine. Page 19

I heard about the musicianship and personality of Mr. **Cliff Juergens** ever since arriving in Tucson, Arizona five years ago this month. All of those five years I had been hoping to meet him or meet someone who could introduce me to him.

I wanted to meet him because I was looking for work and was trying to meet everyone who might possibly use a resurrected vocalist. I had a bad case of insecurity about my singing at that time. So, I didn't meet up with Mr. Juergens until a few months ago.

"If you can't play for all the people all of the time," Cliff remarks, "you play for some of the people as often as they'll pay you to do it," which is mostly based on the support you receive from the public. We had quite a talk about that as both of us feels the public in general, at least that part of the public that represents our age group, seems to be a little lukewarm in their support, yet loud in their protest that there is not enough of "our" kind of music around.

Cliff Juergens is one of our most talented local bandleaders, an excellent musician, a warm affable MC, and speaking for myself, I found him a pleasure to work with. Realizing his favorite pastime, big band leadership, is as nebulous as Ghost Riders in the Sky, he remains flexible enough to head up a quartet, quintet or sextet. His light has been dimmed as aforementioned, by a general lack of support. Times haven't changed that much folks, when it comes to payday. The musician still likes to get paid for his effort and the restaurant or the club owner still needs to make a profit to pay for the music you like to hear or dance to.

What was one of the funniest things that ever happened to you, Cliff was asked. "Well, once upon a time they used to have what is known as a Dollar and Drown Dance. The draft beer was furnished and you brought your own set up if you wanted anything else. With everyone chug-a-lugging along, you can just about bet before the night was out a few skirmishes would break out. If this happened, usually the playing of "The Star Spangled Banner" would calm things down. This particular evening, I was playing with a six piece band at St. Bonaventure Hall in Cincinnati, and the band was on a stage about three feet high when some pretty good bassing started going on. So we started playing "The Star Spangled Banner," figuring it would calm them down. We played it again and again and about that time, it was like a steamroller and the mob just creamed the stage, the musicians, the instruments and everything in their path. It was probably pretty scary at the time but looking back at it, it was really pretty funny."

Yes, looking at it through your memory it sounds like a very funny scene. What about today? What is your basic or fundamental philosophy for coping with today's world?

"Do your best. Give one hundred per cent and if you accept a job, never complain about anything." Not a bad philosophy I'd say. So, when you name Cliff Juergens or any other professional musical entertainer, stop and say to yourself, "I'm happy to help pay for these excellent and talented musical performers who are still playing professionally and bringing me my music the way I want to hear it."

Photo: A young Cliff Juergens, from December 1989, *Entertainment Magazine*. Page 19.

Disco fever heats Tucson teens

By Hilary Bass and Veronica Rivera
Autumn 1978 – Youth Alternatives. Page 11

Once disco was limited to people 19 years and older, but no longer! Many of Tucson's finest nightclubs have set aside one or two nights a week for teens to get into the disco scene. Now, it's for anyone who likes to get down to any kind of music, from rock to disco, live bands or the Top 40.

The manager of **Bogarts**, **Joe Bono** says, "There is a lot we can do to keep teens interested. If they can't dance, we will teach them." Bogarts is offering free dance lessons on Thursday nights from 7:00PM to 9:00PM. If Bogarts is not convenient for you to take lessons, there's always the **EI Dorado Disco**, which is offering dance lessons on Tuesday from 7:00PM to 8:00PM. **Steve Somerman**, banquet manager of the **Ramada Tucson Resort** has arranged a Ramada Trans Disco Club.

Many of the discos have regular customers. At Bogarts, "There's a different group of people every week," Joe Bono told us. But, the situation at **After The Gold Rush** is different. According to **Sean O'Hayre** "The same 120 come every week. Now, we get 700 people. But there's a regular group." The Ramada Tucson Resort's Trans Disco has grown from 113 teens to 911 teens since the disco started, Somerman added. The El Dorado disco gets 100 to 200 teens, and usually it's the same 200, but that may vary.

O'Hayre, part owner and manager of After The Gold Rush, says that to keep teens dancing "We want to have another **Community Food Bank** night and maybe a dance contest."

If you want to dance to the beat of Macho Man, Boogie Oogie Oogie or San Francisco, you know the places that you can get on the Groove line.

Photo: High school disco dancers during the February 1979 weekend teen dances at **Gazebo Restaurant and Nightclub**. The dances raised funds for the *Youth Awareness Press* and provided youth with their own teen nightclub near the University of Arizona. *Youth Awareness Press* archives.

Youth Alternatives and *Youth Awareness Press*

The first newspaper for Tucson youth, *Youth Alternatives*, published two editions in 1978 and as *Youth Awareness Press* (YAP) from the winter of 1978 through 1981. The newspaper then published as *Tucson Teen* from the summer of 1981 through the autumn of 1990. Each month, up to 20,000 free copies were distributed into public schools, libraries and hundreds of businesses. The publications were created by **Robert Zucker.**

Teen dance launches new teen paper

A free Disco-Swim Party was held on September 30, 1978 to celebrated the first teen newspaper in Tucson. The first edition of *Youth Alternatives* was printed in the summer of 1978. The non-profit publication produced numerous entertainment events to raise funds for printing and staff.

The launch party was held at the **Tucson YWCA**, 302 E. University Blvd., north of downtown and west of the **University of Arizona** campus. The four-hour event was hosted by **KTKT-AM** radio station.

Guests enjoyed free swim in the YWCA's Olympic-sized swimming pool, free beverages and disco music filled the pool and patio.

The event attracted dozens of teenagers and was attended by a representative of governor **Bruce Babbitt's** and congressman **Dennis DeConcini's** offices. **Kalil Bottling Company** donated beverages.

Disco music was provided by disc jockey **Jim Bednarek**. Jim started at 990 KTKT-AM in 1976 at the end of his junior year in High School. He worked his way on air and spent the next decades working for just about every radio station in Tucson and Phoenix. Jim now coordinates and hosts music, entertainment events and special occasions.

Disc jockey Jim Bednarek spinning records at the Tucson YWCA disco swim party for *YAPress*.
Photo by Donny Newman, *Youth Alternatives*, October 1978.

Disco: A fad of the '70s

By Ilaina Krauss
Autumn 1979 – Youth Awareness Press. Page 8

In the '50s the music scene was Bill Haley and the Comets, The Crew Cuts, the Platters, and the Mellow Kings. And of course the '60s– Jan and Dean, The Yard Birds, the Kinks– and let's not forget the Beatles. Then came the '70s… In Tucson, the '70s started out dull and slow.

There were no other fads and little fun. Inflated prices were beginning; also the mini skirt era was ending. Then disco began. Discos opened all over. Rock radio stations converted to disco music, and stores began to fill their racks with various disco fashions such as satin pants and jackets, slit dresses and spike shoes. Peaches and Herb blared through huge· stereo speakers and disco lights flashed. The '70s turned from dull to dynamite!

When tomorrows' generation has their own fad, "disco" can be added to the list of nostalgia. Disco is getting bigger and better. It is spreading all over the country. Some cities even have teen discos now for the younger set. They're a perfect place to meet people, socialize, and also dance the night away. It's an inexpensive way to spend an evening. All it takes is a cute outfit, a will to get down with the music and a smile on your face.

Teen dances at the Gazebo

Tucson teenagers had their own disco nightclub in the spring of 1979 at the downstairs **Gazebo Restaurant**, 831 N. Park Avenue, on the northwest at University Blvd.– right next to the UA Main Gate.

The weekend dances were hosted by the new youth newspaper, *Youth Awareness Press* (formerly *Youth Alternatives*). Local radio stations helped promote and local businesses provided give-a-ways to the hundreds of teens who would gather each weekend. Radio stations **KRQQ** and **KTKT** held dance contests and gave away free albums. Local radio disc jockeys met listeners and played the latest disco hits. **Steve Rivers**, KRQQ DJ, hosted a live show on Friday and Saturday nights at the Teen Disco.

Teens dancing at the Gazebo, February 1979, *Youth Awareness Press* archives.

Teen dances at the Gazebo

The Gazebo is a combination restaurant upstairs and a nightclub downstairs. The basement disco features a sparkling light show and pushily decorated to set the mood.

Since liquor is not served to youth under 19, or allowed in the downstairs disco lounge, acceptable identification must be shown to prove legal drinking age to be served beer or wine upstairs in the restaurant.

The weekend disco dances ran from the end of December 1978 through May 1979.

The teen disco dance fad continued through the summer as the *Youth Alternatives* newspaper helped organize and operate a series of summer teen dances throughout Tucson.

The building that housed the Gazebo (a former **Hardy's Hamburger Restaurant** in the early 1970s) was razed in 2005 for the new Marshall Building. [31]

A dazzling light show was presented at the Gazebo to project laser images in tune with the disco music. Photo by Bill Greener, *Youth Alternatives* archives.

[31] **Robert Zucker**, who organized the 1979 teen dances at the Gazebo and produced the *Youth Alternatives/Youth Awareness* newspapers, had also worked in the newly built Louis Foucar Marshall Building in 2005 for the University of Arizona Department of Journalism (now School of Journalism). It was an odd feeling being in the same space two and a half decades later.

Disco dancing faze

The disc jockey's box, at the Gazebo Nightclub west of the University of Arizona, stocked with LPs and dual turntables needed to bring "state of the art" entertainment to the dance floor during the disco dance craze.

Photos: *Youth Awareness Press* archives.

Cruising Speedway is a well-traveled tradition

By Laurie Robinson
Autumn 1979 – Youth Awareness Press. Page 7

I t's like clock work– decade after decade. When the weekend rolls around, so do the cruisers. Up and down Speedway Boulevard they make their trek until the wee hours of the weekend mornings. Hanging out while watching cruisers is a favorite pastime as well. It's a sort of special gathering for young people to meet others on neutral territory. Everyone checks out any displayed hot rod. It's part of the show and the tradition.

Well, here we are. Entering into the twenty-first century while confronted with a worldwide energy crisis. And, well, let's fact it, the gasoline shortage will be around for a spell.

The gas squeeze has many folks, worried sick about the young people who just might be hit the hardest by it all. What is going to happen to the American teenager's favorite all-around pastime?

What will happen to all of those cruisers?!!

Well, if you happen to be among the concerned crowd, don't fret.

Cruising has been around since your Algebra teacher was in elementary school (yes, horse and buggies did it, too), and today's generation isn't about to kick the habit now.

The cruisers here in the Old Pueblo seem to take the whole situation fairly lightly. One cruiser related his motto, "Conserve five days of the week and blow off the other two by cruising!"

Another put it this way, "It scares the hell out of me; but if there's gas around I'll use it for cruising." And you wonder why it is nearly a dollar a gallon.

In case you have never been cruising– or have just been wise enough to detour from Speedway Blvd. during the cruisers' weekend rush– the following is a novice guide to what a fun-filled evening cruising is all about.

Within a half hour to forty-five minutes after the sun sets at the week's end, creatures that appear to be normal high school students, and even college students, by day, are transformed into what the connoisseurs call *"animal weirdoes"* (Wild animals).

Before even considering to go cruising, one must be completely furnished with the required paraphernalia. This includes:

A car. This does not mean just any old junk heap with four tires and a steering wheel. No Sirreee! If one wants to be just noticed on the strip, they must be seen driving a high powered, chrome covered piece of machinery ready for the Indy 500. However, it is acceptable for the females to roll around in anything no less savoir-faire than a Volvo, if what is driving it really belongs in a Porsche. Also, it is not permissible to borrow Mommy's station wagon.

A license. This can be anything from a marriage license to a hunting license, since everyone on the strip drives like a baboon-on-the-make, anyway, TPD only recognizes official driving licenses, though, so be cool.

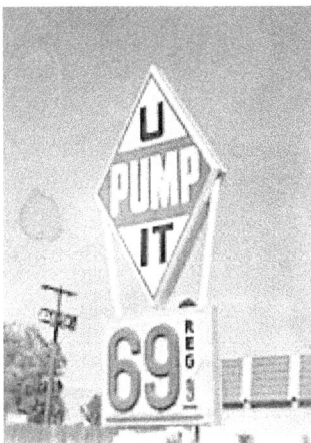

In 1978, the price of a gallon of gas in Tucson was only 69¢,
Sign from U-Pump-It on Speedway Blvd.
Photo by Robert Zucker, 1978.

Gasoline. This is probably the most crucial on the list. Due to the recent gas shortage, many cruiserologists believe this should be added to the endangered species list, for without this precious petrol, well– let's face it– have you ever tried to cruise on a Schwinn?

Okay, let's take a look, The chrome's a shinin' the tank is topped off– well at least half way between the E and the F; the radio is blasting; your hair is combed; and awaaayy weee goooo!

There you are! Cruising about 25mph down Speedway Boulevard. You're going ten miles below the speed limit so as to get a good look at all of those lovely landmarks.

And what landmarks they are! The opposite gender positioned all around you; seated on the hoods of their cars in the empty lots; purchasing munchies; and even cruising along right beside you.

Hmmmm. Take a look at that cute member of the opposite sex hanging out at **Jack-in-the-Box**. You're feeling on top of the world, right? So pull over and lean out the window.

"Hi babe, how's it going," you inquire. "Pretty good," replies the blood beauty. Heh, heh, you'd better believe it! You begin to chat with your new discovery about her name, age, curfew, when you have to return the keys to Mom, and the general rundown.

As visions of sugarplums (that make wild cherries) dance through your head, you don't notice the mean looking Jumbo Jack that just barreled his way out of the fast food joint. He's grasping a Pepsi in one hand and a lead pipe in the other. You finally perceive the moose. Hm. He has an angry look on his face. Hmm. He's shuffling your way. Better burn rubber! SSCCRRRREEEEEEEECH!!!

Whew! Once the smoke clears you get a look through the rearview mirror. Uh, oh. King Kong is hot on your trail. Quick! Turn right, up here… now, take a left through this alley. No good, he is still right behind you. Okay, do ninety degrees right after the oak tree. Yeah, you're losing him. Now, turn left just before the little old lady walking her dog … oh well, the poodle needed a hair cut anyway. Whew!!! You lost him.

Let's see, it's almost 1:00AM. Better be getting home. Hey, take a look. There's a Mustang just like yours. His is a newer model, though.

The driver is angrily watching you eye his hot rod. He's getting a bit perturbed. Quick, look the other way. Too late. He wants to drag. "Oh well (sigh), what better way to end the evening, right?"

Your dragsters are lined up at the intersection of Speedway and Swan. RED light, GREEN and they're off!

At first, the race resembles that of a hare and tortoise. But wait, don't lose all hope. You're catching up with him. It's neck and neck – er, bumper to bumper – er, well shiny chrome grill to mangled up taped together headlight. You watch as you pass him up. You're smothering him in dust. You're gaining speed… Crash! Bang! Crunch! "&$%%!!"

As soon as you scrape yourself off the front windshield, you realize that what you just smashed up was no ordinary black and white Chevy Nova. No, no, you had to total a police car!

Well, after two hours of explaining, begging and whimpering for your life, you are handed a not-so-little citation and end up having to take the, ugh, bus home. Then, after a few other episodes you came upon the fellow Mustang. It is too bad that you didn't win. But face it, his midnight blue '79 model was no match for your hot pink '66 in the first place.

Which brings us to your unexpected encounter with Tucson's Police Force. By the way, those little pieces of paper he gave you are not just little tokens by which to remember your first drag race.

So, how did you like your first Speedway cruising escapade, eh? You have covered just about all the training it takes to be a professional cruiser in Tucson.

Speedway Boulevard weekend cruisers and car photos by Byron McClure, August 1979, *Youth Awareness Press.*

Turning on to KTKT

KTKT/99 disc jockeys Don Beetcher, I.W. Harper, Jim Bednarek, Kirk Russell, Kacie Sommers, Bill Murry, Ed Alexander and the KTKT van. Photo by Robert Zucker. Summer 1979, *Youth Awareness Press*. Page 9.

By Bryn Bailer
Summer 1979 - Youth Awareness Press

From the outside, top radio station **KTKT-99 AM** appears to be nothing more than a one-story, adobe-colored building in the middle of desert scrub and surrounded by a ring of five towers. But it isn't the building that has earned KTKT a prime position on the ratings charts– the people have.

According to **Mark Schwartz**, KTKT's the pipe-smoking general manager, "KTKT represents to Tucson a lot of history, a lot of actual trendsetting. "We're alive. We're today. We're the lifestyle that people are leading."

But the KTKT Tucson relationship doesn't stop here. Schwartz stresses the great commitment KTKT feels toward southwestern Arizona, Tucson in particular. "We're in a city that we feel is a tremendous growth city, a city that has been very good to us," he says. Tucson has been so receptive, in fact, that KTKT has plans for a new contemporary station, **KTKT-FM**.

KTKT-AM and FM will be separate stations, each having its own image, format and approach. But that's the future. What are the reasons behind KTKT's present success?

"We like to be first." Schwartz says, gesturing with his pipe for emphasis. "We feel it's our responsibility. If you're going to call yourself a leader, you have to lead." A few of KTKT's "leadership firsts" include a fund-raising basketball team, a referral service (Call for Action), a station van, and Tucson's first full-lime female Top 40 disk jockey.

Don Beetcher, sporting a mustache, boots, and electric blue eyes, is the 10:00AM to 2:00PM air personality whose show is living proof of KTKT's ability to keep up with the times. It was originally a "strictly female-type show," but then it was discovered that quite a few of the afternoon listeners are "househusbands" who stay at home while their wives work. "We try to play a mass-appeal type of music on the show because we're reaching almost everybody who has access to radio– young adults, men, as well as women."

How does Beetcher, also operation manager of KTKT, prepare himself to 'appeal to the masses?' "A lot of people think you just walk in, play what you want, say what you want, do what you want." He grins at the thought. "It's not like that at all . . . I try to recollect a whole bunch of thoughts early in the morning, write 'em down, and prepare them for my show." He goes on to say that ideas often come to him while he's in the car, and he'll end up driving with one hand while writing with the other. "You should be in a good mood when you go on the air," he comments, "And you should be ready to do four hours of work."

A big part of Beetcher's show is entertainment. But, just like the records they play, KTKT has a flip side. Beetcher explains, "we feel it's important to do something for people other that just giving them music ... you see us actively taking part in the March of Dimes, Multiple Sclerosis, Walk-a-thons... The list goes on. We try to do and to help as much as we can."

KTKT/99

Tucson's Favorites

Don Beetcher, Bill Murry, Kirk Russell
Jim Bednarek, Kacie Sommers, Ed Alexander

Playin' the Best Music
Tucson's Ever Heard

Call us 880-KTKT. Anytime

KTKT Joins the El Con
So. Arizona Values Energy Exhibition
This Sat. 11 a.m. - 3 p.m.

Ed Alexander [32] (whose name is synonymous with The **March of Dimes**, KTKT's programming director, and the 6:00AM to10:00AM morning show) is not quite as big as one might expect from hearing his voice, which has the same rich quality off the air as it does when he's speaking into several thousand dollars worth of sound equipment.

Referring to the benefits of his profession, Alexander cites such things as "all the concerts you can go to, and all the records you can eat" but he also mentions that he gets to meet a lot of interesting people, from superstar celebrities to "just neat people that you meet."

Alexander has been an aspiring D.J. since he was about nine years old (despite his parents' first reaction: "Oh, my God! A disk jockey? When is he going to get serious?") He was in a few bands in high school, and reputedly did a great Mick Jagger imitation, but eventually moved into the announcing field. "The best thing about it is that there's always something new," he says, taking a swig of Dr. Pepper, "news, music, audience reaction ... it's ever-changing. "

One thing that doesn't change much is the limelight– it always seems to be focused on Alexander– and at the same time, on the station. Described by general manager, Mark Schwartz, as "the single most received personality in Tucson. Alexander has plenty of stories to tell about being recognized at baseball games, McDonalds, and the like. "I've been around for a while now, and people know me by face."

---

[32] **Ed Alexander** was KTKT's program director and is now Operations Manager of Tucson radio station KVOI and KCEE.

Ed Alexander broadcasting at KTKT-AM.
Entertainment Magazine photo, March 1986, page 3.

Alexander's future looks like it will involve a lot of "public image," especially if he achieves his ambition to become a television producer. For the present, however, he'll be kept busy enough with the new FM station, and, of course, also with KTKT-AM.

What is Alexander's personal success formula? "A lot of hard work, and caring about my job, caring about the audience, and caring about the people I work with. It only makes the station better." He grins. "And if I don't do it, I won't be able to sleep." Now, that's either insomnia, or Dedication with a capital "D."

Until a few months ago, **Nancy Reynolds** was sales manager for KTKT. She now has another title to her name– station manager. Nancy, blonde and freckled sees KTKT as "fun radio," and recognizes its long-term success of 30 years. She attributes KTKT's success to a dependable image.

"People know what to expect from KTKT," she explains. "We've been planning the same kind of music for many years and people can depend on KTKT." When asked how she feels about the station, Nancy's response was immediate and predictable: "I love KTKT," she says. "I love our music– we have a great blend of music. I like our personalities, and enjoy our news, I like the fact that when people need help, they call on KTKT . . . it makes you feel good."

The newest member of the KTKT clan is 22-year old **Kacie Sommers** self-described as "unpredictable, always talking, and Norwegian." In person, the 6:00PM to10:00PM lady jock radiates happiness through an ever-present smile.

Sommers came very close to being in the Navy. Holding her fingers half an inch apart to show how close she actually did come, she says, "people just didn't think it would be possible for a female disc jockey on Top 40 AM radio. They almost discouraged me." Almost, but, not quite.

Sommers has been in the radio business for about three years. She worked in both Montana and Washington, before Tucson. "I'm not in there to be any kind of a sex symbol," she insists, "I just happen to be a female who's doing a Top 40 job."

"Radio people are insane," Sommers suddenly announces, a sinister look in her eye. "We claim no sanity. We have to project an audio picture to the listeners, and they turn it into a visual picture." She wraps her fingers around a bottle of Tab cola and brings it to her lips. "When you're that good," she continues, "you get paid 100,000 bucks a year in Chicago or LA."

Station manager Nancy Reynolds, revealed the secret behind the station that "makes a difference" when she said that KTKT "is a combined effort from all the people that work there ... a group of good, solid people working together for an overall sound."

KTKT radio station playbill, courtesy of Jim Bednarek. Circa 1979.

The crew at KRQ

KRQ jocks pose for *Youth Awareness Press*. From left to right (standing) Steve Rivers, Bob Majors, Jim Gillie; (sitting) John Stevens and Dan McCoy. March-April 1979, *Youth Awareness Press*. Page 10.

By JoAnn Mesa
March-April 1979 - Youth Awareness Press

"We want to be part of Tucson." is a phrase stressed by **John Stevens**, program director for **KRQQ**-radio station. He speaks for all the jocks that have successfully brought KRQQ a number one rating over other local radio stations.

KRQQ – popularly known as just KRQ – has reached Tucson's young population with their "community service" style and by providing the country's best contemporary music for Tucson.

KRQ is constantly doing one type of community service or another. They have been active in the **Easter Seal Walk-a-Thon**, the **Community Food Bank**, **Toys for Tots**, **Jerry Lewis Telethon** and **Casa De Los Niños**, just to name a few.

KRQ jocks also spend their time playing basketball with high schools and other non-profit agencies. Proceeds are given to the groups, courtesy of KRQ. Since January, KRQ has heavily promoted the Weekend Teen Disco Dances and other benefits sponsored by *Youth Awareness Press*. Nearly $1,000 dollars was raised through KRQ's constant promotions.

Why is KRQ so involved in the community? The station crew agreed with John Stevens when he replied, "We think it's worth it and it's lots of fun." KRQ's five full-time jocks all have their own individual ambitions and purposes. But a few goals they have in common are to inform, entertain and stimulate listeners with the power of music. Captured in the middle of a Tuesday afternoon, KRQ jocks shared comments about their job.

"I know how hard it is to wake up in the morning, so we'll wake up together," says **Dan McCoy**, music director and morning energizer for KRQ. McCoy is on the air from 6:00AM to 10:00AM getting people out of beds, to school or work.

"I do what I love to do– and I love what I do," states **Jim Gillie**, KRQ's mid-morning and afternoon jock. On the air from 10:00AM to 3:00PM, Gillie shares a lot of time with women (housewives) and businesses, filling his listeners in on special events of the day and keeping everyone aware of things going on in the evenings.

"I'm a companion to the people coming home," says Program Director, **John Stevens**. John is on the air from 3:00PM to7:00PM, riding around with the rush hour crowd. Caught in between laughter and a joke or two, Stevens manages to say, "KRQ is like McDonald's– "We do it all for you." Stevens has been in radio broadcasting for nine years.

Steve Rivers, [33] KRQ's evening jock says, "I want to relate to people as my friends and I want to be their friend." Rivers is on the air from 7:00PM to 12:00AM. He enjoys doing a lot of entertaining during this time. To Rivers, the prime importance is music, or anything that relates to music, such as concert information. To keep us all musically cultured, Rivers provides disco sweeps, record sweeps and mini concerts. All three areas consist of good continuous music. In his spare time, Rivers is involved in the community. He hosted the *Youth Alternatives Press* Disco and he visits high schools to discuss broadcasting with interested youths.

"I want to be on a one-to-one basis with my listeners. These are the ones that keep me energized, so in return I do the same," says **Bob Majors**, the early morning jock for KRQ. Majors works from midnight to six in the morning. According to Bob, the night world is a totally different world. Majors tries not to stick to a pattern during his program. He would much rather freelance and joke around with his listeners. Majors concentrates on sports, news and important information that might be a matter of interest to his listeners. Majors has been "into" radio broadcasting for three years.

(Above) Drawing courtesy of Ted DeGrazia, [34] DeGrazia Gallery in the Sun, cover of the first edition of the Winter 1978-1979 *Youth Awareness Press*, drawn especially for the introduction of the *Youth Awareness Press* newspaper. (Below) Ted DeGrazia signature.

[33] **Steve Rivers** (**Bobby Rivers** a.k.a. **Steve Boker**) passed away February 9, 2005 in Lafayette, Indiana.
[34] **Ettore "Ted" DeGrazia** died of cancer on September 17, 1982. He was 83.

Disco fever spreads around Tucson

KTKT radio station personality Ed Alexander hosts one of the Summer 1979 Teen Discos at Santa Rita High School where over 230 teens attended. Photo by Robert Zucker.

Autumn 1979, Youth Awareness Press. Page 9

The next summer of 1979, a teen disco show traveled through Tucson to bring ten neighborhood dances to nearly 1,500 teenagers from June to August. School gymnasiums, cafeterias and meeting rooms were turned into discothèques on six Thursday nights, three Fridays and one Saturday evening those three months to provide youth a place to dance during summer break.

Several community groups sponsored the teen dances, including the **Tucson City Parks and Recreation, Kalil Bottling Co., Tucson Police Department**'s School Resource Officers, five Tucson schools, three neighborhood centers, **Pima County Collaboration on Children & Youth,** the **Southern Arizona Youth Athletic Association** and *Youth Awareness Press*.

KTKT DJ Jim Bednarek (with baseball cap) hosts one of the summer 1979 teen disco dances on August 6th at Rincon High School where 250 teenagers traveled across town to dance. Photo by Robert Zucker, *Youth Awareness Press* archives.

The dances were scheduled to reach all sides of the city: on the south side at **Santa Rita High School** (June 21st), the west side at **El Rio Neighborhood Center** (June 28th), the north side at **Amphitheatre Junior High School** (July 5th), the south side again at **Sunnyside High School** (July 12th), the far east side at **Sahuaro High School** (July 19th), in mid-town at **Rincon High School** (July 26th); at the centrally located **Tucson YWCA** (Aug. 3rd) and on the west side at **El Pueblo Neighborhood Center** (Aug. 10th). *Youth Awareness Press* publisher **Robert Zucker** and the staff helped organize and operate the disco events.

Mark Schwartz, general manager of **KTKT** radio station agreed to be a co-sponsor and provide, at no cost, public service promotions, disc jockeys to host the discos, prizes and promotional give a ways like vinyl records, movie tickets, t-shirts, etc. KTKT DJ's **Ed Alexander** and **Jim Bednarek** took turns hosting the dances.

KTKT-FM: New 96 Rocks Airwaves

By Bryn Bailer
Autumn 1979 – Youth Awareness Press. Page 9

Tucson has a new radio station. Tucson also has a new music format. They are both found on **KTKT-FM (96 Rock)**, Tucson's only pure rock and roll radio station. Explains **Ed Alexander**, program director for KTKT-AM and FM, "Whenever I listened to rock and roll (stations), it's been watered down with pop, disco, jazz ... On this format, if you want rock, you get rock."

The format is described as "album-oriented rock and roll," and is the brainchild of the Burkhart-Abrams firm, which programs stations nationwide. 96 Rock will sound like Tucson, however, not like Phoenix, nor any of the other 50-plus cities that Burkhart-Abrams handles. The Tucson sound is attained through KTKT-FM's ongoing music and audience opinion surveys, local promotions and a general involvement with the community.

Best representing the station's community-oriented image is the news department, headed by **Rob Ritter**. In addition to the hard-core stuff, the news offers public service programming such as a calendar of events, Mexican-American programming, talk shows, and "lifestyle news" geared to 18-34 year olds, which are the station's target group. The key word at 96 Rock is, of course, music.

Not a day goes by without some music highlight, be it artist and album features, top album countdowns, guest disk jockeys and upcoming concert information.

Tying everything together is the 96 Rock air talent– **M.J.** (6:00AM to 10:00AM); **Ziggy** (10:00AM to 3:00PM); **Allen Browning** (3:00PM to 7:00PM); **Bryan Miller** (7:00PM to midnight); **Ted Carradine** (Midnight to 6:00AM); and **Robin Wells** (weekends). They all are very enthusiastic about the station, its audience and new format.

As Alexander puts it, "If you want rock and roll, you know where to come. We won't chase you away with the other stuff." Alexander has been elected to the Board of Directors of the **Southern Arizona Chapter of the March of Dimes**. He continues to serve as chairman of the annual **Superwalk**.

Disco Inferno– the beginning of the end

The beginning of the end of the disco phase began abruptly on July 12, 1979. The Disco Demolition Night at Comiskey Park in Chicago, Illinois was a baseball half-time promotion that got out of hand. A crate filled with disco records was ignited on the field in protest of disco music. The explosion, and stampede of tens of thousands of rowdy patrons, damaged the field and the Chicago White Sox had to forfeit the second game of the doubleheader to the Detroit Tigers. Disco was on its way to fade away.

The Desert Springs Concert Event

May 1979 – Youth Awareness Press

The **Desert Springs Rock Festival** was a 1979 Memorial Day weekend outdoor music event that brought six local bands and 1,500 people together for 10 hours of rock, jazz and soul at the **Pima County Fairgrounds** from noon to 10:00PM on May 27th (1979).

The Fairground's newly built band shell served as the main stage for performing local bands such as **Summerdog**, **Jeff Daniels**, **Airtight**, **Ambush** and the **Epics**, a four-man Motown vocal band. **Tom Weeks** of **Rampage**'s three-member band smashed his guitar on stage in a grand finale to end the show.

In late April 1979, representatives from **Culturecraft Int'l.**, a concert promotion company, offered to tie in a *Youth Awareness Press* fundraiser with its upcoming concert.

Although the turnout was lighter than anticipated, the publicity provided on the radio helped increase visibility of the *Youth Awareness Press*. The shows promoters, who had a loss, picked up the entire tab. Tickets were only $3.50 in advance and $4.00 at the gate. Standing back stage, it was disappointing to look over the large empty field that was suppose to hold up to 10,000 anticipated concert-goers.

Ambush performs during the Desert Springs concert on the new Pima County Fairgrounds stage.

Desert Springs performances at the Pima County Fairgrounds

Bluegrass with Summerdog

Rock with Airtight

eegee's frozen drinks

The **eegee's** truck has been a familiar sight at many high schools after classes during the 1970s when it would park across the street serving its trademark "eegee's drinks," a slushy mix of lemon flavored frozen drinks.

Founded in 1971 by **Edmund Irving** and **Robert Greenberg**, the two men combined their initials (lower case "e" from Edmund and the lower case "g" from Greenberg) to form the company name– eegee's. The vending trucks eventually made way for the chain of restaurants throughout Tucson and Casa Grande. In 2006, eegee's ™ was sold to CEO Foods, Inc.

eegee's refrigerated truck serves fans during the 1979 Desert Springs concert at the Pima County Fairgrounds.

KHYT's disco machine

By John Engle
Autumn 1979 – Youth Awareness Press. Page 9

It is 9:00 in the morning and **Rich Brother Robbins** is busy checking prep sheets, answering the request line, pulling and cueing records, turning dials, flipping switches, and stacking commercial tapes. Sounds tough? Not really, Rich enjoys it. He's been at it for 21 years.

Most people get into radio by hanging around the station. Rich first got into radio in Los Angeles. He and a friend received a job at a station called 10-Q and from then on he stayed with it. Rich looks like a jet pilot when he puts on his earphones and sits behind his console taking off for three hours of Disco Boogie. And you can bet that three hours keep him busy. Most of the commercials are on what look like 8-track tapes.

All the record reports are on an LP. Rich takes meter readings every two hours to see how the transmitter is functioning. *Youth Awareness Press* asked Rich if **KHYT-1330AM** was really trying to compete with other stations. His reply was, "No, we like to work in harmony with other stations." KHYT has done very well in the ratings: they moved from 16th to 3rd place this last season. KHYT first went Disco in March 1979 and has been doing very well considering it is only a daytime station. But that is going to change. Beginning the end of October KHYT goes 24 hours.

Six new 16-story radio towers are being built for KHYT near the Sabino Canyon area. KHYT's new broadcasting station will move to Tucson's south side. These advances allow KHYT to better serve its Tucson listeners and continue to make KHYT the best Soul Disco Boogie machine around.

Skate Country advertisement, Autumn 1979, *Youth Awareness Press.*

Raffle's dazzles with lasers and DiscRock

Winter 1979 – Youth Awareness Press. Page 11

Steve Rivers is at the controls of Raffle's Disco computerized light show during DiscRock dances for *YAPress*. The YAPress logo is featured to the left of Steve. Photo by Robert Zucker, November 1979.

Remember when, after all of the fan fare, **Steve Rivers**, evening disc jockey at **KRQQ-FM** had to leave his air shift because of a problem that interrupted his golden radio voice? He lost it, the voice, that is. Now, he's back.

After a half-year from doing Tucson's top rated evening popular music show, Steve Rivers made his comeback to the airwaves December 1st (1979). His show is planned to keep you tuned to the radio.

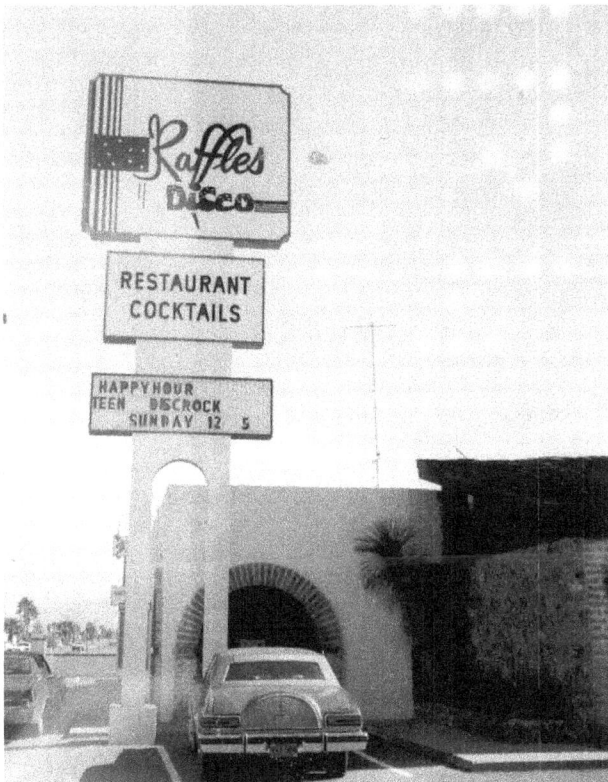

Rivers is hosting **DiscRock** dances at **Raffles Nightclub**, 5632 E. Speedway, as a benefit in November to raise funds for Tucson's youth newspaper, *Youth Awareness Press* (YAP). DiscRock is a music format developed by Rivers. It combines popular rock and roll with top disco hits and previewed music selections.

The management of Raffles offered *YAPress* use of the club for the Sunday dances. Rivers operates the computerized light show that he programs into a spectacular splash and mix of colors across the large dance floor.

Rivers also writes a monthly music column for the teen newspaper.

Raffles Disco Club on Speedway announcing the Teen DiscRock Dances. November 1979. Photo By Robert Zucker.

Games Around Town: Video, pinball, pool and Flash

By Tracy Landers
Autumn 1979 – Youth Awareness Press. Page 10

If you like to race, the **Malibu Grand Prix** is your place! They have formula cars that go up to fifty miles per hour on a winding, professional track, and they also have a large game room with over one hundred action machines. "Everyone comes here," says **Michael DiGiovanni**, the manager. The most exciting night at Malibu is Saturday when all the teens come to play the machines and race. "More people play the pinball machine, "Flash," than any other game we have," says Michael. Malibu Grand Prix is open from noon till 2:00AM seven days a week and is located at 4002 E. 22nd Street.

The **Gold Mine** is another exciting game room located in **El Con Mall**. Assistant manager **Joe Kelly** says they have fifty-nine machines including one called Space Invaders and the popular pinball machine called Flash– two of the most played games. The Gold Mine is open from 10:00AM till 10:00PM seven days a week.

Photo: Golf 'n Things has miniature golf and video games.

Do you like a choice of things when you go out? Then why not try **Golf 'n Things**. They have golf, games and bumper boats. It's fun for families, and teens of all ages. "More people who come here also prefer to play Flash more than any other game we have," says new manager **Ted Williams**. "We have one hundred and fifty machines that you can play anytime Sunday through Thursday, nine a.m. to midnight and Friday through Saturday, 9:00AM to 1:30AM." Golf 'n Things is located at 6503 E. Tanque Verde Road.

Have you checked out the **Fool Around** lately at 940 E. University Blvd? "You can play our fifty machines including pool for only thirty-five cents," says manager **Gary Eastman**. "More people play video than anything else. Among our seven video games is the popular Space Invaders." Fool Around is open seven days a week: Sunday through Thursday 8:30AM to midnight and Friday through Saturday, 8:30AM to 2:00AM.

Do you like pool and pinball? **Old Pueblo Billiards** at 3825 E. Speedway has pool and games featuring Tornado Foosball. You can play their games any time, seven days a week because they're open twenty-four hours a day.

Green Acres Golfland is located at 6118 E. Speedway. They have a large game room of Pinball, Air Hockey, Foosball, and many other skill games. You can play their games seven days a week from 10:00AM till midnight. Call 745-0810.

Step into the wonderland of **Magic Carpet Golf.** They have two skill golf courses you can play, along with their Cameroon featuring a shooting gallery, seven days a week from eight a.m. till midnight. Magic Carpet is located at 6125 E. Speedway.

Sports: A new season with the Tucson Toros

By Anne Griffin
Winter 1979-80 – Youth Awareness Press. Page 15

The 1978-79 season started out well for the **Tucson Toros**. [35] For most of the first half, it looked as though the Toros were to win the first title in their division of the **Pacific Coast League**. The Tucson Toros were doing great until they played a three game series with the Albuquerque Dukes. The Dukes swept the series and cut the 6-½ game lead the Toros had over them to 3-½ games (The Dukes eventually won the title).

The Toros, however, were still in the race until the parent club, the Texas Rangers, began to make trades and call up players. A trade sent the Toros' starting catcher **Mike Heath** to the Oakland A's; another sent one of Tucson's top hitters **Gary Holle** to the Chicago White Sox; and the Rangers called up second baseman **LaRue Washington** and pitcher **Danny Darwin**.

The trading of Holle and Heath, and the calling up of Washington and Darwin, led the Toros to call players up themselves. They called up two from Class AA: Tulsa catcher **Fla Strawn** and second baseman, **Ron Gooch**. Strawn was here for only a month, but Gooch remained.

In July, there was talk of a trade that the Rangers wanted to make. This trade would have sent **Mickey Rivers** from the Yankees to the Rangers. In exchange, the Rangers would have sent **Mike Hart**, **Gary Gray** and two other players to the Yankees. However, the trade was voided by Baseball Commissioner Bowie Kuhn because Hart and Gray did not clear waivers. The trade between the Yankees and the Rangers did go through, however, with **Oscar Gamble** going to the Yankees and Mickey Rivers going to the Rangers.

A dispute between the Toros and Rangers concerning exhibition games played here led to the severing of the contract between these teams. After negotiation with all of the Major League teams, the Toros narrowed their choices to ten teams; then, finally one. Happily, the Tucson Toros are now the top farm club of the Houston Astros.

"It's an exciting organization," comments **Jack Donovan**, general manager of the Tucson Toros. "We thought it was the best move for the City of Tucson."

"I think Tucson is great. It's a pleasure to be here. This is a good place for the kids to play in and live in, they won't have to worry about things they shouldn't have to worry about," said Bill Wood, Minor League Director of the Astros who was present during this interview.

The Astros are the fourth parent club that the Toro's had– the others being the Chicago White Sox, from 1969-1972; the Oakland A's, from 1973-1976; and the Rangers, from 1977-1979.

The Toros had a tremendous Booster Club headed off by **Fred Kalat**, "Freddie the Toro." The booster club was doing something for the players, their wives, the reporters, and were always helping the management. General Manager of the Toros, Jack Donovan, summed up the season, "It was a great year, enthusiasm stayed even though Tucson didn't win the pennant."

---

[35] The Tucson Toros was a professional baseball team founded in 1969. The original Tucson Toros were a Triple-A Minor League baseball team in the Pacific Coast League until 1997. In 1998, the team became the Tucson Sidewinders. In 2000, the Sidewinders were purchased by **Tucson Baseball, LLC**. Owner Jay Zucker also revived the Tucson Toros for two seasons in 2008 and 2009 at Hi Corbett Field.

Goodbye '70s, Hello 80s

By Ilaina Krauss
December 1979 – Youth Awareness Press

Just think, very soon we will be in a new era! It seems almost like yesterday when it was 1969 and everyone was looking forward to 1970 and saying goodbye to the '60s. The 1970s were the beginning of a new world. Everything changed: music, clothes, hairstyles,

It was 1970 when Elton John came out with a new hit "Your Song." He was a new star then. Mini skirts and long hair were still the height of fashion and flared pants were the "in" thing to wear.

The Jackson Five, The Defranco Family, the Osmond Brothers and the Partridge Family were popular in the early '70s.

Then mid-seventies things changed, Skirts got lower, flared pants began to narrow and Led Zeppelin got popular. "Black Dog" and "Misty Mountain Top" were only a few of their popular songs.

Rock became louder and had less romance to it. The Rolling Stones were popular again, changing their style. Their old "Time is on my Side" type music changed to wild songs "Miss You" and "Some Girls" songs. Their album was a smash. Their concerts drew tens of thousands of fans.

The fate seventies brought ERA, otherwise known as woman's liberation. Women demanded equal pay, equal treatment and equal job opportunities. Women became career professionals in place of housewives.

The 1970s also brought a new thing called Disco music. Tight straight leg satin pants with satin jackets, slit dresses and spike heels were the latest in fashion.

Discos opened up all over the country, including teen discos in some areas. Big disco speakers blared pounding music and guys and girls boogied. A really big disco hit was "Le Freak" by Chic, "Get Off" by Foxy, and Rod Stewarts "Do You Think I'm Sexy?" Another popular Disco hit was "Instant Replay," by Dan Hartman.

Then a shock to everyone a Disco Single album! One long-playing song on an album only ten minutes long. "Disco Singles" sold like crazy. But then a lot of people disliked Disco and held anti-disco demonstrations where they actually burned disco records! Will Disco dance its way into the '80s? Only time will tell.

From the 70s, the Knack, the Cars, Rod Stewart and ELO are just a few of the group singers we're leaving behind. But then of course, who says they are leaving anyway? All these groups will continue into the '80s!

Draft Exxon photo by Robert Zucker, circa late-1970s.
ERA rally in Phoenix on January 8, 1979, photo by Connie Leinbach.

Jim Anderson: Tucson icon

For decades, every day a familiar face is seen running down Speedway Blvd., near the **University of Arizona**, always trailed by his faithful followers. **Jim Anderson**, the Pied Piper of the group, is the well-known owner of the infamous bar **Some Place Else**, 1239 North Sixth Avenue.

Anderson is always found running with his trademark staff– a solid gold facial replica of Anderson's head. Anderson unsuccessfully ran for Tucson mayor in 1979, 1983 and 1987.

The bar lost its liquor license in 1986 due to numerous violations. Anderson denied the complaints– 60 charges in one day.

Jim Anderson campaigning for Mayor of Tucson, circa 1979.
Youth Awareness Press archives.

1980:
Technology
becomes personal

Disco died a quick death.

It was only painful for those
who had a closet full of bellbottoms.

Disco-vision, cable and home computers

By 1980, Tucson– home to about 330,000 people– would soon receive cable television service. The Tucson City Council would be granting a license to one of the many companies vying to serve the city residents– among them were **Cox Cable**, **Tucson Cablevision** and **Warner Cable**.

Ed Alexander, local radio personality and new program manager of **KTKT**/96 Rock, predicted that we can look forward to our "own personalized communications system for home security and instant communications with portable transmitters/receivers (the extension of the "beeper" pager) that you can carry with you to let you check phone messages, make calls and many other things from wherever you may be."

"To predict what kind of music or movies we will be receiving on these newly designed systems for the '80s is pure speculation. We can safely assume that there will be enough varied entertainment to please everyone's personal taste…much more than we can imagine today!" [36]

The Compact Disc (CD) became commercially available in October 1982.

Disco-vision, cable, home computers

by
Ed Alexander

What's on channel 375?

This is one question you may likely be able to answer in the next few years.

Communication and entertainment is becoming an evolving and integrated process. Macro-mini electronic and laser technology promises great leaps for your entertainment pleasure in the 1980's.

I have no crystal ball, but the pressure of a $2.00 a gallon gasoline and escalating movie prices will only reek more havoc on our consumer dollars. We will find ourselves at home much more often, though, to choose our entertainment in revolutionary ways.

Look for *Disco-vision* to bring your favorite entertainers right into your home by way of synchronized audio/visual playback modules. These machines are already being made and refined. Just as the home video tape recorders *(VTR's)* let you capture TV shows on tape, the Disc-oriented system may make your latest Pink Floyd album obsolete.

Record companies are gearing up to sell these "floppy discs" sound recordings with video. Your favorite rock group can be caught live, in the studio, or laying down their own interpretation of their music for you to hear and see.

[36] "A new age of entertainment for the 80s," by Ed Alexander, KTKT/96 Rock Program Manager. *Youth Awareness Press*, Spring 1980, page 5.

What's on channel 375?

By Ed Alexander
Spring 1980 – Youth Awareness Press. Page 5

What's on channel 375? This is one question you may likely be able to answer in the next few years. Communication and entertainment is becoming an evolving and integrated process. Macro-mini electronic and laser technology promises great leaps for your entertainment pleasure in the 1980s.

I have no crystal ball, but the pressure of a $2.00 a gallon gasoline and escalating movie prices will only wreak more havoc on our consumer dollars. We will find ourselves at home much more often, though, to choose our entertainment in revolutionary ways.

Look for Disco-vision to bring your favorite entertainers right into your home by way of synchronized audio/visual playback modules. These machines are already being made and refined. Just as the home video tape recorders (VTR's) let you capture TV shows on tape, the Disc-oriented system may make your latest Pink Floyd album obsolete. Record companies are gearing up to sell these "floppy discs" sound recordings with video. Your favorite rock group can be caught live, in the studio, or laying down their own interpretation of their music for you to hear and see.

Speaking of video, cable television will bring movies, specials, cultural and sporting events, concerts and public access from Tucson and around the globe. This will give a much broader choice of entertainment than what is currently available on network and independent stations.

But, wait. The picture on your screen in the future (the next few years, that is) will bounce from around the world to your own mini-satellite receiver on your rooftop. At anytime, you can receive, with the proper decoding equipment, broadcasts from around the globe.

With a bit of extra effort by broadcasting companies in foreign countries, you will hear the dialogue in any language you choose. A major nationwide store chain is currently developing such a satellite receiver dish for about $500. This, along with extended cable service, will bring you clear, distortion free radio signals through your TV system.

For Tucson, HBO is a start. In most major U.S. cities, cable is already a reality. Tucson will be getting a cable system soon after the Tucson City Council grants a license to one of the many companies who wish to serve the city. This will happen late this year. Cable TV will change the way we watch television and will provide much more to see and experience. Major TV networks are very low keyed about the future if cable. Now, they are the only show in town. Soon, they will be like fish in a huge ocean of electronic entertainment.

Look forward to your own personalized communications system from home security and instant communications with portable transmitters/receivers (the extension of the "beeper" pager) that you can carry with you to let you check phone messages, make calls and many other things from wherever you are.

The combination of electronic entertainment and home computer systems (which will become more inexpensive in the coming decade) will tie together a world we never knew before, but will soon become a vital part of our lives.

To predict what kind of music; or movies we will be receiving on these newly designed systems for the '80s is pure speculation. We can safely assume that there will be varied entertainment to please everyone's personal taste– much more than we can imagine today.

Lee Joseph – most motivating musical force of the '80s. *Newsreal.*

Rockin Tucson in the '80s

By Constance Commonplace
February 8, 1985 - Newsreal

I returned to Tucson in July '79, from a two-year desert break in Boston. Music in Bean Town was already at a rapid boil in terms of the "new wave" thing, and it was hard to leave knowing what hard rock and country comforts awaited my now aurally expanded ears, but the call of the cactus was too great.

The musical climate was calm with an electric edge to it– kind of like the end of winter with snatches of spring no longer at the wishful thinking level - almost there, but not yet. People were looking a tad different and when I went to **Pearl's Hurricane Bar**. I knew it was just a matter of time before this ripple would rip through town like a tidal wave.

The **Pedestrians**, **Suspects** and **Z-Nine** were playing. **Dissonance** became the bottom layer upon which songs were built.

Black was the only color you were caught dead in and those hippie locks of the '70s were shorn. The sleepy, creative, energy hanging around the Old Pueblo was replaced by a youthful zeal and was raising its fists, making a joyful noise.

It was late '79/early '80 when things began to jell. Bands were forming and developing consistent styles. Remember **Romeo and the New Deal** on 36th Street? Bands were labeled as New Wave, in **Night Train** club listings, so those die-hard rockers would know what they were getting into.

There was loads of animosity on 4th Avenue between the wavers and hippies in those early days. **Tumbleweeds** was staging bands like **Channel 88**, **Memory Product** and the **Serfers**.

By June '80, **Pearl's Hurricane Bar** was booking blues, the **New Deal** had gone Hispanic, and **Tumbleweeds** was bulging at its threadbare seams with "new music!" **White Pages** was playing regularly with various out-of-town punks. The summer of '80 was no time for those kind of blues as the air was filled with the music of The **Pills**, **Giant Sandworms**, The **Erotics** and **Ménage a Trois**. One end of this new era was the closing of **Pearl's Hurricane** in July.

October was a month of major changes. On September 29th at the **Contractions** and **Pills** concert, it was announced that **Tumbleweeds** would close. The **Serfers** left for L.A. to find fame, and sometime during this period **Memory Product** had been signed with **Subterranean**. **Loudness One** is formed and brings a unique concept to Tucson entertainment.

The Christmas season begins on a sad note as Tucson mourns the death of John Lennon with the rest of the world. **Tumbles** opens where Tumbleweeds once was and continues its new music format. **Ménage a Trios** becomes the **Phantom Limbs**, while other Tucson bands are moving to Phoenix and beyond. In the new year, the **Assassinators** and **Suzie Caruze** are new acts in town.

I would like to mention something about promoters and this spot seems as good as any. Incredibly good acts continue to be brought into town by **Feyline** and **Evening Star Productions**. ESP filled **Dooley's** with some of the top touring acts.

Jonny Sevin performing at Reid Park Bandshell, circa 1985. *Newsreal.*

The spring brings us **Jonny Sevin**, a band that had Tucson music lovers at a fever pitch just knowing they were practicing at Broadway and Columbus. **Tumbles** does just that and closes its doors.

In May, just as the shortage of venues becomes oppressively apparent, **Club Europa** opens on North Stone Avenue. Although great acts are being booked, the scene seems to have taken itself on vacation to another part of the world. The **Giant Sandworms** are sending tapes from the Big Apple, **J7** is in the studio with **Bill Cashman** recording on his **Art Attack Records** label. Frequenters of the **Pawnbroker**, club for the elite dealers in town, start roaming **Yanks**, home to the ever-popular **Bob Meighan Band**. The fall of '81 is actually quite boring except for the opening of the **Backstage** that was formerly Tumbles.

In early September, **Green on Red**, from L.A. (who were the **Serfers** when they left Tucson) played at the Backstage and gave a sweet and sour performance. The FM radio stations are as bland as cold oatmeal and lacking in texture– it's like they sent our ears to Siberia. The **Chromatics** and **Les Seldoms** are finding it difficult to be different in this musically unsettling time. People are becoming apathetic and not supporting music as they had in the past. As '81 slips away, so does the direction of Tucson's music scene, and one more club bites the proverbial dust, **Club Europa** closes.

Trout Unlimited forms with ex-members of the Serfers and the Chromatics, they have abandoned the wave and put out no frills rock and roll. R&B gets a boost with the Salt and Pepper band and Straight Up. All around groovy musician **Lee Joseph** produces two cassettes of his own weird brand of tunes on his **Iconoclast** label. The **Pills** have returned from N.Y. and add **Barry Smith** of **Loudness One** to the line-up. And, radio closes the door further on originality– **Bob Cook's Bezerko Lounge** is off the air.

On March 27, 1982, **Whistling Shrimp Records** hosted a Smash-a-thon to boycott the corporation influence in radio programming. **Chances** Night Club gives Tuesday a new lift with recorded new music and live acts on Sunday. **Jonny Sevin** is changing personnel and **Ned Sutton** puts together some new **Rabbits**.

Photo: Ned Sutton
(2nd from right, top row) and the Rabbits. *Newsreal*, February 1985.

Spring '82 has a new club featuring country-rock. **Nino's** opens on First Avenue. **Jonathan L** and **Bob Bish** get an hour to air new releases on **KLPX**. **Lee Joseph** is at it again with a compilation tape including: **Pink Dancing Elephant, Conflict, Jacket Weather, Stainless Steel Kimono, Urban Guerillas, Cowgirls, Les Seldoms** and **The Chromatics**. **Virgin Vinyl** begins on KLPX. Downtown, **Moda Modeling Studio** features live new music.

Photo: Chris Burroughs and the Nationals

The next six months are pretty unearth-shattering. **Eighty Go Ninety, Chris Burroughs and the Nationals** and **Clean Dog** make musical entrances on the scene. **Nino's** starts booking new music. A major loss to the music scene of Tucson occurs in August when DJ **Bob Cook** is shot and killed in a church parking lot.

'83 has **Dooley's** changing its name to the **Stray Cat. Stainless Steel Kimono** becomes **The Freds** and **Evening Star Productions** [37] is booking at **Cowboy's**. The **Night Train** becomes the **Midnight Express** and it seems that nothing stays the same.

As we enter '85, three clubs have been felled by fire– The **Stray Cat**, the **Backstage** and **Chances. Rainer (Ptacek)** and **Naked Prey** are making an impression at **Jack's Pub. Gentlemen After Dark** (formerly the **Pills**) had hooked up with Alice Copper, gone to L.A., and have since returned wagging their tails behind them.

Photo: The Chromatics

Major acts being book in town are at an all time low, but **Evening Star Productions** keeps trying to keep us musically informed. Radio has plummeted to its most nauseating level of garbage as **KWFM** turns to adult contemporary to raise ratings and **KLPX** isn't sure what it wants to do. **Los Lasers** have put out a fine little album and other locals will soon be following suit.

Maybe it's me, but it feels like the mid-70s again, with a lack of innovation from the music-makers of Tucson. Fortunately, I remain optimistic and sense this period as one of transition, a calm before the musical storm, so to speak, for if Tucson's musical history repeats itself ... the beat will go on and the song will not remain the same.

Photos from *Newsreal*, February 8-March 18, 1985.

---

[37] **Danny Zelisko** has been bringing shows to Arizona since 1974. He founded and ran Evening Star Productions up until 2001 when he sold his company. Zelisko returned to Phoenix to present more shows, including at the Celebrity Theatre, and hosts a weekly radio show, "Phoenix Finest Rock," every Thursday night at 8:00PM and heard locally on 93.9 FM or on the internet at www.KWSS.org

Video Games: Buzzes, whirls and pongs

By John Noyce, Cholla High School
March 1982 - Tucson Teen. Page 7

You see them everywhere you look ... in stores, airports, theaters, Laundromats and in hundreds of arcades around the nation. They beep, buzz, zap and zing their way into the hearts of the American people who spend $3-9 billion a year on them. About 50-75 percent of these Americans are 18 years or younger.

What can create such a stir? Electronic video games! The billion-dollar industry that has invaded us from inner space is possibly the biggest, most popular past time for American teens, who pop millions of quarters into slots of their favorite computerized boxes.

It all started in 1972 with Atari, one of the biggest video game industries that brought us "Space Invaders." Atari moved into the home shortly thereafter, followed by Mattel Electronics' Intellavision and "Odyssey."

Video players soon moved into the living room with millions of dollars of home video games bought this past Christmas alone.

But video isn't the savior of our youth, as some communities now declare. In a town called Mesquite, Texas, an ordinance was passed to prevent anyone under 17 years of age from playing these games unless a parent or guardian is present.

Ronnie Lamm, leader of the crusade against video games, says, "We hear unacceptable language, and see anti-social behavior in the arcades. Only the bad kids go to them and we worry about the young children not old enough to make value judgments. Those without strong moral codes can be drawn in."

Lamm claims, "They drive our young people to crime ... children snatch purses and gold chains for money to put into these machines." Despite growing opposition, thousands of teens still flock to the local arcades to play their favorite games. **Ernie Aguirre**, manager of the **Supercade** on Ajo Way doesn't feel the games are harmful. "They help the coordination of the eyes, hands and concentration. It also helps relieve frustrations." The most popular games, he says, are Pac-Man, Defender and Tempest.

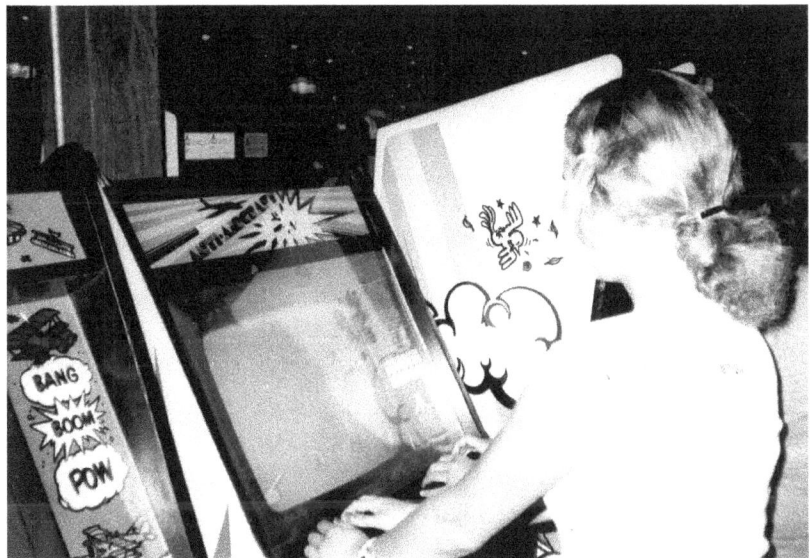

Graphic by John Noyce, Cholla High School. Video games photo, *Youth Awareness Press* archives.

Surge forward

By Bennie Jasinowski
September 1980 – Youth Awareness Press. Page 9

There is a versatile band in town called **Surge** featuring Ms. **Joie Jaye**. They're personable, entertaining, and most of all, a lot of fun.

Joie is lead vocals; **Lupe Rodriguez** is lead guitar and backing vocals; **Mike Quine** on keyboard and vocals; **Steve Watkins** on bass and vocals and **Jimmy Spencer** on drums.

Joie, born and raised in Canada, joined a band there that eventually ended up in Michigan. She later joined a recording group from Ohio, called the Big Beats, playing towns like Tahoe, Vegas, etc. Being a woman presented a slight obstacle in her younger years, Joie recalls, "A lot of men club owners had it in for women. But they weren't all that bad. You just have to make them understand that if they wanted to deal with somebody, they deal with you, because there's a lot of jobs out there."

The band, based in Dallas for a while ended up in Tucson thanks to Steve, their bass player, who's from Tucson. Originally from Los Angeles, Lupe Rodriguez comes from a musical family. He first became interested in music by watching his Dad play.

Mike Quine is one of the two members from Dallas, Texas. He has a peculiar habit of donning things like cowboy hats and ghoul masks during performance. He's been playing keyboards for about eight years. "I first started in junior college. I used to play guitar originally, but switched over to keyboards because a friend needed a keyboard player."

Jimmy Spencer is the newest addition is Surge, having been with them only a couple of months. He also hails from Dallas. Jimmy started playing the drums when he was sixteen. After a brief stint in the Army, he decided to make music his career. He started in clubs in Dallas. In February he met Joie, and, as they say, the rest is history. Steve Watkins was born in Munich, Germany. Steve started playing music in 1966. "Everybody in my family took piano, and by the time it got around for me to take it, I didn't want to.

Mike Quine probably summed-up the overall feeling of the group best: "It's been real good. Of course, we're talking about family, now. How do you feel about your family? It's the same thing. I love everybody in the band. And there's lot of respect too. Joie's been an inspiration in a lot of ways. They've all been a lot of help to me. They've all helped me grow." Joie Jaye & Surge can be enjoyed Tuesday through Sunday from 8:30PM to 1:00AM at the **Somerset**, 5150 E. Speedway.

Joie Jaye & Surge, Cabaret Attractions & Talent. September 1980, *Tucson Teen - Limelight*. Page 9.

"First Wave" concert splashed out

Winter 1980-81, Youth Awareness Press. Page 8

The Serfers excite TCC fans that rush the stage to pogo with the band at the New Wave concert, November 13-15, 1980. Winter 1980-81, *Youth Awareness Press*. Page 8.

The first local New Wave concert was held at the **Tucson Community Center Music Hall** November 13-15, 1980, over three nights as a benefit for *Youth Awareness Press* teen newspaper. The surprise of the event was a new local reggae band called the **Upsetters** who just recently began playing in public. The other standout performance was by the **Serfers** who came back from Los Angeles for the weekend to play at TCC. Their extra dose of music brought many of their fans jumping on stage.

Straight Shot, Subterranean Blues Band, Backstreet Boogie Band, The Pills, Loudness One, Phantom Limbs and **Giant Sandworms** also performed during the three evenings.

Publicity was provided by **KWFM, KHYT, KLPX 96** Rock, **KTKT, KRQ** and **KZAZ**, the *Newsreal, Arizona Daily Star* and *Tucson Citizen*. The **Record Room** booked the bands and sold tickets with **Zip's Record Traders**. A light turnout of fans, though, did not stop the energy pulsated by the nine local bands who had performed.

Doc Holliday's Records & Tapes advertisement, September 1980, *Youth Awareness Press* archives.

1981: Evolving Music Trends

KTKT's new sound: Music changes trend

By Carol Tepper
September 1981 - Tucson Teen. Page 2

The new format of **KTKT** 99-AM radio station will no longer be rock and roll music. From now on, it is known as "adult contemporary music" station. This type of music is geared towards people in their mid-20s to early '40s. KTKT's program director, **Ed Alexander**, and the operations manager **Bobby Rivers**, have been planning the change since January (1981).

Until recently, KTKT was at the top of the Arbitron radio ratings. But, in the most current ratings, KTKT was shown to have fallen lower on the list. On the other hand, **KLPX**, the FM sister station of KTKT, had risen to become the Number One rock station in Tucson, Arizona. In a recent interview, Alexander told *Tucson Teen* that there was no sense fighting KLPX for the Number One rock slot.

Audience reactions to the change are mixed, according to Alexander. He said that the teens are "not crazy" about the change, but listeners aged 20 and older seem to like it.

Mike Cutchall, the general manager of **KRQQ**-FM radio station, said that it was too early to tell how KTKT's format change will affect KRQQ. He would guess, though, that the teenage listeners would go to KHYT and the older ones would come to his station to hear rock music.

The "American Top 40," *Billboard Magazine's* list of the top 40 hits of the week, will continue to be aired on KTKT every Sunday morning. Alexander said that the Top 40 show gives listeners a chance to hear current hits and to find out which records are being bought in America.

Royce, the assistant manager of **KHYT**, said that if his station were changing formats, he would have made a more definite change– like a shut down of the station for a few hours so people would realize the change.

Tucson's Favorites

Don Beetcher, Bill Murry, Kirk Russell Jim Bednarek, Kacie Sommers, Ed Alexander

Playin' the Best Music Tucson's Ever Heard

Call us 880-KTKT. Anytime

KTKT Joins the El Con
So. Arizona Values Energy Exhibition
This Sat. 11 a.m. - 3 p.m.

KTKT-AM playbill, 1979. L-R (kneeling) Jim Bednarek, Kacie Sommers; (standing) Don Beetcher, Bill Murry, Ed Alexander and Kirk Russell. Courtesy of Jim Bednarek.

Cox gets nod for Tucson cable TV

By Curtis Dutiel
November 1981 - Tucson Teen. Page 5

D o you ever want to watch two television programs that are on different channels at the same time? Then you may become very frustrated within the next few years. When Tucson gets it first cable TV service, the choices will become overwhelming.

Cox Cable, winner of the exclusive Tucson City cable contract, has promised to have some parts of Tucson wired for cable television within one year. The entire city, including Davis Monthan Air Force Base and South Tucson should be wired within the next three years.

For the basic 65-channel service, subscribers will pay a $6.95 monthly fee plus a $35 installation fee. For $9.95 a month, cable subscribers will receive 95 channels, according to Cox Cable's plan presented to the Mayor and City Council.

Subscribers will eventually be able to get helpful services, such as bank-at-home and shop-at-home for an additional fee. All movie and all sports channels will also be available, along with several public access channels for anybody who wants to make their own television show.

Simply Samples (Letty Zucker, owner), KTKT and the Workshop Music Store advertisements, *Tucson Teen*, September 1981, page 2.

Jonny Sevin: rising success

By Donna Morgan
December 1981 - Tucson Teen. Page 2

Jonny Sevin successfully completes their sixth performance by opening up for the **Romantics** on November 15th (1981). The crowd was pleased with their show, thus; giving Jonny Sevin the feedback that was so welcomed.

Jonny Sevin photo. *Tucson Teen* archives, December 1981.

In a personal interview with Jonny Sevin (bass guitarist), **Lee Joseph** describes the show as an "hour in heaven" while **Mark Smythe** (Lead vocalist-guitarist) said, "the lights, the crowd, and the applause were great."

Joe Dodge (guitarist and vocals) says, "The people are our fuel, they're what makes us run." The Jonny Sevin album will be released in the very near future, Jonny Sevin's influences are both different and alike.

Lee enjoys punk rock, rockabilly, early '60s and psychedelic music. Joe relates to the Sex Pistols and early Rolling Stones, with an influence of Keith Richards. Mark enjoys early blues music, the Sex Pistols and Alice Cooper. Joe loves Roxy Music and has been influenced by Tommy Ramone and Keith Moon. Jonny Sevin is made up of four completely different personalities that built the popularity they have achieved only after their first few performances. Their advice to struggling local bands is: unite, plan, practice and set goals.

White Lightning strikes innocent audiences

By Bennie Jasinowski
November 1981 and December 1981 - Tucson Teen. Page 3

It could happen to anyone. Even you. It's a Friday night and there's really not much to do in Tucson. You get together with some friends and head out to a few local establishments. So far, there's nothing too interesting; a band here, a band there ... You think they were live, but, you're not quite sure. Then suddenly, you walk through a door and ZUZAAAAAPPPP! You've just experienced a rare phenomenon, first hand, **White Lightning**!

White Lightning is **Mark Newland** on lead vocals, **Milton Cox** on rhythm guitar, **Jeff Stowe** on bass, **Brian Stowe** on lead guitar, and **Mike Davis**, on drums.

White Lightning is a select sampling of some of Tucson's veteran bands– **Oasis, Viper** and **Volts**. And let there be no mistake, White Lightning is heavy metal. In the December edition of *Tucson Teen*, this reporter will present an interview with the members of White Lightning. They gave some very electrifying answers to some very probing questions.

White Lightning, December 1981. *Tucson Teen* archives.

*This reporter was able to catch most of the band members of the local group **White Lightning** together at **Mike Davis** house one evening. Between **Mark Newland** (vocals), **Milton Cox** (rhythm guitar), **Mike Davis** (drums), (**Jeff and Brian Stowe** were missing), a 6-pack and Mike's laundry, it was a most memorable evening:*

TT: How did you come up with the name White Lightning?

Milt: We ran through about 50 names, and we all thought, "Nahhhh, no way." It's hard to get five people to agree on a name.

Mike: Once you get a name, you have to stick with it. If you keep changing the band's name, your following won't know who you are after awhile.

TT: How about some past history about the band members who played, where? Who does what?

Milt: I've been in this band for about two years, a yea year and a half, a year, somewhere around there. I've been in a couple of bands before this one, **Viper** and **Heavy Axe**. I've been playing mainly rhythm (guitar), not that much lead.

Mark: I'm formally from the band **Oasis**. I play some guitar and I sing ... I try ...

TT: How did you get into the band?

Mark: How did I get into this band? Pure luck.

Mike: We drew straws and we lost (laughter).

Mark: Brian said they were getting rid of Scott and I got in.

Mike: I used to play with **Volts**, a three-piece band that was around town for quite a few years. After that band broke up, I went into playing (clears throat and mumbles) country western, six nights a week. After that, I was approached by the Stowe brothers, and well…

TT: What's the band's view of drugs?

Mike: In the band, it's OUT.

Milt: Nobody in this band get high.

Mark: There's no drugs involved. We're serious about rock and roll.

Mike: I don't think anybody who plays music should do drugs before they get on stage. If anybody thinks that it makes them better, bull. They may think they sound better (laughter).

TT: What's your opinion of the clubs in Tucson? Places to go, things like that?

Mike: There aren't too many rock clubs, are there?

Mark: There's nothing to do here. Nothing. Music in Tucson is a drag, 'cause there aren't any good, hot, bands that have an image. But, we're trying to change that.

TT: Where do you see the band White Lightning in the future?

Mike: In the White House (laughter).

Mark: We want to run the White House!

Milt: Actually, our first step is to leave the city limits.

TT: What goals does the band have set up?

Mike: Millions of dollars (laughter).

Mark: We plan on turning on as many people as we can. Get a good name.

Milt: Our first goal is to get our name known throughout. Arizona. After that, I guess to get a couple of songs on record. Mark: To make a living at what we do, really. Our ultimate goal is to make some good rock and roll!

1982:
Revolving musicians

Tucson Teens– some bands bite the dust

By Mark Newland
February 1982 - Tucson Teen. Page 2

It seems that local bands are having a harder time than ever trying to make it, especially the teenage bands around Tucson who hardly ever get exposure. So, (as of February, 1982) this is the Tucson teen music scene: Bands like **White Lightning**, **Izia**, **Nitro**, **Harvey's Boys** and the **Pills** have bit the dust. As it settles, other bands like **Heavy Axe**, **Antariez Rayen** and **Jonny Sevin** are sweeping into the spotlight. **Rampage**, by the way, has gone off to L.A. to seek stardom.

A new mystery band is in the forming ready to dazzle Tucson teens. Keep an eye on this column for developments. This reporter, **Mark Newland**, formally from White Lightning, has a new song and will begin recording in a few weeks. **Randy Orange** seems nowhere insight, but *Tucson Teen* managed to get some comp albums from **Westwood Recording Studio** to give away to readers.

There is another band getting ready to play around town made up of high school students from Tucson. They are called **Base Six**. They plan to be opening with the *new* **Pills** soon. Base Six members are working towards a studio four track recording they want to market. The group plays all original music and is eager for Tucson teens to relate to their music. They will be playing at **Sahuaro High School** in March. Base Six was interviewed by *Tucson Teen* on **KHYT**'s "High School Hotline."

"High School Hotline" is a Sunday morning radio alternative show presented weekly by *Tucson Teen* during the spring. The informative program was taped on KHYT, Sundays at 8:00AM, with a wide variety of entertainment interviews, events, news and features, prepared by teens for teens. Interesting people like Bob Weir, Dana Hill, Devo, **Giant Sandworms**, The **Pills**, **Planned Parenthood**, *Tucson Citizen* film writer **Chuck Graham**, and others are featured. Concert and movie reviews are also included in the programs.

A pizza eating and video game contest was held as a fundraising event at **Chuck E. Cheese's Pizza** on Broadway and Camino Seco Blvd. on March 17, 1982.

Thanks to the efforts of the event, Chuck E. Cheese's, the **Tucson Zoological Society** and the **Tucson Youth Sports** athletic teams, a new elephant would once again stalk the cage at the **Reid Park Zoo** the next month.

The new elephant was named in a contest after its arrival from North Carolina. The elephant replaced **Sabu**, who recently was put to final rest because of a painful ailment from an injury.

Tucson Teen staff member **David Moskowitz** (left), with the winners of the Pac-Man video game competition, **Ricky Rivera** (not pictured) and runner up **Michelle Rivera**, at the Chuck E. Cheese's Pizza Parlor fundraiser. David, a Catalina High School student, joined the *Tucson Teen* newspaper staff at the end of December 1981 and was active for several years helping out at events, distribution and writing. Photo by Bob Jasinowski (3/17/1982).

Good news for local musicians

February 1982 - Tucson Teen

I f you've been wondering where the local music has been hiding, you might tune into 1330 **KHYT** on Sundays at midnight. Starting March 6th (1982), **Rick Medran** and **Jack Green** will co-host an hour of Tucson's talent.

"Of course, we'll be playing groups such as **Jonny Sevin**, **Chuck Wagon and the Wheels**, and **Street Pajama**," says KHYT's 19-year-old public affairs director and disc jockey Rick Medran. "But, we want to play some new local material as well."

"Local groups submitting records or tapes should make sure they are licensed," adds production manager and disc jockey Jack Green. "What we really want is to play original Tucson music."

Rick Medran, KHYT Disc Jockey, opens the music set for "Eighty Go Ninety" who performed during a *Tucson Teen* sponsored segment at the Pima County Fair.

Photo by Bob Jasinowski. February 1982. *Tucson Teen*.

Pills: Return to Transition

By Timothy Gassen
March 11-April 9, 1982 – Newsreal. Page 7

I know what I see
I see the tears
Of a burning tree
Of a tropical day

The Pills, circa 1982,
during a performance at
Sahuaro High School.
Entertainment Magazine photo
by Bob Jankowski.

"It's like we all got into a car accident two weeks ago," said **Robin Johnson** of the reincarnated **Pills**. [38] He was referring to the near fatal car wreck that put drummer **Rex Estell** into the hospital just one week before the band's opening show. The patient, well-rehearsed group was suddenly without a drummer, and it seemed that their spirit was broken.

"Music is a hard business," observed keyboardist, violinist, and sax man **Barry Smith**. "We've got to bounce back when things go wrong. The band quickly decided to do the show, and **Snowblind** drummer **Winston Watson** stepped in to handle the chore. The new Pills played with determination to the second largest **Night Train** audience ever. (Only the Blasters had a larger turnout.) Luck was against the band once more, however, as the sound system leapt out and crippled the performers. Mikes and speakers faded in and out, if they worked at all. "Sometimes it seems like things that are simple for other bands are almost insurmountable for us," lamented singer **Brian Smith**.

The faulty sound system could not blanket the fact that these new Pills are perhaps the most musically ambitious band ever to hit Tucson. Along with bassist **Fred Cross**, the band members are vocal in their assertions that their sound will break barriers. As Barry Smith points out, they are interested only in music "that comes from the heart."

The band is also vocal in its amazement and joy over Estell's rapid recovery. "He fell asleep at the wheel . . . and ran into the biggest cement pole possible at 50 miles an hour without waking up. But he's a healer," grinned Johnson. "Now he can talk when he holds his finger over his tracheotomy. It's like an intercom button or something."

---

[38] The **Pills** changed their named to **Gentlemen After Dark** in September 1982.

112

*The fatal winds
Of changing times
The fatal winds
Of modern times*

The Pills backstage at Sahuaro High School show. (R-L) Brian Smith, Barry Smith, Robin Johnson, Winston Wilson, Fred Cross. March 1982, *Entertainment Magazine* photo by Bob Jankowski.

Incredibly, Estell could be back playing drums within two or three months. He is recovering from numerous broken bones and a massive facial reconstruction. Still, he is apparently taking the trauma in stride. "He was playing the Talking Heads in intensive care on a ghetto blaster," said a chuckling Johnson.

It is unfair to compare the old Pills with the new. True, only one member is different, yet their musical approach is completely reversed. "Songs about girls, going on the road, drugs ... it's such a cliché, a thing of the past," contends Brian Smith. "To us now it's such a comedy what we used to sing about," added Johnson.

Certainly Barry Smith's role is one that sets the new Pills apart from the old days. His home designed keyboard and his saxophone bring great color to the band, but it is his violin that is perhaps the most impressive. Smith explains that, "A violin has personal character. It's hard to get an individual feeling with a synthesizer." That desired spirit of individualism is important to the entire band, he said.

Perhaps the most scrutinized member of the band is singer Brian Smith. He was much maligned for his vocals with the old Pills, and the criticism continues today. Smith is weary of the question. Johnson said strongly, "Brian is about ten times better than he was in the old band. He can sing and he's getting better and better." Brother Barry added that "Our style is much more important than if we sing perfectly or if I play my violin perfectly on key."

The group has also been criticized for retaining their old name. Not to worry, they say, because they're searching for a new title. The band contends that they needed the instant recognition of "the Pills" to get started, but it will soon be put to rest. These new Pills are going to be a powerful musical force once they overcome injury and insult. Time is on their side.

*I know what I hear
I hear the tune
Of a weathered dance
In a broken heart*

(Lyrics from "The Fatal Winds" by Brian Smith.)

Larry Miles: Spinning records for a living

By David Moskowitz
March 1982 - Tucson Teen. Page 15

L arry Miles, disc jockey at **KLPX/96 Rock**, has been interested in radio since he was a kid. "When I was eleven," Miles says, "in a little radio station down the street, there were these DJ's who would do these dances at night at the local playground and I got to talking to them. The guys would say, "Come on down, hang out." They would let me run the records. I'm running a radio station and I'm only eleven!"

"When I graduated out of high school," Miles told this reporter in a recent interview, "a friend of mine knew the DJ who was on a very prominent rock station in my home town in Pennsylvania. He got me in the studio a couple of times and I watched him do his thing. He said, "If you're that interested, go get yourself a license and then we'll make a tape and maybe get you a part time job here," which, in fact, I did. After a year and a half of part time jobs, I went into doing full time, nighttime, rock gigs there. It was like a Top 40 type of format." One of Miles favorite groups is Dakota, a group that was the warm up band for Queen.

Miles said, "Working in a radio station, you have to have a broad music interest in different bands and an open mind to flew music. I definitely do not like New Wave. Fortunately, it's dying the same way disco has. You're always going to have New Wave fans, but I don't get down on anybody for what they like, because everybody is entitled to their opinion."

Tucson Teen staff member David Moskowitz (right) talking with Larry Miles, March 1982. *Tucson Teen* archives.

"I find myself making tapes for listening in car that have various material on them. It's almost like a radio format: where you're playing hot tracks from band to band." Styx was Miles favorite band when he was a teenager.

"Equinox is probably Styx best album," he says. "That was the turning point in their career. It was also a favorite between me and a very special girlfriend in high school."

Miles once played Frisbee with Nancy Wilson of Heart, met Geddy Lee of Rush, interviewed the Cars and talked with Loverboy when they opened for April Wine. He says that musicians are just like normal people.

"Unfortunately, today its gotten much tougher for those of us in radio to even obtain backstage passes for concerts, because in the beginning of the tour, somebody from a radio station gets backstage and makes a real fool of himself," remarks Miles. "Instead of treating someone as a normal person, they treat him as like a big star."

His immediate goal is to be a program director of a radio station. He wants to be the person who can claim responsibility for a successful radio show, such as 96 Rock/KLPX. "The program director is the person who is basically responsible for what the station sounds like, and what music is being played. The program director picks the air shift and is pretty much responsible for the promotion the station does. Basically he runs the show."

For a teenager who wants to be a disc jockey, Miles suggests, "We had an amateur hour for awhile which a lot of high school students got involved. We are probably going to get back into it in the near future. That is a real good way of seeing a radio station, getting somewhat of an idea of how it works, and what is involved. There are a number of paths to take."

"The one thing people don't understand about disc jockeys is that we do have freedom to playa lot of music, but at the same time there is a systematic way of doing things as far as music is concerned. A typical Top 40 station plays a hit track within two hours. We aren't like that. We have a lot of music to expose that is news. There is a lot of old material that we like to expose. I get about five requests every five minutes. You take fifteen minutes of requests and that's an hour and fifteen minutes worth of music. We try to get everybody's request."

Reporter Chuck Graham on work and music

By Richard Whitmer
March 1982 - Tucson Teen. Page 16

A two-part interview with **Chuck Graham**, [39] music writer for the *Tucson Citizen*, will be featured on "High School Hotline," **KHYT**, Sunday, March 7th and 14th (1982).

What does the entertainment writer for a major daily newspaper do? What is it like to review concerts, albums, plays and movies or the media?

Graham gives his views as a music writer and critic in this special career-interest interview series. He discusses his background, the Tucson radio and local music scene and their directions. Graham graduated high school and college. Interestingly, he majored in Psychology. Graham finds it a valuable asset to his journalistic abilities.

Much of Graham's teenage years were spent wearing the "right" clothes, driving the "right" cars and hanging out with the "right" crowd. He said much of that has worn off and become less important to him.

Graham spoke to the *Tucson Teen* entertainment staff mid-February and discussed reviewing, interviewing, writing for a newspaper and the music scene. The staff learned new techniques to increase their reporting skills in this series of educational/training programs provided for the youth newspaper staff.

---

[39] **Chuck Graham** now publishes online "Let The Show Begin" at http://tucsonstage.com

Rick Allen: Radio as a career

Rick Allen, KWFM Music Director and afternoon announcer, shares his job experiences with the *Tucson Teen* Entertainment staff during a recent meeting. People from the media meet with the youth staff to help in their coverage and skill development in the newspaper and radio program. Other visitors as Chuck Graham from the *Arizona Daily Star*, Jill Shensul from the *Tucson Citizen* and DeeAnn Sheehan from KLPX-KTKT have spoke at the newspaper staff meetings. Photo by Bob Jankowski. April 1982, *Tucson Teen* archives.

By Lori Hornback and Neil Costin
April 1982 - Tucson Teen. Page 13

Rick Allen is the new kid on the block at radio station **KWFM**. His voice is heard every day from 2:00PM to 7:00PM.

Allen comes to Tucson from Steamboat Springs, Colorado, or as he put is "from oblivion to the 66th ranked market in the country." Not bad for a small town kid, a native of Thermopolis, Wyoming.

Allen was first on the air at age 14, full time, anchoring the TV news at age 16. As far as specific broadcasting training, Allen remarks, "I went through absolutely no schooling, yet had research work with a journalism class in high school plus community resource training.

However, not to put college training down, he did say, "I applied for college (to study radio) and was overqualified, having already met half of the requirements on my own, just by working in the business. I consequently went after a radio career."

One wonders about the longevity of a radio personality and how long one can keep going at such a pace that's needed for such work. In Allen's case, he wants his lifespan on the air, somewhere, to be "as long as I have my voice." However, the pressure is there. "When 1 was 16, 1 got two ulcers (and working on one now)."

His on-the-air roots include, "the only wind powered commercial radio station in the whole world (Steamboat Springs)." Allen's last place of employment in Steamboat Springs was a really small town. How small was it? "The kinds with only two stop lights, no pinball or hamburger joints for the kids to hang out." Allen is glued to music, "I once worked in a grocery store for two days," he remarked, "and couldn't handle it because there was no music. You name it and I'll listen to it– everything from classical to country music."

"As a long time listener to music, I think I can sense when an announcer is enjoying his work or just doing it because it's a job. " Fortunately, at KWFM, according to Allen, "all the DJ's are music fanatics." Comedy is an integral part of his program. Not out of necessity, but because he enjoys it. "I write my own material," he said, "and I've always been a fan of the top three, Carlin, Pryor and Williams."

September 1982: Local musicians release new tapes

By Joel Schenkenberg
September 1982 – The Magazine [40]

Lee Joseph, local record dealer, mover on the punk music scene, and bassist extraordinaire (**The Suspects, The White Pages, Suzan and the Erotics, Jonny Sevin, Audience Abuse, Sin of Detachment, E.S.S.**) recently formed Tucson's first independent punk label, **Iconoclast International**. So far, all the releases have been on cassette tape, but a release of a **Jacket Weather** EP and one from E.S.S. is on the way.

Seldoms: "What I did with my friend" (IC 8202). Two young punks meet up with an electronic drum unit, and with Lee Joseph producing, create one of the few truly original sounds in Punk.

Valley Fever. A Taste of Tucson's Underground (IC 8204). A double-length compilation type of the best of Tucson's new music bands. Runs the full spectrum from adolescent rage noise/punk, to more sophisticated avant-garde material. All the groups turn in good performances with Seldoms "Nothing Is" (Not on their tape), **Sin of Detachment**'s, "Greenworld" (not on their tape), **Pridy Stryange**'s "Jonestown," **Three American's** "I Never Did," **LJ's** "Worthless," and the **Phantom Limbs** "Blasé" being the standouts.

Jacket Weather: "It's A Wonderful War" (IC 8205) **Timothy Gassen's** lyrics are provocative. **Howard "Slitboy" Salmon**'s flashy pseudo-tribal drumming is superb. The synthesized music often seems perfunctory and not completely thought out. "Set Ajar" and "Statement" are the best tracks.

TV at your fingertips

September 1982 - The Magazine. Page 2

The merging to television, computers, the typewriter and video technology, inevitable as Eve and the apple, will personally wire each of our lives to the television tube.

Predictions for the beginning of the 21st Century, less than two decades away, foresees about 40% of Americans working from their television sets at home instead of going to the office. Schooling, banking, shopping, and other new possibilities will be brought to the home via home information systems.

"Videotex" will make its appearance in many households as cable TV will soon be introduced into Tucson by **Cox Cable**. The combination of current, and soon to be developed technology, will make it possible to conduct most of our daily activities without walking out the front door.

The phrase, "No more pencils, no more books..." may be a more than just a nursery rhyme.

---

[40] The *Magazine*, is a sister publication to the *Tucson Teen* also produced by **Robert Zucker** through **Southwest Alternatives Institute, Inc.** (SAI). The first edition was published in September 1982. The *Magazine* later published under the title the *Entertainment Magazine* beginning in April 1985.

Leanne McCabe: singing her heart out

By Aaron and Diana Rey
December 1982 – The Magazine

Seventeen-year-old vocalist **Leanne McCabe** has put in a lot of hard work and dedication since she started singing at the age of five in Cortez, Colorado where she began her singing career in church.

When McCabe came to Arizona with her parents ten years ago, she began harmonizing with other girls and eventually a church youth group was formed with the help of her mother, **Leora McCabe**, church members and Leanne's undeniable enthusiasm.

Her Sister, **Freda**, originally helped with arrangements of the music, practice sessions and her appearances.

This **Amphitheatre High School** junior is able to carry a song even when she jams with a group that doesn't know her music. Without loss of rhythm or beat, she knows her music and pulls the show through.

Last March (1981), **KIKX** radio station sponsored the "Wrangler Talent Search Contest" in Tucson where McCabe, singing her country-pop songs, placed and went to the state finals. Another contest at Mr. Lucky's in Phoenix brought her first place in September (1981).

In competition with professionals and seasoned talent, she continued to go on to the finals in November. Although she did not win the finals, she has had many band members and businessmen in Phoenix and Tucson states that she definitely is star material.

Throughout the summer, she jammed with different bands and sang with a group, called **Desert Show** for a few weeks. Most recently, she appeared at **Las Margaritas Restaurant Lounge** with her own band **Persuasion**, Singing those crystal clear notes and belting out sounds like "Silver Threads," "Delta Dawn," "Rocky Top," and "Nobody." With her charisma, her heart and soul seemingly in each song, her expression and feeling flow as if she lives each one.

"Not being old enough to go into different places and have friends be able to come, is definitely a disadvantage," said Ms. McCabe, also having to "give up Friday nights and dates when I have to work," she explains. Benefits include "making more money than in average jobs like my friends and I will be more prepared for this field when I am older. I am young right now and a novelty."

Where does McCabe want to go from here? "The top ... naturally," she said smiling. There was never a clear time of decision as she grew into this entertainment profession. "I guess when we started to get a band of my own," responded Ms. McCabe to the question of her career choice timing.

When asked if she had ever been discouraged, she empathically stated, "No." With more experience, connections and a lot of luck, the talent and stage presence of this young adult from Tucson will undoubtedly put her in the limelight for years to come.

Leanne and band member **Buddy Johnston** (lead), **Rob Eads** (piano), **Jimmy Epps** (drums) and **Cat Blue** (bass) are packing folks in at the Stockman's on Friday, Saturdays and Sunday, but only for those ages 19 and up.

(1st photo) Leanne McCabe photo by Mrs. Leora McCabe. The *Magazine*, December 1982.
(2nd photo) Leanne McCabe, EMC Entertainment, Tucson.

"Desert Tracks"
Tucson's best– together on one local album

By Elizabeth Bellamy
December 1982 – The Magazine

Every city has its own unique music scene with plenty of top bands hoping to make it big. In the past, most of these bands didn't get much notice on the radio and have had to stick to performing in nightclubs and out of the way places. Producing an album wasn't always as easy as it sounds. But lately, many radio stations, including country stations, have been devoting much time to local music. It has proved to be very popular.

One radio station is producing its own album to feature Tucson's best musicians. **"Desert Tracks"** is the name of the album in production by **KLPX** and is scheduled for release sometime this month. Over 150 songs were submitted to the stations "Rock to Riches" contest. The winning entries made it on the LP. The album features 10-13 songs each representing a wide variety of local music. Some bands include, **Troupe Deluxe, LFB & the Apocalypse Horns,** the **Moon Men, Crown Glass,** the **Randy Orange Band, Eclipse,** the **Night Rider,** the **Uptones** and **Fetish**.

Many radio stations across the country are producing such local music albums. Included with each album will be a ballot to vote for your favorite band on the LP. The band with the most votes will be the winner of the local contest and move on to the regional contest. That winner will then move on to the finals.

Tucson's 1982 Punk Rock Scene

By H. "Slitboy" Salmon
January 14-February 11, 1983 - Newsreal

Change is good, and so is growth and Tucson's punk underground showed signs of both. It was a year that started off real wide– the scene was disjointed and so diversified. Some bands were real serious, they'd left town to do well, and Tucson was behind them. That is, until most came back with unhappy confessions that were in stride as real life lessons.

But all of a sudden the bar scene was aching for some people to scrape off the mold that was caking on the teen-punk thrills for which their stages were made 'cuz the year started off with a scene that was jaded.

But don't get me wrong, it wasn't that bad. It's just that Tucson's nightlife has always had a tendency to be kinda slow– the scene needed more kids in order to grow! '82 (the early part) was working with the ghost of some "new wave" fun that had once been the most about 2-3 years ago, when it all started here, that was all in yesteryear.

We were groping for direction, we wanted some action we had three different bands, and three different factions!

(And the bands I'm talking about are the bands that have played most of their gigs at "that bar" on 4ᵗʰ Avenue!) They were **Sin of Detachment**, the **Seldoms** and **Conflict**– the latter being Tucson's token punk outfit and the former being more dirge-like and not as fast. They both released tapes on **Iconoclast International.** The label was young at the time and still forming, but the fires of inspiration they indeed were warming, for if they did anything, they focused our attention on the small-time garage bands who usually go without mention. And, just for background, between January and May there was the short-lived **Trout Unlimited** and **S.S.K**.

Jonny Sevin were briefly the big band but soon turned out to be a flash in the pan, the **Limbs** came back from San Francisco, and "new wave nights" were happening at discos, and that sounds kinda gross - you could hope for more, when not too long after Tucson goes hardcore! It was the hardcore uprising that provided the glue, it was fast and exciting (though it wasn't that new) and bands began thrashing toward one common vision: a world without supervision!

But the end of the summer is when the real fun began because Tucson sported three hardcore bands. There was **E.S.S**, **Civil Death** and **Conflict** and a great new faction of bands: psychedelic!

And, of course, there're the bands that are arty like **Clean Dog**, **Chromatics**, and **Yard Trauma** party (!) (Y'see the art school faction has always been around. It's just that they're the most underground!)

And there are also the new bands the scene's got in store, like the **Hecklers** and the **Corporate Whores.** The last four months have been the ones of most celebration while the previous eight were the ones of preparation! The scene's now got fanzines, some radio, some indie cassettes and visits from Black Flag, and Dream Syndicate, the Circle Jerks, the Necros, and Channel 3, and isn't it sickening reading all this in poetry? You might think that it's all just ego inflating when actually it's myself that I'm really nauseating– I like to make all of these gross generalizations, but enough of this song-song-like masturbation let's just hope that for the New Year the underground scene will shift into high-gear, that the punks will grow and the word will spread, that there'll be lots of great shows– enough said?

1982 Punk Chronology (a close-enough idea)

By H. "Slitboy" Salmon
January 14-February 11, 1983 - Newsreal

JANUARY-FEBRUARY (1982): **Giant Sandworms, Pills,** and **Loudness One** back from New York and laying low. **Jonny Sevin**'s album is out. **S.S.K.** (formerly called the **Jewels**) are gigging, **Conflict, Sin of Detachment** and **Seldoms** only bands in the punk (i.e. **Backstage**) scene. **Lee Joseph** starts **Iconoclast** International label and releases tapes by Sin of Detachment and Les Seldoms. **Phantom Limbs** get back from San Francisco. **S.O.S.** fanzine runs for one-ish. **Teardrop Explodes** plays the **UA Cellar.**

MARCH: **S.S.K.** leave to Oregon. Limbs' **Jim Parks** puts out one of his nameless fanzine's. Phoenix's Soylent Green, J.F.A., Grant and the **Geezers**, and Tucson's **Conflict** play big gig. **Whistling Shrimp Records** has radio smash-a-thon. **Virgin Vinyl** starts with **Jonathan L.**

APRIL: **Iconoclast** releases **Jacket Weather** and **Jim Parks** cassettes. **Voodoo Godhead** releases cassette single. Gigs: April 10th– **Sluts/Conflict**; April 23rd; Party Boys (L.A.)/**Jacket Weather**; April 24th: **Wasted Youth/Social Distortion/Conflict. Bad Brains** play at UA Cellar.

MAY: **Sin of Detachment** breaks up. **Chris Burroughs and the Nationals** form. **Jonny Sevin** breaks up. Gig with The **Cowgirls** on May 28th.

KLPX advertisement,
December 1983-January 1984, The *Magazine*.

1983:
Alternative Music
Scene Emerges

LeAnne McCabe: Taking it to the Top

By Diana Fuller-Rey
March 1983 – The Magazine. Page 4
March edition cover photo of LeAnne McCabe, by Ed Wagner.

Colorado-born bundle of joy and energy **LeAnne McCabe** is continuing her rise to popularity in Arizona and Colorado.

The drive and determination by both **LeAnne McCabe**, a student at **Amphitheatre High School**, and her mother **Leora McCabe**, has brought to life the dreams in their souls. Jamming around Tucson and entering contests brought her from the cocoon of her talent into a real butterfly of a show business bug.

"Music is an art and the most beautiful form of communication," seventeen-year old LeAnne said, "Music is something you have to live 24 hours a day and it makes me feel fulfilled."

What music has done for LeAnne has changed her life from an average teenager to a lifestyle that includes living in the almost totally adult world of professional artists and hard work.

"Sometimes I get real excited to go up and do the show, but It's not a matter of being nervous…just excited!" LeAnne remarked in a second *Magazine* interview.

What's it like for this talented Tucson youth to be on stage?

"It feels like you are there to relay a message to everyone in the audience and a little bit of me is in each song." she replied. "I feel that's the only way to get the songs across. You live a little part of each song at some point." Audiences are the most important part and LeAnne feels strongly that "If there are two people or five hundred you should still put on the same show."

When LeAnne came to Arizona with her parents ten years ago, she began harmonizing with other girls and eventually a church youth group was formed with the help of her mother. She started singing at the age of five in her hometown in Cortez, Colorado.

She plays a wide range of songs with her talented band **Persuasion**. Ranging from country, country/rock, pop and rock and roll. She brings a special flavor to the music. A song written for her to sing, "Look Out For Me," stirs emotion and feeling as she belts out the chords.

LeAnne currently performs at the **Old City Jail** weeknights and Saturday nights and will be in Colorado at the end of March. In April, she will be singing at the Festival '83; Nashville on the Desert and will do a show at the **Pima County Fair** on April 16, 1983.

LeAnne will appear for a special fundraising concert/dance at the new north side young adult club. **Sundance West** on March 20th. The event benefits *Magazine* and is sponsored in part by Sundance West and **KLPX**.

For aspiring young vocalists, LeAnne hesitantly explains, "It definitely depends on who would ask me. You have to look at it as a business, but you have to also want it badly enough to put up with the low parts because it is a hard life to live. If you want to move to the top and not just play the same gigs all the time. It really depends on your goals and if it is going to be just a side job to make money, you're going to stay at the same place forever." This is not LeAnne's goal...her plans are to take it to the top.

Sundance West advertisement from March 1983, The *Magazine*. Photo by Ed Wagner.

Singing her new hit: "Look Out For Me"

Magazine presents Tucson's own

LeAnne
in concert
with the **Persuasions**

at the all new young adult nightclub
Sundance West
3820 N. Oracle

Sunday, March 20th

One show only!
9-11 pm
Proceeds benefit "Magazine"

SUNDANCE WEST   KLPX

Sponsored by "Magazine," Sundance West and KLPX
FREE Record & T-Shirt
Giveaway from "Magazine"

Young adult club opens

A new young adult entertainment nightclub opens March 18th (1983) on Tucson's northwest side south of the **Tucson Mall**. **Joe Tofel**, owner of the new **Sundance West**, says the club is designed to provide a quality entertainment atmosphere.

Concerts and live bands will be featured throughout the week, as well as recorded dance tunes. Music videos will be projected onto a 14-foot screen inside one of the two gigantic rooms in the club. Sundance West's concert and dance side can hold over 1,000 people. The other side offers pool tables and video games. Non-alcoholic beverages and exotic drinks will be available with a wide selection of food. The club also hosts, an adult only After-Hours until 4:00AM, Local music will be showcased.

Sundance West is located at 3830 N. Oracle Road. Sundance West, in conjunction with **KLPX**, will host a *Magazine* benefit featuring Tucson's rising young star, **LeAnne McCabe**, in a special performance. Records and T-shirts will also be given away on this Sunday, March 20th evening event.

LFB: A sound looking for a name

LFB photo by Bruce Schockett. February 11-March 11, 1983, *Newsreal*. Page 7.

February 11-March 11, 1983 – Newsreal. Page 7

A band looking for a name. Indeed. The above six musicians who've been calling themselves lately **The New LFB** have undergone personnel changes since the departure of lead vocalist **Cecilee Streetman** and drummer **David Perry**. Streetman wants to go into other musical directions, as does Perry who left the avant-garde **Chromatics** earlier this year. Perry might rejoin Chromatics and **Clean Dog** guitarist **Steve Kennedy** to do some new projects.

Replacing the departed are vocalist **Andrea Munoz** who's past credits include the **Breeze** band. The new drummer is **Bryan Stewert** who has worked with **Pete Fine** and **Susan Kennedy**.

Also, the addition of keyboardist **Franz Thuringer** will inject a "higher energy, more of dance sound mixing funk/R&R/ jazz," says vocalist/bassist **Rick Pegram**. The two other remaining players besides Pegram are **Av Musiker** (guitar) and **Phil Krawzak** (sax and flute). This newer edition debuted at the now temporarily defunct **Yanks** on Friday, January 21st (1983).

A quick history check on LFB and The **Apocalypse Horns** (as they were known for quite some time) shows that a local doctor, **Stephan Scappa**, who long ago left for the scenic confines of Los Angeles, co-founded the big band (at times as many as 8-9 players) just about three years ago. In that time span almost thirty musicians have been a part of one of Tucson's oldest bands.

February 1983: Short Music Notes

February 11-March 11, 1983 – Newsreal. Page 7

Currently there are only two extremely arty bands in town, **Clean Dog** and now the **Swamis**. Multi-talented **Lawra Steelink**, the little lady with the jet black Mohawk hairstyle (also a Clean Dog), and **Lance Kaufman**, who recently jumped out of his "pajamas," along with **Nationals** drummer **Tom Larkins** (who seems to get faster every time I see him) and **Jimbo Miller**, also no longer wearing "pajamas," have a unique sound bearing no description. Their song list ranges from a haunting industrial original, "Hiroshima Maiden," in which Lance takes the lead, to a spastic dance number "Gloriani" with all the players making this a memorable piece. They will be making an appearance at **Nino's** (can you believe it?) on February 13th (1983). It's one thing to see them in a nonalcoholic environment. To see them in the atmosphere of a nightclub, I have a feeling it's going to be double the fun.

The Freds: Don Dalen and Richard Bade.
Entertainment Magazine photo by Fonda,
January 1, 1983.

Brace yourself! **Stainless Steel Kimono**– move over and make room for the **Freds**.

Citing personnel problems and musical self-definition in a much more competitive market (?) like Portland, Oregon, drummer **Spam** together with **Richard Bade** and **Don Dalen** are returning soon to the Old Pueblo. **Criss Dalen** is back east (NY) and **Steve Ferrart** is in New Jersey. Gaining a good learning experience from up there, the trio will regroup here, play some gigs and then, who knows? As Spam put it, "Les **SSK** est mort, vive le **Freds**."

Look for a new **Bob Meighan Band** soon. … Happy 3rd Anniversary to the **Los Lasers** who partied down with an over packed crowd at the **Country Club Lounge** ... Two clubs closed, hopefully temporarily in lieu of new owners, **Yanks** and the **Oxbow** ... A new club like the **Riverfront Inn** (the old **Cowboy Steakhouse** on 1st Avenue) seems to be holding their own, appealing to the 25-plus set. ... The **Stray Cat**, formerly **Dooley's**, now under new ownership, says it will have live music. No word on whom yet … **Lee Joseph** still hard at work on some new Tucson compilations. … **Westwood Recording Studio** has installed a new video playback and editing room. The **Hecklers** are about to release a nine-song cassette. **Jacket Weather's** LP in the pressing stage.

KOLD-TV advertisement, March 1983, The *Magazine*. Page 3.

Uptones return "home"

The Uptones, *Newsreal* photo by Bruce Schockett, February 1983. Page 10.

By Jane Jerome
February 11-March 11, 1983 – Newsreal. Page 7

The **Uptones** are one of Tucson's oldest reggae bands. They first played together on Halloween of 1980, and in the time since, the Uptones have become Tucson's favorite reggae band. Here's a brief rundown on where the Uptones have been and where they are likely to go.

The Uptones had their beginnings in a jazz group called the **Chameleons**. **Gerry DeMers**, bassist, and **John Sferra**, drummer were part of a house band doing jazz and rock numbers down at the **Chicago Bar**. Sometimes the Chameleons played reggae tunes, and then the crowd would pack the tiny dance floor. Seeing all those people move was a turn-on. When the time came to select a theme for an upcoming bash, it seemed natural to rehearse several sets of reggae. **Wes Lawson**, Gerry's roommate, was asked to play along on rhythm guitar, and the Uptones were formed.

Actually, the band was originally known as the **Upsetters**. They first started playing around town with **Jon Browning** on keyboards, **Zebo Miller** on percussion, and **Moses Smith**, who's currently vocalist with the **9th Street Checkers**. Shortly before appearing as the opening act for Steel Pulse's Spring '81 performance, the

Upsetters added **Mark Wilsey**, lead guitarist, to the ensemble. Then, prior to a date with Peter Tosh, the group started calling themselves the Uptones, since a Jamaican group had already laid claim to their old name.

As the **Uptones**, the band built upon the following they had attracted from concerts by appearing frequently at various Tucson clubs. In the autumn following the Tosh show, Zebo and Moses quit the group. The band's five-member core went into the studio with the **Big Roach Horns** and laid the tracks for a four song EP of original music. The record came out in the spring of '82. The Uptones were, by then, the toast of the town. Colorful posters advertising their shows decorated street corners and enthusiastic reggae fans crowded tighter clubs dates than proverbial sardines in a can.

At the height of their popularity, the Uptones left town and headed for the road. "Young Wesley" explains, "We wanted to travel and see what it was like back East. We didn't want to limit ourselves to one town." The Uptones played Santa Fe where, contrary to rumor, all went well, and then Knoxville during the World's Fair.

They took the tour to the Jersey shore where the band had some connections, and started out playing Rick's Café in Long Beach. Gerry says, "It was like starting over. Nobody had heard about the Uptones, though more people had heard about reggae." Things went well. The EP got airplay in the metro areas, and the Uptones could afford showcase performances in the major markets by playing the New Jersey club circuit. Although most towns in the East don't have as many reggae bands as Tucson, reggae music is a viable cultural force there. In fact, John's first serious exposure to reggae happened several summers ago, listening to WLIB-AM (New York), a commercial station that broadcasts reggae all day long. Still, the scene back East gets stale, especially when winter ventures along. After eight months on tour, the Uptones decided to go home, although the keyboard player, Jon Browning, chose to stay in NYC to pursue a career.

The Uptones think the energy in Tucson is great. John "Youth" Sferra comments, "I've never seen a better reggae crowd than in Tucson. There's nothing like it anywhere else. I don't know if it's the sunshine or what. Everybody's just feeling good all the time. You don't find that back East ... this town is hip to reggae more than any place we've been except Brooklyn, which is 60-70% Caribbean."

The Uptones returned to Arizona with twelve new songs, which everyone in the band helped to write, new equipment, and positive energy. Every member of the band thrives on performing reggae. Maybe Mark defines their philosophy best. "When we start playing reggae, first thing people start feeling is the beat in the music, and once you start dancing and getting into that groove, all of a sudden the words start coming through. There are great messages in reggae music. I personally love it. We're not Rastas, we're not Dreads. We belong to American culture. We try to apply reggae to the American culture and try to present some of that positive energy, the great love, and the great messages that are universal…we feel the messages of peace and love are for everybody."

Gerry adds that the Uptones music is "Reggae plus. We're sympathetic to Rastas in a lot of ways. We translate doctrines into our specific situations here in our culture, which is different." A more intuitive explanation is given by John, who says, "We're using all that we learned playing rock, jazz, and the blues, playing reggae… reggae gives you a more positive outlook. It puts you on the track– like seeing the paths better. It eliminates confusion…we love it, and people enjoy it."

The Uptones will be performing here with occasional appearances by special guests including the Big Roach Horns, a section of trombone, trumpet, and alto sax, and **Greg Armstrong** who is a sax, flute and keys player of **Ron Devous Revue** renown. While the group is preparing to play Tucson and Phoenix area clubs, The Uptones are planning an outdoor show that allows amply-sized dancing areas.

In May, the band will return to tour the Atlantic Seaboard seeking cooler summer days, exposure and new fans. Concert tapes, videos and more recording may be possible. But, the Uptones say, "Tucson always will remain home."

Serf's up for Green on Red

Green on Red
Tucson's loss — LA's gain

Green On Red. April, 1983 – *Newsreal* Cover photo.

February 11-March 11, 1983 – Newsreal. Page 10

Having evolved from the seeds germinated a year ago, the **Serfers** are now in their toddler stage and about to break into a run toward a successful musical future … is where we left off in August, 1980. They ran to L.A., changed the name from Serfers to **Green on Red** and after doing some roller coaster rides through reality, the band seems headed toward musical recognition.

"Recognition" seems more appropriate than "successful" because even though their debut 12 inch EP has been favorably reviewed in *Creem, Bam* and the *LA Times*. **Jack Waterson** (**GoR** bass player) is still on the bus at 8:15 to do warehouse work 'til 5:00. "Success" on the other hand seems to mean one can skip the 9 to 5 slide and cruise on the revenue generated by the creative endeavor and, according to Jack, the band hasn't reached that phase– yet.

Early Green On Red return to Tucson. *Newsreal* photo, February 8, 1985, Page 29.

Musically, it was a magical period for Tucson with a communal, innovative energy abounding in **Pearl's Hurricane Bar** and **Tumbleweeds**, but for the Serfers the sequence was coming full circle and burnout was setting in. Days were spent drinking beer and seeking smoke 'til stage time.

"We had kind of gotten down to the very depths of humanity living gig-to-gig… REAL, distraught. You reach a point when Halloween has gotta end," reflects Jack in a recent phone conversation. There were many doubts, but the intuitive feeling of the band was to move on and make music for a larger audience and although at times the obstacles seemed insurmountable, Jack (speaking for the band) says, "We're all glad we did it."

When they first arrived in L.A., Jack, **Chris Cacavas** (keyboard/vocals), **Dan Stuart** (guitar/vocals), and **Van** (drummer), lived in a studio apartment on Vine with some mice and a few other people. Only Dan was working. Van left L.A. on the same day Darby Crash OD'ed and John Lennon was shot, leaving a trio of Serfers behind. They didn't play music for a year.

In February of '81 a friend of theirs gave them money and told them to do a record. At that point Green on Red had no drummer, so they recruited **Alex Mac Nicol** for the sessions and he eventually became the permanent fourth member. Jack looks at the record project as a learning period, "you're aware of what only experience can teach you. You see all the truths ... and you see all the lies, and you know when somebody's trying to give you the knife."

They knew it wasn't worth playing gigs without "the ace up our sleeves," which was vinyl. In L.A., "very few bands become well-known without having a record behind them." The 12-inch EP was released in June. In the period between February and June they played as a trio and became "solid as hell." They also met "Comet Man" in the hall of their apartment building.

He was a black, funk bass player who played a left hand bass with his right hand and it was "like he was trippin'" when he played, his eyes would roll back in his head and sometimes he drooled. He used to tell us the only problem we had was we didn't have any soul. So he kinda gave us soul lessons."

They hung-out with Comet Man for about a month and then moved from the studio into a house. Alex began getting them music jobs that they played for free. In mid-August they landed an X gig and played with Lydia

Lunch the following night.

It looked as if the band was finally beginning to roll. But, by November the band made no progress and Alex became disheartened and left for New York. The sputtering stops and starts left the remaining members in a sad state. They didn't interact with their instruments and they had little to say to one another.

Alex returned from the Apple and although they hadn't practiced at all, they came and played in Tucson (February 1982) and were "flipped-out" by how good it sounded to them. Sometime after, they put out a demo tape and on May first they played in L.A., meeting members of the Dream Syndicate, which became a turning point for GoR.

They decided to have a barbeque and invited Dream Syndicate and members of other bands they had grown to respect. A communal feeling began to develop, as those Sunday parties became regular events. During one of those gatherings, GoR played their tape for Steve Wynn of Dream Syndicate and he decided to put out GoR's first album on his Down There label.

The gigs just started happening and they began playing an incredible amount of dates. They recently did six shows in four days, while doing their day jobs in between...crazed! Musically, Jack describes the band as an "electro-folk-combo" and they are as rebellious as ever. As in the **Serfers** days, they are still "revolting against everything we see as normal."

Dan Stuart sees the seeping of societal desperation from the urban landscape, then, lyrically etches his impressions onto a background of neo- psychedelic and the naive urgency of the folk era. Dan's voice lyrically conveys raw reality juxtaposed with Chris' sweet, almost lilting harmonies. Chris renders his organ riffs with Doors-esque textures while Jack and Alex provide precise rhythmic support.

Having suffered and squirmed through the head-reeling realities of rock, Green on Red is now headed onto the L.A. freeway toward musical "success." They are working on a second 1-inch EP to be produced by Steve Wynn and have several labels quite interested in them. Word is, these former desert rats will be bringing their anxiety ridden dance music to Tucson sometime next month– a party NOT to be missed!

A Limited Pressing 4-Song EP from Giant Sandworms and Chris Burroughs and the Nationals, "An Evening at Wildcat House," Sunday, May 1, 1983. The *Magazine/Entertainment Magazine* archives.

Burroughs & Sandworms: Rock and roll on a budget

By Roxanna Alday [41]
April 1983 – The Magazine. Page 8

If it is true that the best way to be successful is to act successful, then two local groups are well on their way. With their ambitious slogan, "Go National," **Chris Burroughs and the Nationals** display an optimism not often found among Tucson's rock and roll scene. And, rather than submitting to a flagging economy, the group has cut recording and distribution costs by teaming up with another locally acclaimed group, the **Giant Sandworms**.

Chris Burroughs and the Nationals.
Entertainment Magazine archives,
Steve Rabinowitz Productions.

Each group recorded two songs, producing an inflation fighting, four-song, EP of original music. The record will be available two nights only May 1st (1983) at the **Wildcat House**, and April 24th at Tempe's Devil House.

Although the words to the songs are cloudy at first listen, the musical/vocal mix is pleasing enough to guarantee the listening necessary for lyrical understanding.

The Giant Sandworms' "Cross of Wood," a song about the painful habit some people have of "crucifying" themselves, is especially beckoning. It's one of those tunes that seem instantly familiar. "Coalwalker," a song composed by the entire band, is about fire-walking High Priests.

Chris Burroughs composed and sings both "Last Call," a tune that chronicles the bar scene, and "Under the Ladder," a song about making a good impression.

While most bands become rich and famous before their early work becomes "collectable," these bands hope to reverse the process. Basic economic reasoning says that because the offer is limited, the EP will gain value as an "Instant collectors item."

Fortunately, there are more solid values offered in their music elements like effort, talent and experience ... and a sense of humor.

Audio cassette courtesy of SeMi-Round Records

---

[41] **Roxanna Alday**, former editor of *The Magazine*, passed away August 5, 2010 at age 52.

Teens in middle of Sundance West feud

By Roxanna Alday
May 1983 – Magazine. Page 7

In mid-March, a northwest side nightclub opened its doors to more than a thousand teenagers. The quarter-million dollar entertainment center, **Sundance West** at 3830 N. Oracle Road, originally intended to sell alcohol, but the neighbors organized their Neighborhood Watch group to successfully protest the club's liquor license application. Sundance West could not serve alcohol. Instead, it serves teenagers.

Within one month of opening night, the neighbors lodged 18 sworn complaints about noise and carried their feud to fuel the media. They said that the club attracted too many undesirable people, caused too much traffic and threatened their security. Many hours of interviews with the neighbors, who did not want to be quoted, gave conflicting statements about their feelings and motives towards the club.

In between stand the teenagers, who have found a new place to be on weekends. Unless it is at a school dance, the TCC or someone's house party, a minor has no place to dance and listen to live music. Those who do manage (reports from those as young as 15), usually slip into nightclub s with fake ID's.

Although Sundance West now caters mainly to a 13-18 year old age group, the club's owner, **Joe Tofel**, continues to seek a liquor license. The neighbors adamantly oppose the liquor license, and admit they would rather have it as a teen club if it can be well controlled and supervised.

After the first complaints were lodged, Tofel began remodeling immediately. More than $25,000 was spent to increase sound insulation and parking lot security. Tofel said that if given his liquor license, and an okay from the City, the club would be open for teens one night per week.

While the teenagers are enjoying their newfound dance hall, the City Council was bombarded with complaints. City authorities have suggested ways to enforce curfew violations of minors and have considered reprosecuting a law prohibiting dance halls within 500 feet of a residence. Everyone agrees that teenagers need a place to go, especially with summer approaching. It was a fluke that Sundance West opened as a teen club, but the response from thousands of teenagers who frequent the club demonstrates the need for this type of place in Tucson whether north, south, east or west. A nightclub for teenagers is a greatly needed idea...

(Editors note: For several weeks, the *Tucson Teen* newspaper hosted several teen dances at Sundance West and were caught up in the controversy.)

Curfew law to be enforced

May 1983 – Magazine. Page 7

The thirty-year old curfew law will be heavily enforced this summer (1983), according to Tucson authorities. Faced with another summer of very little for teenagers to do, the City Prosecutor's Officer is sending letters to all establishments where young adults frequent informing them of the curfew law and its enforcement.

According to Tucson City Ordinance 11-34: It is unlawful for any juvenile...to be, remain, loiter, or cruise in any vehicle, in, about or upon any place in the city away from the dwelling house or usual place of abode... between the hours of 10:00PM and 5:00AM if the juvenile is under 16 years old; and the hours are between midnight to 5:00AM, if the person has not yet reached his eighteenth birthday.

Sandworms: Desert Sophistication

Giant Sandworms members Scott Garber and Howe Gelb.
Magazine cover photo by Lydia L. Young, December 1984. Not pictured: Billy Sed and Dave Seger.

By Constance Commonplace
July 15-August 12, 1983 – Newsreal. Page 10

It's summer. The heat of the day can be assessed before ever opening a blind in the morning by sensing the quiet of the outdoors. A silence, broken only by the mating songs of the cicadas whose life span is so short they can't afford the luxury of waiting 'til the sun goes down.

'Yeah, but it's a dry heat,' is a true enough statement to an east coaster used to the moisture making-humidity. But, no matter how dry, at 101 degrees Tucsonans still sweat. We may moan about the cultural drought existing in our environment as our energy is being zapped by the sun– yet, we stay.

So why are we here? There seems to be an attraction about Tucson that seeps in and never quite leaves the bloodstream. Perhaps it's a matter of learning to survive on so little– like the saguaro growing in grains of intensely hot sand, getting minimal amounts of water yet greening and stretching their arms toward the sun. It is not all so bleak as we sip margaritas and tequila relaxing in our cultivated mañana attitudes or experiencing the wonder of a desert night with gnomes and UFOs dancing in the silhouette of mountains under spectacularly starry skies.

Tucson is a healthy incubating environment that allows us to stretch out and take risks. We are surrounded by an inexplicable energy that somehow nourishes the spirit– something magically magnetic that keeps sucking us back from wherever it is we go when we say we're finally getting out of this bloody town. Ask the Sandworms– for it is from this Sonoran desert that **the Giant Sandworms** were spawned and ran from only to return.

It has been three years this August (1983) since **Rainer Ptacek,** [42] invited his friend **Howe Gelb** to return to the desert and make music. "My first picture of the city's music scene was in June (1980). The **Pills** were playing on a Monday night and I went down with Rainer to see what was going on. We had left and come back as everybody was leaving the place. This car rolls around, does a u-turn and a guy gets out of the back rear window with a semiautomatic and starts opening up on the crowd. It was then we knew that people weren't happy with what was going on and needed something new," wryly recalls Gelb.

A few days later, drummer **Billy Sed** went to Howe and Rainer for a jam bringing guitarist **David Seger** along. Seger and Sed had been playing together for six years in this desert town. They tried to loosen up with the old standard, "Louie, Louie," and just couldn't do it. The next attempt was "Me and My Rocker" which "was awful, but there was a magic there."

The band (which was not yet the Sandworms) definitely had some beginning of a 'sound' yet was rather amorphous. Rainer's influence was felt in the rhythm and blues aura conveyed in some of the covers played by the band. There was no one arranger for the music. "Somebody would say what flavor they thought they wanted, but everyone would interpret that flavor differently," explained Howe. Somewhere along the way Rainer left the band and the remaining trio decided to make the musical move to New York. "We wanted to see what was going on," cites Howe, "which meant leaving the desert, making us very sad."

The cross-country trip was "wild" by their own description communicating via walkie-talkies and running out of money and gas. Settling in a rural New Jersey town close to the city limits, they practiced in what was once the lion house of the Ringling Brothers/Barnum and Bailey circus. The owner turned-out to be a bit of a maniac– "he had a nasty habit of shooting at werewolves and vampires in his house"– the Worms made the city move. Dredging through New York's outrageously priced apartments for two weeks while crashing on various friends' floors they met Larry, a red-haired Irishman who said with a bit of a brogue, "It's a great little place, you guys."

In a recent *Rolling Stone* article, reference was made to Toilet, a renowned scoring place on the Lower East Side. It was in a cubbyhole occupying the fifth floor of this building on Avenue B that the Sandworms called home. Once settled, they immediately began hitting the clubs and tried to find a place to play music. Appropriately enough, they connect with a Mexican man who rented practice space for a fee that seemed to vary with his mood but averaging about ten dollars an hour. Many of the popular neighborhood bands played there– popularity being determined by neighborhood demand and the amount of time put into the music. The Sandworms were not a popular band but began accumulating the necessary hours to become contenders for the coveted title of best band on Avenue B. Dropping off tapes and making continuous club cans consumed much of their time. Meanwhile...

Scott Garber, who currently plays bass with the Giant Sandworms, was not a Toilet resident (didn't even know the Sandworms existed), was doing the same dance with a more visually oriented beat. A landscape photographer from Rochester, New York, Garber was in the city hustling his portfolio around art galleries. Seems the thing was more S&M oriented. Success was contingent on who you knew and Garber never met the right ones. He wanted to photograph…the desert. So, Scott ran to the desert while the trio of Sandworms were running around the city he was running from.

The Sandworms played a few of the lesser known clubs and were told they had a "western sound," a definition they never quite understood. The first time they played "Mad City" (a popular Sandworm song) in CBGBs the

---

[42] **Rainer Ptacek** passed away on November 17, 1997 from a brain tumor discovered in early 1996. He was born on June 7, 1951 in East Berlin.

person at the board added echoes on the drum and vocals– it was a major awakening of what Sandworm music could become. They experienced an incredible high and felt that the dream freeway may be clearing a lane for them.

Reality and time tends to pale the techno-color quality of dreams and after months of slum living– the dream was over. Howe was in Atlantic City gambling, David was an x-ray technician in Jersey, and Billy was doing the city slide of trying to get by. At their various locations they learned they were booked at CBGB's for that night. Howe who was the farthest away arrived first with ten minutes before they were due on stage. Mishaps and breakdowns had to be dealt with and while they were setting up, Billy and David were ragging at each other. It was not a great gig. Though they persevered through the sequence of obstacles– the Giant Sandworms heard the call of the desert. David and Billy left the city slums and saw saguaros forty-two hours later. Howe stayed a bit longer selling Indian artifacts and pots in an American Indian art gallery and met someone who had connections at **Trax**– a coveted club date– but it was too late. Truly, it was a matter of just not the right time for Sandworm success.

Early photo of Giant Sand, sans Rainer, in New York before returning to the Old Pueblo. February 1985, *Newsreal*. Page 29.

Back in the desert the guys took a summer sabbatical ... from each other. The city scene had frayed some wires weakening the connections. Howe played with **Ned Sutton** in the Black Hills (South Dakota). Billy and David continued to play together.

Around July, Scott was introduced to David and the three began jamming on a regular basis. He was interested in joining the band as bassist that would allow David to get back to his preferred guitar. The only thing left was to talk to Howe about it when he returned from playing with Ned. "I remember the first time I met Howe," Scott conveys, "It was like the decision had come into town." Scott became a Sandworm.

Retrospectively, Howe feels the effects of the city on their music, "exorcised all of our demons toward each other and because of that we can perform and create together a lot better." The music that left the desert had become sophisticated, with crisp edges and a city strut enriched by a fourth member. Scott holds down the backbeat freeing Howe to interact with David and to play his keyboard more often. The band's original music has no real game plan. Each tune has a structure that each member builds his own sound around: Howe, the great experimenter; shy David, popster who lets his lyrics convey his message; Euro-techno is Scott's addition; and Billy is Mr. Soul himself.

The idea of an identity caused a bit of discussion as they felt they don't have one. Scott felt that the urban experience has been ingrained in their music, "the whole idea of cacophony, of everything happening at once is very much like the way the city is. For every city block there are at least five stories going on; someone trying to pick your pocket, people in business suits and folks with no arms or legs– all aspects of life occurring at the same time."

There have been four stages of evolution since the inception of the band and with Scott having been with the band for almost a year, Gelb feels they are moving into a fifth. No matter what phase of progression, the Giant Sandworms is one of the most exciting bands around. Each performance is fresh because they are free to interpret the song for that moment and the delivery conveys commitment to their craft. A Giant Sandworm's gig leaves you dripping with dance sweat and the satisfaction of being able to say, "I can feel the passion."

Lee Joseph: This man wants your tape!

By Brian Schottlaender
August 12-September 8, 1983 – Newsreal. Page 6

I n late 1981, two Tucson musicians, **Lee Joseph** of **Jonny Sevin** and **Chris Holliman** of the **Seldoms**, collaborated briefly under the name of **Sin of Detachment** and, eventually, recorded an 8-song cassette called "The Beauty Within."

Though not perhaps for general consumption, they thought it deserved a wider audience. As no local independent record/cassette label was likely to be receptive to Sin of Detachment's dark, alienated vision, Joseph and Holliman decided to form their own label. "The Beauty Within" then appeared in January of 1982 as the first release of the newly constituted **Iconoclast International**.

"A breaker or destroyer of images." Iconoclast. Though the name was Holliman's, the company very much turned out to be Joseph's, as Holiman (better known as **Chris Seldom**) soon returned to life on the other side of the recording console. Iconoclast International, however, kept on and continues to.

On the subject of that first release, Joseph is quite frank. He and his collaborator/former partner simply wanted others to hear their music. No rhetoric, no ideological statement: just get the music out. Already "in the can," moreover, were enough tunes by Tucson's **Seldoms** to comprise a 30-minute cassette. The music, in other words, was already there; now a mechanism for bringing it to an audience, however limited, was too.

Sin of Detachment, **Seldoms**, **Jacket Weather**, **Lance Kaufman**, , **E.S.S.** – all have appeared, in addition to several others, on the Iconoclast International label since its inception 18 months ago. The label's high output thus far (on the average of one release every 6½ weeks) is, at least in part, attributable to Joseph's apparent mastery of the art of keeping costs down. The *Arizona Daily Star*, in August of last year (8/22/82), reported that, "The way the Iconoclast artists do it, anybody and his dog can make a recording for as little as $20.00." The dollar figure may be a little low today, but the basic fact still obtains where possible, corners are cut (people's homes sometimes serve as "the recording studio." Live takes are often recorded on hand-held recorders or "ghetto blasters," often under dubious ambient conditions, etc.). The intent is always the same, however, get the music out.

To this end, Joseph, within boundaries defined by financial necessity and reality, expends no small amount of energy in the promotion and distribution of Iconoclast's products. Already, Rough Trade and Greenworld carry the label's offerings in their own, (much) larger distribution catalogs. Dutch East India, an East Coast distributor, will shortly do the same. The result, of course, is that the music *is* being heard. Various releases have been reviewed in *Maximum Rock and Roll*, *OP*, *Phenis*, and the aforementioned *Star*, generally favorably.

Currently, Lee Joseph is concentrating his efforts on raising capital in order to promote and distribute the artists signed to Iconoclast International even more widely. Not that the company's output shows any signs of diminishing. On the contrary, in the last six weeks alone, three new Iconoclast releases have been made available to the independent market: one each by **Yard Trauma** (Joseph's current band), **Jim Parks** and the Seldoms.

Lee Joseph photo, *Newsreal* archives.

KXCI to fill void

By Roberta Glick
July 1983 – Newsreal. Page 11

A local non-profit community radio station has been officially recognized by the Federal Communications Commission and has adopted the call letters **KXCI**. The station operates at 91.7 FM and will be on the air sometime in August, said **John Cannon**, director of development for the Tucson-based **Foundation for Creative Broadcasting**. [43]

Station Manager **Frank C. Milan** said the station will fill a void in Tucson radio. "The idea is not to compete with other stations but to complement them by programming things which aren't being addressed," he added. Since KXCI will have a wide variety of music ranging from morning meditation music to punk rock, a program guide for listeners will be printed and will be distributed at **7-Eleven** stores and local record shops. Programs will move incrementally from one musical format to another to avoid unnaturally abrupt changes in format. For example, the station may start out with classical music, then move to jazz and gradually go down the line to rock and roll or more progressive forms of music.

Milan said KXCI already has an extensive jazz collection donated by the wife of Tucson resident **John MacBride** after he died. The collection is said to contain nearly every jazz album released between 1940 and 1965. In addition to music, the station will broadcast public affairs shows and old radio programs such as "The Shadow," which was also donated by a Tucson resident.

The station is especially interested in producing opinionated and controversial programs. Commentaries will be no longer than eight minutes and will often include music relevant to particular issues. KXCI also encourages musicians in town to perform live concerts on the air.

"Anyone who wants to be on the air, live or on tape, must come to the station and fill out a program motivation sheet," Cannon explained. "The Community Advisory Committee will then consider it and ask whether or not the community needs this." Cannon said if enough musicians come to the studio and do the paper work there is a possibility of having a live rock and roll show aired regularly. "There is a lot of responsibility on these bands to take the initiative," expressed Cannon. "If there is a big request for this type of show, it is evident there is a need in the community for it." Milan said KXCI will feature personality shows in which disc jockeys can relax and "be themselves." They will be encouraged not to copy the voice of disc jockeys on commercial stations.

"We want our DJs to talk as if they are in your living room instead of talking to 500 people in a studio. We are not interested in voice training," he added. In addition to radio broadcasting KXCI will run a radio production school. Volunteers who want to work for the station will receive a free training session that will total 10 to 40 hours. This training session begins sometime in July. Funds for KXCI have been obtained primarily through benefit concerts, donations, and grants. The station recently received a $75,000 grant from the City of Tucson in order to train low-to-moderate income people in radio production.

KXCI will use production equipment donated by easy-listening station **KJOY (95 FM)**. The rest of the equipment, that Cannon said totals about $65,000, was purchased with money from fund drives and donations. The station hopes to have all the equipment paid off in five years, he said. KXCI's station building is located at 265 E. Congress St in Downtown Tucson.

---

[43] **The Foundation for Creative Broadcasting** co-founder Frank Milan was also one of the co-founders of *Southwest Alternatives Institute, Inc.* in 1977. SAI became a sponsor for the *Tucson Teen, Magazine* and *Entertainment Magazine* newspapers in 1982.

Radio Free America

July 15-August 12, 1983 – Newsreal. Page 10

T he previous claim that the alternatives of **KXCI** and **Virgin Vinyl** are both concrete and symbolic extensions of democracy beyond the confines of the radio dial rests on the fulfillment of community responsibilities. There are responsibilities attached to the privilege of making a profit from radio– whether it's advertisers or station owners– responsibilities that extend far beyond a few late-night public service announcements.

KXCI and Virgin Vinyl are examples of those responsibilities being taken seriously after years of neglect and/or condescending arrogance on the part of certain radio station owners and other powers that be, an arrogance that continues today in some circles. To preserve these alternatives to corporate rock radio is an act extending and rooting basic freedoms and rights as citizens of this nation. Freedom of speech, the pursuit of happiness, the right to know and freedom of expression.

Radio was so exciting in the '60s– with Chuck Berry, the Beatles, Aretha Franklin, Smokey Robinson, Desmond Dekker, the Supremes, Dylan and the Who all airing in the same show– not because the programmers were more public minded than those today; but because the possibility of such narrowly defined programming as Arbitron and the other computerized formats hadn't been realized. Now, with new developments and possibilities in data processing and profit making comes the need to review and debate accompanying responsibilities.

And, if established, most often conservative stations can't "justify" some specialty programming among their many broadcast hours (as with Virgin Vinyl), the community has a right to expect - and in many cases has received - other forms of cooperation and access, financially, or with the donation of equipment, or the sharing of expertise to help secure the "amazing variety" and diversity of KXCI.

Several stations have taken up this challenge, and the response is often more than a simple expression of good will. On commercial radio **KLPX** broadcasts a fine example of the rewards to be reaped by opening things up for new and local– "non-commercial"– talent to be heard by the public. The experiment has been so successful that they've repeatedly expanded the Virgin Vinyl show. Wonder of wonders, the target of the corporate advertisers– young, white males– more than tolerates listening to something new, and different from what we're told they enjoy. There's a lesson here that only the most jaded corporate heads should have trouble learning.

The Golden Age

W hen rock and roll itself was more diversely represented on the radio, listeners could hear what turned on other people. Tolerance for the music of others was bred. More open-minded attitudes tended to educate everyone in more healthy social relations. A perfect example is Aretha Franklin's "Think"– "think what you're trying to do to me." (Atlantic) Consider the effects of "Do right woman/do right man" or "Try a little tenderness."

Then, there was far more appreciation of the responsibilities that accompany freedoms. Today Billy Joel's "Tell Her About It" and Donna Summer's "She Works Hard for the Money," are relatively isolated examples of previously more prominent views. Whether or not they're our favorite style, they teach understanding as they entertain. Many hard rock programmers and DJs promote just the opposite outlook, fostering a closed view that excludes all but the chosen sound. Now, when more and more understanding is necessary between the sexes to chart a pleasurable course through the pitfalls of changing sexual roles; narrow formats breed intolerance and make it harder to find satisfaction … (I, can't get no ...)

All this is not to say that hard rock is bad. But there is tolerant rock and intolerant rock. Neither is it to say that there is no place of repetition and continuity, nor even a degree of conformity. It is to say that narrow, exclusive radio formats shouldn't stand alone. And in an ever-changing world, the bottom line can be seriously affected. Though the Arbitron stations were guaranteed their narrow market, other stations have had a chance to expand with creative programming. Experiments in Los Angeles, New York and Detroit with quite varied formats have blown the formula stations right out of the water.

But even if there isn't a rush to expand formats across the dial, we in Tucson have unique alternatives that deserve our active support. And while the experiments at **KXCI** and **KLPX**'s **Virgin Vinyl** offer a change of pace as true alternatives, they are also supplements to the dominant programming. KXCI and Virgin Vinyl shouldn't be heard as threats to established programmers as much as they are important parallel elements of our local culture– the new kids in the family of our growing community. Co-existence is fundamental. What makes **KWFM** or **KHYT**, or even **KXEW** popular doesn't directly affect KXCI, and vice versa. It is the existence of alternatives that makes everyone's lives fresher and easier, and makes radio listening a creative pleasure.

Other radio stations have a very direct interest in flourishing alternatives. KXCI and Virgin Vinyl are a testing ground for new music. If a tune airs on the alternatives and gets hot locally, such new hits can be picked before the conservative stations, and the national radio network can be influenced.

With the alternative shows staying up to date and a step ahead of the listening audience, established programmers and DJs have another resource from which to draw to enliven their attempts to lead and follow public opinion in the market place. KXCI also trains people in broadcasting skills, and is contributing to the development of an effective local labor pool.

From KXCI's First Newsletter

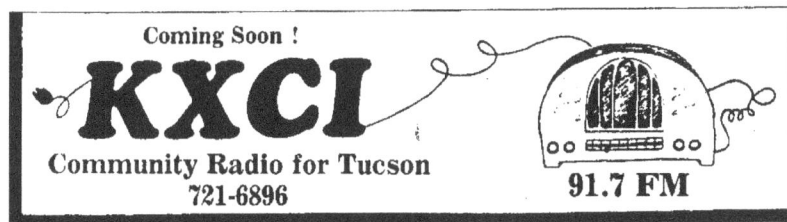

The origins of KXCI-FM go back to 1978 when seven community-minded individuals started the **Foundation for Creative Broadcasting** and began the long process of organization and federal approval. The first breakthrough was in May of 1981 when a new frequency was assigned to Tucson at 91.7 FM. The Construction Permit, for authority to build the station, was approved in October of 1982. Then in January, we moved into our new Downtown studio location at 145 E. Congress Street. We're on our own!

There is more to the ears than currently meets the airwaves. Radio today is an exercise in minimalism. The rule seems to be minimum overhead, maximum adherence to marketing formulas. Unique music, live performances, drama, children's programming, comedy, cultural critiques or simple new ideas while easily adapted to radio are almost never used in radio programming. Many of the sounds that add to the listener's quality of life sounds that lull, inform, excite, thrill, appeal, please or infuriate, never get broadcast. Community Radio KXCI-FM can change all that!

We have room to program everything. Imagine the return of eccentric DJ's, a locally written and performed radio play, an educational and entertaining hour for your children, cultural news, and airtime for special interest groups that would be otherwise without a forum. The station is engineered to play like a seismograph of its listeners. The station is a medium. We are the message (and in stereo, too!). We will complement what is currently on Tucson radio.

KXCI newsletter logo and content, March 1983, The *Magazine* archives.

Confused is all right

By Vicki Tama
August 12-September 9, 1983 – Newsreal. Page 14

The band at first glance appears to be slightly younger than the majority of bands here in Tucson. Clad in casual attire (including some vintage items dating back to the mid '60s), the band takes to the stage with a pleasant modesty.

Mark Mellinger and **Mark Houseknect** both play guitar, switching the lead and rhythm sections. **Rick Aikens** is on bass. **Rambler Kenton Aikens**, the youngest member of the group, plays drums. All of them are 20 years old except Rambler who still attends **Amphitheatre High School** and is but 16. Together, these young upstarts make up The **Confused**, a band that materialized little more than nine months ago.

Perhaps, you'd remember them better as **Chain Reaction**, a short-lived band that took shape about three years ago. While they gigged at high school dances, they were financed to produce one tape under the title, "No Wave." Two 45's were also released by **Chain Reaction** including "So Long John," a tribute to John Lennon, which received airplay on the **Virgin Vinyl** program.

The Confused. TOP: (L) Rambler Aikens. (R) Rick Aikens.
BOTTOM: (L) Mark Mellinger, (R) Mark Houseknect.
Photo by Vicki Tama. August 12-September 9, 1983 - *Newsreal*.

Page 14.

Mark Mellinger spoke about the somewhat naive attitude of Chain Reaction: "We thought we were going to make it because we were clean cut. We were more than clean cut. We were sterile."

"Yeah, and we did all covers. Beatles, Rolling Stones," Mark Houseknect voiced. "We wondered why we weren't the biggest thing in town, why people didn't take us seriously."

At this point, trying to classify their own music is something The Confused won't do because they're "still learning to write." For all intents and purposes their music maintains a late '60s mood with some '80s nuances tastefully placed throughout. Their originals contain a heavy influence of early Who music and bands similar to the Who. The songs themselves provide a wide range of moods and tend to talk about conflicts with people, with one person, with one's self.

Handling the performance is well done by The Confused. The two Marks combine their efforts as guitarists to create a good variety of changes within the songs. Rambler maintains his unique reputation of using busy drum rolls, as did the late Keith Moon. Rick throws in his punchy, creative bass licks and holds the sound together well. Most importantly, they don't pretend to be heroes on stage. Instead, they prefer to make a statement with their music without being overbearing. Rick commented on the band's respect for the '60s. "We respect the truth of it. That's the era when people were actually writing what they wanted to write."

"The old farts kept their hands off the music then," Mark Mellinger added.

Versatility is probably the band's strongest asset right now. With these writers and three vocalists on their front line, the band has the creative freedom needed to experiment with their songs. Consequently with The Confused you'll never get the same show twice.

Mark Mellinger confided, "If we only had one writer you would not be doing this interview. We would be boring as hell."

Ever changing, each of the band members has gone through some sour stages in their music careers. When things weren't so rosy, Mark Houseknect went through a period in which he wanted to offend his audience. Being so upset by the commercial, moneymaking sound, he wanted to play the complete opposite of pleasant. Rick left the band completely to play cover material (for financial reasons, of course), only to return immediately. Inevitably, through the sour stages The Confused have managed to pull together, developing their sound and doing some maturing in the process. Still they'll readily admit, "We're learning all the time. We're definitely not the band we're gonna be."

All of the band members have lived in Tucson most of their lives. They're not blinded– Tucson, in their eyes, has a few major faults although its music scene is moving in the right direction. The biggest complaint seems to be a common one as of late. Very few clubs in Tucson are willing to support modern, original, local music. **Nino's** and **Midnight Express** came to mind as the most supportive clubs. All the other clubs are "heavy metal" or "cover" bars.

"People just go there to get wasted ... the music hasn't progressed," Mark Houseknect stressed.

The Confused is a band to watch within the next few months. Their sound is refreshingly young and creative, This summer, The Confused are the opening act for the **Giant Sandworms** at Nino's, upon the Sandworms' request. The Confused were happy to find a supportive band to give a little spotlight. Mark Houseknect had this to say:

"If we make it big in Tucson within the next six months, the Giant Sandworms will have a lot to do with it. It says so much about a band when they have enough confidence in themselves to help out another band."

The next move for The Confused will be California, not to make it, but to learn more. Tucson is one big practice. The band wants to make their primary mistakes here and then move to a "better musical climate" where "cover bands are outcaste and original bands are getting a chance."

(Phantom) Limbs ready for 'romance'

By Jane Jerome
September 9-October 14, 1983 – Newsreal. Page 6

"You don't have to get metaphysical, baby, and pin me to the mat with your mind
No I hate it when you get metaphysical, cause I'm down for the count every time. . ."

With these cautionary lyrics from "Dead Languages" by **Jeff Keenan** of the **Phantom Limbs** ringing in one's ears, it seems best to stick to the facts.

Tucson's Phantom Limbs have been referred to as an analytical cowboy despair pop group passing themselves off as new wave dance musicians. It's an unusual description of the band's efforts, yet hardly a full accounting of the Limbs' activities.

The Phantom Limbs are, without a doubt, unique. The group is primarily a three-piece outfit– guitar, bass, and drums– yet they are extraordinary even in this. Melodies are usually played by **Jim Parks** on bass, while the rhythmic accompaniment is executed by Jeff Keenan on guitar. Variety is added since Jeff and Jim frequently exchange guitar and bass, and the Phantom Limbs occasionally use horn sections. Right now, **Linda Person**, a university student, and **Mike Sterner**, comic turned high school trumpeter, fill this role. **Lawra Steelink**, former **Clean Dog** and present-day San Franciscan, had played saxophone with the Limbs. Then too, Jeff has vowed that the Phantom Limbs will never, not in a million years, use synthesizers.

The Limbs are also the only surviving band from Tucson's early "new underground" days. Despite numerous personnel changes, the essential core of the group– Keenan and Parks– has been intact for more than three years.

The band had its beginnings in the heyday of **Pearl's Hurricane Bar** downtown, which many cite as the starting point of the entire punk/new wave scene here. Anyway, Keenan was writing short stories and song lyrics. It was only a matter of time before he began hanging out and playing with various local musicians and gained mastery of the guitar.

A group, **Ménage a Trois** with **Andrea Curtis**, drummer, and **Suzy Wren**, on bass, emerged. When Suzy left for L.A. in late '80 with the **Serfers** (now **Green on Red**), Jim Parks joined the band. They changed their name to the Phantom Limbs. At that time, Jim, before then a guitarist, took up the bass. When Andrea parted ways with the group in 1981 to tour the west with **Ned Sutton and the Rabbits**, an American folk outfit, **Howard Salmon** became the Limbs' drummer. Howie, who's gained notoriety as writer and publisher of the now defunct **Slit** fanzine, was no novice on the drums– he's worked with many local bands– and knew the drum parts to many Limbs' songs before the rehearsals.

The **Keenan/Parks/Salmon** incarnation of the Phantom Limbs recorded a full-length album this spring; the LP should be on sale in independent record stores even as you read this. The album, named "Romance," is in consideration of its several love songs– "Dead Languages," "Suicide" and "Wonderful World"– was recorded on the S.F. label, Modern Masters, and is being distributed nationally by Trotter Records. About 2,000 copies are being released.

Romance contains eleven quick tempo songs that could easily pass for new wave dance music, if not pop rock. The lyrics are, however, perhaps too despairing for Top 40 fodder. Instead, accept Keenan's definition of new wave as music that explores the many possibilities that exist. The **Phantom Limbs** combine different elements in wonder to subvert people's expectations, unlike much pop music that seems to reinforce cliché themes.

Jeff characterizes songwriting as the band's primary activity, saying, "What's always been most important is the material ... We have no reason for existing if we gave that up."

Keenan feels that "a good song, like a work of art or a film, should show people something and make them think about the way things are and the way they should be and can be."

"Psychology Today," released on an **Iconoclast** compilation tape, "Town Without Pity," attacks the insensibility of violence. The lyrics, which refer to **Tanya Robinson**, the murderer of **Bob Cook**, a most talented Tucson DJ, strike deep at the cause of insanity and subsequent crime: "I like thinking alone, and I like dreaming alone, and I like drinking alone, but I feel creepy alone."

Phantom Limbs (l-r) Jim Parks, Jeff Keenan and Howe Salmon. Photo by David Noriega, September 1983, *Newsreal.* Page 6.

The Limbs' lyrics are often quite startling. The songs are narrative and analytical, and might be called cynical were it not for the current of almost absurd humor that shows up constantly. "Bleak House" is a good example of this, its verse "Watch me rock/I go for a walk/Get hit by a truck/And now my friends/Have to leave the party/While they go/Identify the body/Hot toddy-hot-toddy/Identify the body/" and the chorus "Bleak House/It's the home of the human condition ... in the depths, immerse/Call a doctor, call a nurse/Tap his chest, tap his chest, Hope for the best, expect the worse/" are numbing.

Keenan says that lots of the Phantom Limbs' songs "have to do with the idea that life doesn't go the way it should and in general people are better off to wise up to that." Jim Parks' songs also reflect this theme, and in "Let's Party," he sings, "Life goes on and on and on/But that's okay. You're just a pawn/There ain't no right and there ain't no wrong/Let's party."

The arrangements of Phantom Limbs' songs are as unusual as their subject matter. A broad spectrum of musical influences are used with innovation and the results are both interesting and danceable. "Slice of Life" contrasts a dirge melody with a pop beat, while other songs, which frequently have quirky melodies in minor keys, borrow phrasing from twangy country music, surf classics, and sometimes, detective movie soundtracks. Even a cover of ZZ Top's "LeGrange" is transcendental, served up Texas barbeque style– red hot– as Jeff and Jim trade guitar and bass.

So what's the average performance like?

The Phantom Limbs, in vintage plaid shirts, baggy trousers, and dark glasses, doesn't look like the average would-be rock star group. Though unassuming, they command attention without being flashy. Jeff appears striking and remote, not strutful, but reflective. His delivery, at times oddly nasal, recalls the cockiness of Billy Idol, but never the self-indulgence of the ex-Generation X-ist. Jim seems nonchalant and stalwart, yet his "oohs" and "Aahs" give the Motown influence on a somber quality. Howie, intent on the swiftly changing and punched up drumming, allows an occasional grin to sweep across his face. Onstage, the group seems alternately relaxed performing the sassy "Wedding Ring on the Bathroom Floor," anguished during a sinister version of "Suicide," and then buoyant as they rave up a **Serfers'** cover "Get That Girl."

The Limbs plan to tour this fall in support of the "Romance" album. They'll play a dozen cities between San Francisco and Boston. Before then, the band must find a new drummer, since Salmon has decided to devote himself to philosophy studies before entering law school.

Al Perry, **Hecklers** guitarist, will join the Limbs for the six-week tour as roadie. Al sat in with the Phantom Limbs at various performances and can add guitar leads so dynamic that they might best be rated on a Richter scale.

As far as the long term goes, the Phantom Limbs don't want to put out a lot of records. Keenan doesn't want to be like some musicians, who keep grinding out albums with nothing fresh or original. "You get to the point where you repeat what you've said."

The group has no dreams of platinum records, either. Rather than seek international acclaim, the Phantom Limbs believe that "the whole idea of success has got to be an internal measure of you against your capabilities." Jeff is already surprised at the level of the Limbs' popularity within the Tucson nightclub scene. "I've always felt like we're getting away with something." Serious existentialist messages such as the Phantom Limbs routinely dwell upon, do, indeed, seem odd company for energetic dance tunes, but the music works.

In the group's three years together, the Limbs have composed a bevy of songs that sting pop sentimentality, refined their musicianship, and committed themselves to vinyl. Their worthy efforts have enlivened the Tucson rock scene and may, someday soon, reach music lovers across the nation.

KLPX Virgin Vinyl welcomes The Plimsouls with The Resistors and The Confused. Wildcat House, 1801 North Stone, September 22, 1983. Europa Productions.

How to Stuff A Wild Bikini

By Steven M. Rabinowitz
September 1983 – The Magazine archives

FIRST: Take Tucson's newest polished band, a rockabilly group called The **Anglers**, consisting of **Joe Dodge**, former of **Jonny Sevin**, on lead vocals **Al Perry**, from The **Hecklers**, on lead guitar; **Randy McReynolds**, sound man extraordinaire, on bass; and **Lance Kaufman** and **Tom Larkins**, both of **Chris Burroughs and The Nationals**, at the keyboards and vocals and on drums, respectively, and have them play forty-five minutes of the likes of Elvis and Jerry Lee Lewis.

NEXT: Show a half-hour of the best and the worst of the 1965 classic, "How To Stuff A Wild Bikini," starring Dwayne, Rickman, Annette Funicello, Buster Keaton and Frankie Avalon.

Avalon plays a young naval reservist who calls upon the services of a witch doctor (Keaton) to find out if his girl (Funicello) is remaining true to him while he's away. More nonsense than usual in this fourth in the AIP "beach" series– witchcraft, telepathy and astral projection, all in cartoony fashion, are on display here, along with music by The Kingsmen. Songs includes "Give Her Lovin'," "After the Party" and the title tune.

THEN: Showcase headliners Chris Burroughs and The Nationals for two sets of original, danceable rock and roll, laced with energetic cover songs from the '50s and '60s. Play more of the movie between Chris Burroughs sets and finish it off just before 1:00AM.

THEN: Begin all this at 9:00PM, Tuesday, September 27 (1983), at the **Wildcat House**, 1801 N. Stone and charge everyone two dollars to get in.

"How to Stuff A Wild Bikini" logo, Steve Rabinowitz, September 1983

Youth producing TV for the first time

September 1983 – The Magazine. Page 13

The first time a young person gets in front or behind a camera, amazing results can be accomplished. This summer (1983), several Tucson youth had the opportunity to videotape interviews, remote shootings and practice exercises in a public access cable television program operated by the **Youth Cable Consortium** with a grant from the **City of Tucson Cable Office**.

Students from **Tucson Job Corps** spend nearly ten hours a week in the program at the **Tucson YWCA Community Services Building** to develop video skills to produce an agency tape, a pilot variety show and a **Davis Monthan Hispanic Day** tape for military use.

Corps members **Elaine Lopez**, 19, **Cornell Elem**, 17, **Chuck Ellick**, 21, and **Xavier Yberra**, 18, have been working hard all summer long to use Youth Cable's video equipment and studio in this alternative learning class.

Tucson Unified School District One students enrolled in the **Professional Internship Program (PIP)** and seniors from **Arizona Jobs for Graduates** will gain video and journalism exposure this semester. **Chrissie Henderson**, 18, a **Rincon High** School PIP graduate is now Youth Cable's Assistant Producer who works with groups of young people in training and production.

A **Boy Scout's Explorer's Post** also meets to develop their video skills. There are about 20 active youth currently in Youth Cable with all types of talent and potential. They spend many hours each week experimenting and overcoming the mystique of the camera to feel comfortable enough to produce their own material. Many of the programs these youth are developing will be broadcast on **Cox Cable's Public Access Channel.** "VideoWaves," a two-hour teen talent show, is nearing the final editing stages.

Dozens of hours of weekend volunteers– carpentry, financial loans for wood, video equipment and materials have helped to construct Tucson's first, independent, community video studio for young adults, organizations and video producers. Youth Cable-trained students help videotape and assist groups in preparing half-inch VHS tapes.

Operated by members of the Youth Cable Consortium, the studio is used to videotape interviews, performances and presentations for public access cable television and closed circuit viewing. The studio can be rented by non-profit groups and youth in the community to produce video programming. Service exchanges can be considered.

The studio is located at the **YWCA Tucson** and Youth Cable headquarters, 738 N. 5th Avenue.

Crosswind: Local trio kicks up dust

By Mary Simon
October 1983 – The Magazine. Page 7

If talent, drive and determination are enough to make a local band succeed, three local **Santa Rita High** alumni, **Crosswind** (that's singular, folks) are well on their way.

Crosswind in performance, September 1983. The *Magazine* photo by Mary Simon.

Bassist **Charles Faucher**, 23; vocalist/guitarist **Terry Harper**, 19, and percussionist **Ross Smith**, 18, are paying their dues in local clubs with covers of everything you've heard on FM airwaves and a smattering of original songs written by lyricist Harper. All of the members collaborate on the new music with Harper providing the lead lines.

Both Harper and Faucher agree they would like to include more original music in their sets but feel that will come with time and exposure.

"Established bands have followings," explains Smith, referring to the band's preponderance of Top 40 covers, new and old.

"Groups get stale real fast. We get together two or three times a week to practice and learn new music," says Faucher. This in itself supports the professional attitude Crosswind displays on stage. Each band member works or goes to school full time when not playing music.

Because they play for the crowd, not just to it, Crosswind encourages– practically begs– for requests. They clearly want to please their audience. Judging from the small, but enthusiastic crowd recently at **Tequila Mockingbird**, they do.

"I have the napkins people bring up with requests on them at home," says Faucher. "That way, we keep current with what people want to hear what they are listening to." If Faucher is the conscience of the group, Harper is the heart, the diminutive drummer, Smith, is certainly the soul. He flails away at his drum kit like there was no tomorrow. It is in Smith's Solid, kinetic push, coupled with the versatile, crystalline voice of Harper, that makes the band so danceable.

From Dan Fogelberg to .38 Special, the Kinks to Bryan Adams, these guys have it and they give it. Their original songs, "Can't Get You Off My Mind," "Catch a Dream" and "Suddenly" also pack power.

Slit: Underground Notes

By H. "Slitboy" Salmon
December 10-January 14, 1983 – Newsreal. Page 18

Rumor has it that The **Marauders**, a great hard rock garage band, (who never played enough gigs, or the right gigs to make much of a difference) have broken up because the guitarist wants to move to L.A. to start a hardcore band. Too bad for Tucson– the one time that I saw them (at the UofA during lunchtime) they were lots of fun and had lots of energy.

Casio players **Timothy Gassen** and **Debbie Dickey** are driving back to Tucson (from Ohio) this month to record (with some friends) some new **Jacket Weather** songs for an upcoming, self-produced album. Jacket Weather, the "introspective" keyboards dance band (who incidentally have got a cassette release on **Iconoclast**) won a "most requested" band contest on **KHYT's "Tucson Music Show"** a few months ago, when they still had the old D.J.'s. There was supposed to be a gig at **Cowboy's** with the winners of the contest, but because the band was in different parts of the country at the time, the gig never happened. Besides, that was months ago– and now that the songwriters live in Ohio and other band members have other commitments, don't expect to see Jacket Weather playing gigs– but definitely keep an ear cocked for the album, which promises to have some great stuff on it!

I was walking around Speedway and Park, when all of a sudden I hear someone calling my name from a car in the street. It was **David Herbert** of Pre-**Pill**: fame! He's best known for his bass playing in the art funk band **Memory Product** (same band), who two years ago moved to San Francisco, changed their name (to Pre Fix) and recorded a single for Subterranean (which was released earlier this year). He provided early inspiration for **SLIT** mag when it was still a comic book, and, ... gosh! He's come back home! Welcome back to one of the pit stops of Western Civilization, Dave! Meanwhile, **Johnny Glenn**, **Pre-Fix's** guitarist, is living in Chicago, last time I heard.

The **E.S.S.** tape on Iconoclast got a good review in the national *Maximum Rock and Roll* fanzine. (Actually, it was more of a "review" of Arizona's musical open-mindedness, than anything else). Speaking of Iconoclast, Tucson's local tape label has plans for releasing another compilation tape, this one with fewer bands (about six), and with more time (about 15 minutes) given to each band. The bands featured will also be the ones who have shown that they can stay together long enough to have played a number of gigs.

Pen Pendleton, former drummer for frat-rockers **Jonny Sevin**, was in town for Thanksgiving recently. Pen is now living in L.A. and looking for a job. He's not interested in getting another band together (he's had his fling), but ex-guitarist **Mark** is. He's living in L.A. too, and last I heard, he had a band called "The Bystanders." Anyone wanna dance?

Green On Red are now a 5-pieceband, having added **Rain Parade's** guitarist to their line-up.

Even though the flyers were put up nine hours before the show actually happened, the Nov. 12th **Circle Jerks** gig was a huge success! People from Phoenix were down here, but they weren't the fools who like to start fights, so as a result, it was lots of fun. Let's all thank **Nick (Civil Death)** for going out of his way to take care of all of the last minute arrangements!

Silent XChange: Local XChange

By Jacqueline Blancato
December 1983 - January 1984 - The Magazine. Page 6

Record companies receive over 400 tapes a week from bands hoping to top the charts with their "unique sound" or "different style." However, the three members of **Silent XChange**, a rising Tucson band, feel their array of original songs are the element that will initiate their steep climb up the ladder of success.

"In my opinion, what separates us from the other bands is the fact that our songs don't all sound the same," says **Michael St. Paul** songwriter, singer and bassist for Silent XChange, "A lot of bands have one really good song and the rest are terrible. They all sound the same."

The three members include St. Paul from Wurzburg, Germany, **Robert David** from Cleveland, Ohio, and **Phyner Scott** from Tucson.

They began their careers in Tucson with a band called the **Flight**. The four-man band made a tape in 1981. However, they did not gain audience experience because they did not play in public often.

"We didn't play towards success, we just talked about it," Scott remarks.

The Flight separated. With the split came a whole new image for the three remaining members. They changed their name to the **Amerikaans**, but only for one show. They officially became Silent XChange in October 1983 at a **University of Arizona** performance.

"While other bands write about sex and drugs, we write about refreshing things. We try to stay away from negative things," said St. Paul.

Photo of XChange by Jacqueline Blancato.
Musicland advertisement, The *Magazine*.

Los Lasers legend and myths

By Caylah Eddleblute
November 11-December 9, 1983 – Newsreal. Page 12

T he humorously jabbing lyrics songwriter **George Hawke** pens, combined with well blended arrangements and a solid rock and roll base, peppered with **Randy Lopez** upbeat sax makes for a rowdy and danceable time.

Evolving from what was primarily a horn band, members George Hawke (vocals, guitar), Lopez (keyboards, sax), **Danny Cox** (lead guitar), **Steve Grams** (bass) and **Marx B. Loeb III** (drums) decided to bend to a more pop sound, according to Marx.

Los Lasers (l-r) Cox, Grams, Loeb III, Hawke and Lopez. *Newsreal* photo by Caylah Eddleblute, November 1983. Page 12.

There were a number of reasons for that change, he said, one of which was that Hawke had been listening to a lot of music and decided, as Marx put it, "we are not exactly going to kick national ass with blues shuffles. It just won't happen."

Over the years the group has created a part mythical, part real character, practically as infamous as the band itself, the "Los Lasers fan." More on that later. First, a little history.

Most folks who have resided in the Old Pueblo for any length of time know George Hawke has been writing songs for a long while. He has been wise and lucky enough to collect royalties for some of his compositions performed by "knowns" in the business like gut crooner Hoyt Axton. Years ago, Hawke played in a band called the **Dusty Chaps**. These guys played the kind of music **Dancing Dan** and the **Stumble Inn** would capitalize on eons later. Country swing … ten years ago.

So innovation, going for the out of the ordinary, is a big part of what Los Lasers is all about. Like when the band first started playing. They made their home out in the sticks at a place called the **Country Club Lounge**.

"The band started playing The Lounge specifically because it was out of the way and there was absolutely nothing going on," explains Marx. "We had to build that up, and at the time a lot of bar owners in town wouldn't even consider it." At that point, recorded music was the rage for most clubs– one less expense plus that stickler– trying to define their music. The band, wonderfully, fits no mold. That's not to say people don't try to find one for them.

"It's funny," commented Grams, who looks part mountain-man with shoulder length hair and a full, speckled beard. "If you talk to someone in their thirties, they think we're New Wave. If you talk to someone in their twenties, they think we're old farts playing something they have no idea of ... Lithuanian folk music. I was thinking, if we all went back East for punk therapy, if we all came back and weighed 90 pounds, had spiked hair, 43 safety pins in our ears, and holes in our T-shirts, I bet the scene makers would love us - playing the same music but they would love us because we looked the part."

Grams feels that their age (30-ish) is part of what makes the band difficult to label. "Fuck, the guitarist for the Police is 42 years old. Sting is in his mid-thirties," he said. "Those guys aren't kids. Not everyone doing record deals and having hits is 19."

Meanwhile, as the County Club Lounge was in the process of losing its beer and wine license, the band was negotiating to play at **Characters**, "in town," and have been there every weekend for the past several months.

"Actually, we have developed a whole new audience," said Grams. "There are still the same old regulars, but a lot of the people I used to see at The Lounge every weekend, I see now once every couple of months. It's as if they still cling to the mystique of The Lounge ... that had no mystique. We just don't seem to draw a college crowd. I guess we don't have the right haircuts or something." Having stuck it out for so long, the band is obviously familiar with the frustrations of surviving in Tucson's varied musical landscape.

Said Marx, "People will bitch that there is no music here, or that they don't like the bands. Well, if they don't go out and find it, they're not going to know about it! Then, when the bands do break up, people tend to get pissed off and say 'hey, why did you guys break up?' Well, we weren't about to make a living."

"It amazes me," Marx continued, "we were talking last night about this article in *Newsreal* about the **Freds** wanting to start a scene at the **Manhattan**, which is where we drink after rehearsal. Anyway, if they want to start a scene there, if they want to take their lives in their hands or bring in armed guards. That's fine. I could see a lot of these real tough proto-punks stopping down at the Manhattan to rub noses and act bad with some bad ass Indians, and have someone stick a knife in their back."

"The whole thing about starting a scene...there already is a scene." And what about the "Laser fan." Well, according to Grams, the band draws mainly an older crowd– artists, professionals, people that like to drink– and that makes club owners very happy. "Usually a younger crowd will drink beer and nurse it all night, 'cause it's cheap," said Grams. "The people we seem to draw don't drink beer unless they're playing softball on Sunday afternoon." And as Grams said, who at one time played with **Ned Sutton and the Rabbits**, then a non-drawing band, "it's all simple economics. If a band draws, club owners tend to treat its members well. If not ... we know the story."

"I thought the quote about us was real nice," said Marx. ("**Los Lasers** could play in the middle of fucking nowhere and their following would go see them," said Freds' bassist, **Richard Bade** from October 1983, *Newsreal*). I don't know if they meant it or not. The weird thing is that it's not true. People think it's true. But if that were so we'd probably still be playing at **Rockefeller's**." And, what about the six months LL played at the now legendary **Night Train**, and their crowd never showed up. Or the time they played at NT for six people, one of whom was ZZ Top's Billy Gibbons. "He (Gibbons) stayed for three songs and left," said Marx, "because we were so depressed we couldn't handle it."

While Los Lasers play weekends, **L Mondo Combo** (LL minus Hawke) can usually be found jamming on Thursday nights playing obscure R&B tunes. Cox's influence in this facet is evident as he supplies a lot of the material, and sings on the majority of the numbers.

¿Que Onda? Where's the alternative music?? KXCI!

By Mary Simon
December 1983-January 1984 - The Magazine. Page 7

Alternative radio has reared its fragile head in the form of **KXCI** community radio– 91.7 FM on the dial. **John Cannon**, KXCI Director of Development, said the station is now on the air in set format. You can take my word for it that the format is so varied you need a scorecard to get it straight. Programming guides are available at KXCI studios at 145 E. Congress Street and several record stores including **Zip's Record Bar** and **Al Bums**. A veritable licorice feast is being played from 12:00AM to 1:00AM. Name your passion: jazz, rock, classical, big band or blues.

Local music promoter **Steve Rabinowitz** said two programs of purely local interest, "Right in Our Own Backyard," and "Kountry Tucson," will air Mondays from 9:00PM to 11:00PM. Local musicians are encouraged to bring material for consideration for airing on KXCI. If none of this interests you, perhaps Sunday nights at 6:00PM you can tune in to find out what "The Shadow" knows or listen to an avaricious "Jack Benny Show."

Statesboro changes

On other musical fronts, **Don Lupo**, bassist, has retired from the **Statesboro Blues Band**. Bassist extraordinaire **Bob Benedon** has taken his place. Benedon played with the **Subterranean Blues Band**. He now joins two other ex-Subterranean **George Howard** and **Pat McAndrew** with Statesboro. The band occasionally plays at the **Riverfront Saloon** and has a New Years Eve performance scheduled at **Nino's**.

"Subterranean Blues was more on the rock side of blues," says Benedon. "Statesboro Blues Bend is more on the rhythm and blues side." **Brooks Keenan** and **Bruce Tost** are also members of the Statesboro Blues Band. Benedon hopes the blues concept will become as popular as jazz in Tucson.

1983: *Newsreal's* Best of the Year

Best Independent Arizona
Cassette Release of 1983
Howe Gelb

Best Arizona Recording of 1983
4-Song EP (GAD Records)

Most Promising New
Tucson Artist of 1983
Van Christian

From the original layout flat for "Faves of '83." Photos by Maggie Heydt, January 15-February 10, 1984, *Newsreal*. Page 2.

1984:
Rock Reigns
Hardcore Fledges

Updating Tucson Music

By Jonathan L
February 10-March 9, 1984 – Newsreal. Page 14

After near dormancy for the past couple months, a lot of positive changes have occurred among Tucson musicians. **Rainer** has a lot to beam about this month. Through a musical friendship with ZZ Top's Billy Gibbons, who saw Rainer at **Nino's** many months ago, touring *Rolling Stone* editor Kurt Loder interviewed Tucson's guitar wiz last week. Look for a hopeful review of Rainer's independently released cassette "Mush Mind Blues" in a soon to be published issue of *RS*.

Lee Joseph, more than just a musician, is leaving to relocate in Los Angeles. The charismatic bassist (**White Pages**, **Suzan and The Erotics**, **Jonny Sevin**, **E.S.S.**, **Sin of Detachment**, **Clean Dog**, and **Yard Trauma**) is joining a '60s styled psychedelic band, The **Unclaimed**. He will play guitar and keyboards.

As far as his **Iconoclast International** cassette label and his compilation projects with **Bomp Records** are concerned, he will pick up steam on them once he gets settled in L.A.

One Tucson band touring this month was **Phantom Limbs** original members **Jeff Keenan** and **Jim Parks** along with new drummer **Cheryl Graham (Seldoms)**, **Al Perry (Hecklers)** as "roadie," and **Dave Robey (Hecklers)** doing sound, traveled to sunny California.

Beginning in San Diego, the adventurous Limbs plus two opened for the Fleshtones at the Spirit Club (Jan. 28th) before a well-attended audience. Next on the agenda was a show in Los Angeles at Madam Wong's with Urban Gypsy's. Moving further north the Limbs did two shows in the Bay Area. First was a show at Dirk Dirkson's On Broadway in San Francisco, second was Berkeley Square with Perfekt Strangers. Last on the two week agenda was a date at Cathay de Grande in L.A., then back home. According to Keenan, everything went well. The band was interviewed in Berkeley and San Diego, and generally, it felt good to leave for a short time.

New bands on the scene to watch are **Lance Kaufman's Soul Rebels**, **Jack Martinez's Only's**, a revised Animation and **Rick Medran's Suspicious**. The latest cassette to hit the shelves of some local vinyl dens is **Fish Karma's** "To Hell with Love, I'm Going Bowling."

In parting, the **Giant Sandworms** will be leaving mid-month to record for **Bob Lambert** (former owner of **Whistling Shrimp Records**) in Denver, Colorado. All four are looking forward to the sessions and change of scenery. The Worms will return to Tucson in the beginning of March (1984).

January 1984: Jazz, blues, country punks

By Mary Simon
February 1984 - The Magazine. Page 15

¡Oralé, Tucson! ("Listen Up, Tucson!") First, there is an exceptionally talented group of Tucson men who are translating a form of gritty American music seldom heard here – the Blues. To be from Detroit, Chicago or St. Louis and expect anything more than mainstream rock and country in Arizona is to displace hope. To boogie with the **Statesboro Blues Band** is to go home.

The **SBB** men have a good century between them of hard paid dues behind every note they lay down and it shows. Surely the ticket buyers at the **Marriott Hotel**'s 2nd Annual Jazz Wars agreed.

They voted the SBB second place winners in a contest that included the best jazz competition in Tucson offers. First place was taken by **Bitches Brew**, an all female band. All five members of SBB have been involved in music for the better part of their lives. And music is the better part of their lives. All five are also employed full time. Catch their act this month at both **Terry & Zeke's** and **Nino's**. Dates are listed in the Events section.

On February 2nd, **Characters** will host the second Country Punks concert. Up first are the **Hecklers** with their own brand of country punk-country trash a speeded up hardcore approach to the usual tunes.

Next on the stage are **The Good, The Bad and The Ugly** with **Howe Gelb** at the helm. The band also includes **Jack Martinez**, ex-**Chris Burroughs and the Nationals** and **Van Christian** of the **Naked Prey**. They will play Gelb originals and be followed by the **Phantom Hombres**, better known as the **Phantom Limbs**.

Closing is **Jorge Gavilan** and the **Ovalteens**. English translation– **George Hawke** and a country band played by most of **Los Lasers**.

With the **Ovalteens** will be **Neil Harry** (ex-**Dusty Chaps** and **Chuck Wagon and the Wheels** and **Bill Emery** (ex-Chaps and the **Two Bills**). Another fiddle player also will join the band. Some of the shows will be broadcast **KXCI**.

Other local notes: What has been the **Longhorn Saloon** is once again called **Road to Ruin**. It features live rock and in the future may book nationally known acts.

As soon as the **Sundance West** on Oracle Road finally gets its liquor license, which should be next month, its format will be live country music with plans for national acts in concert.

Terry & Zeke's advertisement, The *Magazine*, February 1984. Page 15.

Statesboro Blues Band: Happy with the blues

Photo of Statesboro Blues Band from L-R: Patrick McAndrew, Bruce Tost, Brooks Keenan, George Howard, Bob Benedon, *The Magazine*, January, 1984.

By Mary Simon
March 1984 - The Magazine. Page 19

Editor's note: Last month, the Statesboro Blues Band was introduced in the ¿Que Onda? column which spotlights local music. This month completes a full profile on the band.

The *Magazine* has been dogging the footsteps notes of the five members of the **Statesboro Blues Band** for nigh on to a month and a half and can report that they do indeed have the right amount of funk.

When first seen at the home of harp and keyboard player **Brooks Keenan**, the men in the band were worried about set structure– that is which songs should be included in a particular set and in what order.

Guitarist **Patrick McAndrew** asks, "Aren't we pandering to the audience including (commercial) hit like this?" They had just finished a truly elevating rendition of Jack Wilson's "Your Love (Is Lifting Me Higher)" and were considering what to continue with next.

Professional concern is not wasted on the audiences the SBB performs to **Terry & Zeke's**. As a friend with me commented, "So, this is where all those people go." Those people are the hardcore dancers, jazz and music lovers who populate a good entertainment establishment. They did not look like they would take much pandering.

But, any band with exuberant talent and expertise of the men in this band are probably only equaled only by the **Tucson Symphony Orchestra**.

Comprising the rest of the band are **George Howard** on drums and most vocals; **Bob Benedon** on bass and **Bruce Tost** the omnipresent saxophone player whose loomy presence dominates proceedings.

Howard, from Asbury Park, N.J. is a professional photographer. He says he got burned out working in the finance department of banks for 10-15 years. He has played with Benedon and McAndrew in the **Subterranean Blues Band**, a group that opened for such national acts as the Fabulous Thunderbirds, Roy Buchanan and John Cougar.

Howard does an admirable job combining vocals with percussion that any drummer will attest is a hard job. On B.B. King's "The Thrill is Gone" for example, Howard gives an unique twist drawing the lyric out just a couple of belts longer than "Thrill" listeners might expect. It is appreciable

Indeed, the beat is the message. "I'm real interested in keeping the beat steady and uncomplicated" says Howard. "Maybe that sounds too simple but when I see people dancing I just want to keep it going.

Keenan who contributes to some of the original material ("Midnight Kitchen") is an architectural engineer with a local consulting firm. With a penchant for three-piece suits this unassuming baby-faced keyboardist can give the audience a real goose with his jazz-blues harp playing. Several solos had the Terry & Zeke's crowd hooting while they were hoofing.

Keenan sums up the group's philosophy: "What we're aiming for is playing some of the nation's blues festivals. There's one in New Orleans in April, for example. That's really what we want to do continue to play locally and go to a few festivals."

Playing locally is what the SBB is all about. They are the house band at **Terry & Zeke's**. The club seems designed for them. Owner **Terry Glassman** says he put a couch near the club's dance floor to induce a feeling of home and the band members agree. "It's like playing in our living room."

It must be. We've never seen veteran sax man **Bruce Tost** quite so comfortable. Weaving a knitted cap down to his ever-brooding eyes. Tost actually danced his saxophone into the audience and up to a table or two during their performance.

Seeing Tost let loose is a treat. You've heard him for years as he puts it, "In every idiom from jazz to gospel." He seems to dominate many sets on Sunday nights at the **Marriott Hotel** where Tucson's jazz musicians gather to jam. "Dr. Sax," who shows great facility on all four saxophones, holds an M.A. from Illinois State University (where he also taught.) He is employed as music teacher in **Tucson Unified School District**.

Bob Benedon helping Howard keeps the steady beat displays a frantic marionette approach to bass playing. From Wisconsin, Benedon finds the blues a spiritual medium he has been chasing off and on since the early seventies.

Patrick McAndrew [44] is a teacher. Political science is his medium in Marana and at **Pima Community College**. His music contributions can be found on three albums by **Dusty Chaps**, as well as on movie and on television soundtracks. Like Keenan, Howard and Benedon, he also played with the **Subterranean Blues Band**. But like his band brothers, he is a familiar face to Tucson audiences. He writes ("Working Man's Blues") and props up the band with quicksilver licks that pack a lot of sound. Music, he feels, "is a generational thing."

The Blues has transcended the generations and Statesboro Blues Band in their new living room off Speedway is proving that Tucson has an appetite for this all American art form.

---

[44] **Patrick "Pat" McAndrew** passed away on December 28, 2008 at the age of 61 from a heart attack.

Road Furniture: Born on the Highway

By Lydia L. Young
March 1984 – The Magazine

Road Furniture is a band that began in an unusual, almost backwards, way for Tucson. They started as a concept recording project called **Tony Baloney** and the **Spontaneous Cheesemakers**. In a short period of time the group expanded their line-up, have done tapes that have received airplay made some videos and moved on to performing live. Whatever they are doing, it is filled with originality and humor.

No sooner did the band record than they received airplay on **Virgin Vinyl**. The first recording, "Woman at the Door, initiated a curiosity about the group which was not yet a band. The second tape, "American Cheese," was full of fun about the different uses of cheese. Chris said that "Spontaneous Cheese was done with **David Slutes**, someone who was very instrumental in helping us produce our first songs and giving us a lot of motivation."

The change to Road Furniture, in keeping with the spirit of the band, was spontaneous. Tony, Chris and their dates were going to see the Ramones in Phoenix and happened to see quite a few hitch hikers. "Every time we passed a hitch hiker, we said, 'looks like road furniture,' " Chris said. One night they were goofing around at home and Tony suggested to Chris they write a song about road furniture. Tony said, "We had tape and started writing. Chris would write a line and then I write a line. That's how the song came together." Tony Don worked out the guitar part later and Road Furniture born.

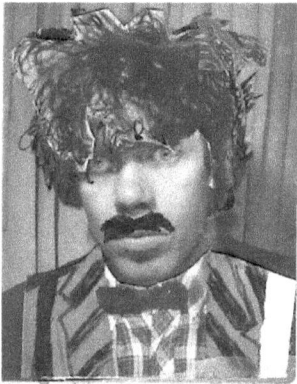

Road Furniture: (Upper left to right) Bruce Halper, Chris Wagganer, Tony Dow and Don Dalen. March 1985, *The Magazine*.

After writing "Road Furniture" the band began extensive work on some videos. To date, they have three on their master tape, all to "Road Furniture." One is a home project they completely themselves. They were limited by equipment techniques, but made up for it in a very funny video dancing cacti and Tony made up as a scruffy 'road furniture.'

One was done live at **TWIT**, but not professionally. The third featured a floating Mr. Potato head and cows alternately moving across the screen. By far, the first set is the best, but the third, conceived by Chris, is fun to watch.

I asked what cows had to do with road furniture when Chris said the cow had become their trademark: "It's the pastures effect of the West Coast," he answered.

They are going to do another home project in hopefully their new "Daddy Can't Dance," my favorite. Road Furniture is beginning to play live gigs now. According to Don, the songs they are playing live are versions. At this point they are concentrating on live show. Each member gave a different reason for deciding to play. Tony said, "It's a logical step." Chris said, "It's a good way to mix audio with visuals," and Don said he personally playing live.

Shagnatty: A Twist of the Jah

By Kata Mapes
April 1984 - The Magazine. Page 13

"Brethren and Sisterern, leave de Babylon cares behind come to Smokey's for a special reggae celebration featuring Jah music of Shagnatty. " – from a poster on back of Shagnatty's bus

Tucson has seen reggae groups come and go over the last several years. **Shagnatty** has been together for about 12 years, but not in Tucson.

Originating in the San Diego area, the group has toured and lived in western Canada, Southern California, Colorado, New Mexico and Arizona.

Now the core members, **Ras Dan**, **Cassie-I** and **Logga**, live in the country 80-100 miles north of Tucson. Nearly every weekend they take off in the Shagnatty bus to play in Tucson, Phoenix and Flagstaff.

Their music is original reggae composed primarily by Ras Dan. Early in their career, they were influenced by Bob Marley and the Wailers, the Toots and the Maytals.

Their first album, "Rejoicing," will soon be available on cassette on the **"Jah Works"** label.

Ras Dan says Shagnatty will produce a second album this summer. The group also contains members **Marcus** on guitar and vocals and **Ed** as the sound engineer.

Smokey's Nightclub advertisement, April 1984, The *Magazine*.

Public Access Cable: A chat with Jan Lesher

By Casey
May 1984 – The Magazine. Page 3

Y ou see her on television asking for **KUAT-FM** donations. You see her behind her desk as the new Executive Director of the **Tucson Community Cable Corporation**. You see her stand up from a table at a meeting of the **Arizona Women's Political Caucus**, which she chairs.

She walks across the room with purposeful steps, talking quietly to friends who slowly drift away.

"Sorry if I'm a little late," smiles **Jan Lesher** as she sits down. The waitress brings coffee and Jan quickly shifts into the interview mode. Her last meeting is still fresh in her mind, "I think the women's movement has been given renewed vigor by the Reagan administration. Women started realizing that they were losing ground." She paused and then continued with candor, "I help women when I can."

The new Public Access Cable Czar, Jan Lesher, talks candidly about her roll in telecommunications.
Photo by David and Kay Fintel. The *Magazine*.

"Your assistant directors at the Tucson Community Cable Corporation (TCCC) are males," I tease.

"Sex should not be a barrier to employment," returns Jan with the alertness of a tennis player fielding a fast serve, an analogy befitting a former member of **Tucson High School**'s tennis team.

Jan still enjoys a good game of tennis, but finds that country swing, which she taught for a year in Flagstaff, also provides a good channel for her energy. Besides tennis and dancing, aerobics and a dash of yoga help steel this native Tucsonan for the whirlwind of meetings she attends.

She keeps track of this busy schedule by listing "things to be done." Lists of "things to be done" to kick off the TCCC adorn the walls of the hall outside her office. "It's compulsive," laughs 28-year-old Lesher, "I make lists in the morning, and at night I update them."

It is perhaps a compulsion that has aided her since she first cut her teeth in the fledgling cable industry at Warner Communications five years ago. After rising to a vice presidency at Warner-Amex, she took the newly established position of Director of **Tucson's Office of Cable Administration** in late 1981.

Her April 1984 appointment as Executive Director of the TCCC leaves Jan the task of administering a relatively new concept, as well as a new program. Forged in the spirit of free speech and press, public access (in Tucson it guarantees the right for citizens to put their own non-profit video programming on cable TV) still faces pitfalls at the national level.

"Some changes can occur at the congressional level," muses Jan, who earned a degree in Political Science at the **University of Arizona**. She quickly shifts gears and looks at in another area. "A recent court decision found that if your city franchise mandates public access, it is no longer legal because it violates the cable operator's first amendment rights."

"Tucson, however, has signed a public access contract that is separate from our cable franchise." Jan lifts her cup of coffee, takes a sip. Her youthful face is accented by dark brown hair splashed with gray highlights. Blue-gray eyes mirror the concerns she feels.

"Control of the media is being centered in fewer and fewer hands. The other day I read that the major daily newspapers in this country are controlled by 14 companies. Public access and other media alternatives help guarantee first amendment rights."

Speaking of the first amendment, what can be put on public access cable?"

"We can't censor," states Jan, "However, certain things are illegal. You can't have lotteries on the public access system. You can't have political cablecasting. The biggie is the obscenity law."

"The first two categories are pretty clear cut. A lottery is a lottery, and politicians are usually astute enough not to do anything illegal." Jan puts her coffee cup down.

"With obscenity, the problem is you are not determining what goes on in public access, but what is considered obscene. And that, she adds, "is based on community standards."

A different community standard that Jan Lesher will have a definite impact on is the growth of public access cablevision in Tucson. "It'll be rough at first," she cautions. "We're working 50 to 60 hours a week to get ready for the July 1st transition. If everyone can show a little patience with us, we can get the system moving pretty quickly."

"Where will that take us? How widespread do you think public access will become in the future?"

"It'll be great," Jan replies enthusiastically. "Every time I think about the future I get more and more excited. I'm convinced this community can easily support our eight channels and eventually expand to fourteen."

The waitress pauses by the table again. "Care for another?" came the question.

"No, thank you," we reply and turn back for the wrap up. "Tell me, Jan, do you have any projects you would like to personally do on public access?"

"Yes, but that's a ways off. First we have to get public access running smoothly."

Care to mention any personal projects? "Not yet."

Tucson's sounds abound

By Jeff Latawiec
June 1984 - The Magazine. Page 6

In response to the *Magazine's* reader surveys, a column devoted to new music will be published from the raw edges of hardcore, the outer limits of art punk, to the more expected and fashionable "new wave" pop.

Tucson's longest lasting hardcore outfit, **Conflict**, has broken up. They played their final show at **Nino's** on April 1st (1984). Drummer **Nick Johnoff** said the split was inevitable because not everyone in the band was willing to put out 100%.

Four local teens have decided to form an all-girl hardcore band this summer. **Kerry Tucker**, guitarist, said the main reason to form the band was boredom. "There's nothing to do in the summer, so we decided to play some music to keep from being bored," she said.

None of the girls have played in a band before. All are still learning their instruments. But that hasn't dampened their enthusiasm in the least. They will receive able assistance from Kerry's mother, **Maureen**, who was drummer for one of the 1960's most popular cult bands, the Velvet Underground. A famous "rock and roll animal" by the name of Lou Reed was singer/guitarist for the Velvets. Three of the girls, **Erin, Charlotte** and **Karr**, attend **Mansfeld Jr. High School**. The other member, **Kiki**, goes to **Tucson High School**.

U.P.S. guitarist **Paul Young** said his band will be going into the studio soon to record a 45.

Community radio station **KXCI** features a hardcore show on Friday nights, 8:00PM to 10:00PM with **Bill Dozer** better known as **Bill Fisher**, ex-singer for the **Corporate Whores**. He sticks strictly to the HC and plays a variety of international selections. Bill is also in the process of trying to start a new HC band of his own. He already has a name **M.P.S. Chunks**. He has hooked up with ex-**Savage Circle** drummer Tom. Savage Circle was one of New York's better known bands.

Barry Smith has left **Gentlemen After Dark**. His brother, **Stewart**, has joined the group that plans to move to California. Finnish HC band Raw Power will play in Tucson around the beginning of September.

Ex-**Jonny Sevin** guitarist/singer **Mark Smythe** is back in town to form a new band with drummer **Rex Estell**. Both played together in one of Tucson's most popular new music bands, the **Pills**. New Music is featured Sundays at **Terry & Zeke's**. Currently, **Ipso Facto** performs with special guest bands.

Hair Shack and Otis Records advertisement, February 1984, the *Magazine*.

A Tost to the Blues

By Jeff Latawiec
June 1984 – The Magazine. Page 8

It's a small nightclub. The band is crowded into a far corner. When the dance floor fills people are elbow to elbow with the musicians. It's packed and personal. It makes for a perfect communication between audience and band. The beat throbs and bodies sweat and bounce to the rhythm of the **Statesboro Blues Band**.

Every Friday and Saturday night the five members of the band gather at **Terry & Zeke's** club on Speedway to play their music.

To play the blues today and have any success a musician has to be good at it. It is a tried and true art form where current performers are judged by the accomplishments of past masters. When the Statesboro Blues Band plays, they leave no doubt that they are good at what they do.

The band is **Bob Benedon** on bass, **Pat McAndrew** on lead guitar and vocals, **George Howard** on drums and vocals, **Brooks Keenan** on keyboards, rhythm guitar and vocals and Bruce Tost on sax.

Saxophonist Tost has impressive credentials, including a master's degree in saxophone from Illinois State University. Tost said he likes playing the blues because it "gets you in touch with your instrument."

"I play a lot more rhythmically than most sax players," he said. "In the Statesboro Blues Band, I get a chance to experiment with my sound." His main goal is to further develop his concept of playing rhythm or "background" sax.

Tost joined the Statesboro Blues Band in September 1983, about a year after they formed under the name of the **Subterranean Blues Band**. Before joining, Tost had his own group, **Desert Slim and the Fistful of Blues Band**. He also played with a blues band in Chicago. Tost began his musical career in grade school when he started playing clarinet. He was influenced by his grandfather who was a successful classical pianist.

In order to make ends meet now, Tost teaches music in TUSD (**Tucson Unified School District**). Currently, he is working on a demo tape for Ray Charles whom he auditioned for this past April. As for the future of saxophone, Tost said he sees a trend towards electronic music that means fewer and fewer horn players are going to be used. With his characteristic optimism, Tost said he doesn't see that as all negative. In fact, if fits rather nicely with one of his ambitions.

"I eventually want to get to where I sound like a whole horn section by myself through electronics."

Photo of Bruce Tost by Rick Aldridge. Cover of June 1984 issue of The *Magazine*.

The Resistors: What are they resisting?

Will   Larry   Kayci   Murph   Squid

Europa Productions

THE RESISTORS

(602) 742-1738

The Resistors press photo, Europa Productions.

By Jeff Latawiec
July 1984 – The Magazine. Page 7

When I was assigned to cover a story on a local band called the **Resistors**, I wasn't too thrilled. I thought to myself, "On, boy, another bunch of old sounding New Wavers." When I arrived at **Nino's** to hear them I had to struggle with myself to maintain a professional objectivity.

That fight lasted about half way through the first song I heard. They were smoking. The individual musical ability of each band member is apparent. Sometimes, that much talent in one group could cause nothing but hassles. Not so with the Resistors.

The Resistors are a five-piece outfit made up of veteran musicians who have managed to survive countless obstacles and other bands finally to wind up in a group they feel has a chance to really go someplace.

Resistors members are **Kayci,** formerly with **Eighty Go Ninety**, on vocals; **Will**, one-time **Street Pajama** percussionist and also a published poet on drums; **Squid**, who studied guitar at the **University of Arizona** on guitar; **Larry**, also formerly with **Eighty Go Ninety**, on bass; and saxophonist **Murph** who has done duty with the **Giant Sandworms** and **Chris Burroughs and the Nationals**.

There are no quick stylistic labels to throw on them. Throughout their sets, one can detect a variety of musical styles, sometimes two or three in the same set-funk, ska, and rhythm and blues. It's jazzed up rock and roll and some new wave sounding material that makes up the elements of the Resistor sound.

One of their standout features is the sax playing of **Murph**. He works his instrument in the same manner of a guitar or bass. What it means is that his sax almost never quits. He uses its sounds to flesh out a song just like the guitars do. Murph's style is similar to **Statesboro Blues Band** saxophonist **Bruce Tost** (see *The Magazine,* Vol. 7, No. 5, June 1984), who is trying to develop a rhythm sax style of his own.

"I want to be more rhythmic, to sound more like another one of the instruments," Murph said. During a song titled "Count On Yourself" he accentuates a particularly sharp and physical sax solo by doing one on the flute.

In another tune, "Breathing the Signals," **Squid** and Murph do a joint guitar and sax fill that is a nice energetic blend of ripping wild into your ears. Visually, the band is stimulating to watch. Singer **Kayci** swings back and forth to the beat of the music, enticing emotions from the audience both with her voice and physical presence. They will be opening the show for Joe "King" Carrasco and the Crowns on Sunday, July 15th at the **Wildcat House**. They perform every Monday at **Terry & Zeke's** and will probably be quite popular on the local club circuit.

The Resistors Story

The band Resistors was conceived on a hot Sunday Afternoon in May of 1983, in a north side Tucson rehearsal room. Bassist Larry, singer Kayci, and drummer Will had just left other bands and were looking to form a new original music group. On a tip from *Newsreal's* **Jon Rosen**, the three arranged to meet and talk at a local nightclub, where guitarist Squid happened to be hanging out. The four set a date for a jam and invited a keyboardist. The jam turned into a no-nonsense session, and when the smoke cleared a half-dozen original tunes had been composed and learned. The five relative strangers decided to become a band on the basis of this immediate creative rapport, and named themselves Resistors quite accidentally that same night while talking about electronics.

Within a matter of weeks the band had written a full set of originals and booked a premiere at **Cowboy's**, a Tucson nightspot. The first gig was a success, and led to a string of engagements at other live-music venues around town. At a grand-opening concert for a new record store the band was approached with a management offer by **Europa Productions' Ron Greatbatch**. The new partnership produced a new direction, the band now concentrating on selected showcase appearances in Tucson and Phoenix while expanding and refining its song list and doing some preliminary recording. The band's sound evolved away from synth/pop into a fusion of new wave guitar rock, reggae, ska, funk, and R&B; the keyboardist left and was replaced by saxophonist Murph, who along with Squid and Larry doubles on keyboard.

The band now plays a list of thirty-six original titles. Typically, the band starts with a tentative lyrical, melodic, and rhythmic composition by one member and then collectively arranges each song into its final form. Some newer tunes have been co-written from scratch by the whole band, and show the positive effects of the band's open minded, experimental attitude toward new material.

July 1984: New Music Column

By Jeff Latawiec
July 1984 – The Magazine. Page 6

On the local heavy metal front, **Rockefeller's** is keeping the faith alive and rock steady. Every night of the week metal maniacs and head bangers can their wild urges with a dose of hard rock sounds. On July 2nd (1984) **Icon** appeared there. Icon guitarist **Dan Waxler** said the band has enjoyed being on the road. He offered his opinion as to why metal is enjoying its resurgence in popularity. "Too much other music was pumped down people's throats and they got sick of it." Bass player **Tim Howell** says his band, **Skyline**, will be ready to play soon– definitely with that metallic sound.

Another Tucson band playing aggressive music is the **Only's**. They aren't exactly heavy metal, but sound something like U2 would if they had a rock edge. Drummer **Johnny Ray** was with one of the hottest local bands ever, the **Veins**.

Guitarist **Jeb Lipson** was with **Spectre** and most recently **Animation**. Singer-bassist **Jack Martinez** played with **Chris Burroughs and the Nationals**. Jeb said their first video will be in *Music Magazine* this month. The song, "Do the Distance," was filmed at **Pima Air Museum**.

U.P.S. has their EP recorded locally at **Tape Techronics**. It is still to be released.

Former **Naked Prey** and **Pedestrians** guitarist **John Venet** is forming a new group. He describes their sound similar to XTC.

Conflict's guitar and bass players **Bill** and **Matt** are now doing the same for **MPS Chunks**. Their KXCI show should start July 14th from 1:00AM to 2:00AM. Two other local HC bands are **Chaotic Allegiance** and **White Super Beings** both of whom, along with MPS share member is common.

KRQ in conjuction with
Creative Entertainment, Corp.
proudly presents
KOOL & THE GANG
with
Shannon
with special guests
The Dazz Band

Get Ready Tucson
for the party of your life!

Sunday, June 3rd   7:30 P.M.
at the Tucson Community Center Arena

Kool & the Gang advertisement, July 1984, The *Magazine*.

September 1984: hardcore, new wave & other punk

By Jeff Latawiec
September 1984 – The Magazine. Page 8

Local hardcore has gained a production company, **Tucson Hardcore Productions**, started by **U.P.S.** guitarist **Paul Young** and **KXCI** HC (Hard Core) disc jockey **Bill "Bulldozer" Fisher**. The other day, while down at local indy record store **Roads to Moscow**, I ran into U.P.S. singer **Lenny**, who let me hear their demo. It sounded great. Intense trash played at breakneck speed, although the mix was too muddy for my tastes. When will the band finally release some often talked about vinyl? Soon, I hope.

Just Us singer **Paneen Call** has left town to go to school. **MPS Chunks** are now defunct. Their bass player **Matt Griffin** told me, "We had a really bad experience the first time we played live (the Nip Drivers show), and it lost momentum." And about his old band **Conflict**'s demise, Matt said, "I don't think the personalities in the band meshed real well." Currently, Matt is involved with a new band, **Los Hamsters**, with **Fonda** on vocals, **Linda Andes** on guitar and **Matt Nass**. He said they are looking for a drummer, and may add another guitarist later, according to him. They aren't going to be a thrash band, but more straight-ahead punk.

Ex-Conflict skin beater **Nick** is supposed to be in a new band called **Triantulon**, with **Woody** on bass, **Al** on guitar, and **Micheline** guitar– and the sound is metal punk?

Bill Fisher is rumored to be having a party Sept. 14th with bands the **Massacre Guys** and **Peace Corpse**. He and I see eye-to-eye on the relationship between heavy metal and hardcore– being that they definitely share strong bonds.

It is my opinion, and I just know it's going to make rock critics worldwide sit up and take notice. HM is enjoying a phenomenal rebirth in popularity, and like the punk HC scene, this is mainly due to a grassroots movement among fans. Fisher said he would like to see **THC** do some joint HM and HC shows.

The metal scene kept hot during the summer, too. Mark, from **Rockefeller's** has consistently tried to put on showcase featuring up-and-coming HM bands such as Phoenix's Icon, who played The **Rock** on July 2nd. Malice, an L.A. black metal outfit, appeared July 15th. Both shows were good, although, Malice played so loud I think they offended their P.A., because it kept quitting on them.

Local hard rockers **Roc Lochner** have been doing some Sunday and Monday nights at Rockefeller's recently. They've been around for a while, and deserve more attention. Unlike many other local hard rock bands, Roc Lochner does not rely on copy tunes.

Robby Lochner told me they are going to record a six-song EP the first week of September at Tucson's **Sound Factory Recording Studio**. It's self-promoted with a tentative release date somewhere around Thanksgiving. He also said that their latest demo has sparked some interest in Atlantic Records who told the band they would keep an eye on them. The group's bassist, **Rick Travis**, has a solo LP recorded. f

Only's, whose video "Do The Distance" has shown on *Music Magazine,* says they plan to send it to MTV. See this month's edition for an interview with Only's.

Gentlemen After Dark returned to town to do some shows at **Nino's**. It seems their relocation to California was only a summer thing.

The blues are alive and well!

Submitted by the Mainstream Blues Society
September 1984 – The Magazine. Page 12

Those of us who didn't escape the Arizona summer survived by countering the heat with more heat– good Mexican food and hot blues. The blues has surfaced at **Terry & Zeke's** Tucson's Home of the Blues. The club, on Speedway near Columbus is also the home of the **Statesboro Blues Band** who can be heard there every Friday and Saturday. Other musicians who have boogied and sung the blues on Terry's stage have included Charlie Musselwhite, **Professor Paul, Denis Offret, Highbeam**, the **Subterranean Blues Review**, the **Cattle** and a string of itinerant and local musicians who have sat in. **Rainer**'s **Das Combo**, the **Boomers** and the **Soul Rebels** are playing their own brands of blues and R&B at various clubs around the city.

Tucsonans were treated to several great live shows this summer from Jr. Walker and the All Stars, Bo Diddley, B.B. King and Charlie Musselwhite, Bo and Charlie were backed up by Tucson's own **Statesboro Blues Band** whose inspired performances showed them to be as versatile and competent as exponents of this genre anywhere.

The local airwaves are becoming notably heavy with the blues and R&B. **KXCI** (91.7 FM), our community radio station, devotes specific time slots to the blues as well as increasing inclusion of this music in its general music mix. Saturday mornings at 11:00AM, **Harmonica Mike** plays traditional blues and occasionally has local blues players perform live during his show. **Terry O** hits the air at 5:00PM with electric blues from its beginnings to the most recent release.

At 7:00PM, Terry turns over the turntable to sister **Cheryl Crews** who treats us to contemporary sound and R&B until 9:00PM. Every couple of weeks, **Kid Squid** puts together a "Roots of Rock and Roll" show Saturday afternoon. Squid's "Doo Wop" show is great.

KUAT-AM produces the Folk Scene, aired at 7:00PM Saturday, which presents some very fine blues programs. Other than this, KUAT plays very little blues. If you'd like to change this situation, call the station manager and make your tastes known.

As I write this article, a group of local blues musicians and enthusiasts are forming an organization that will be bringing a number of Blues artists to the Old Pueblo, and generally fostering more interest in, and disseminating information on the form of music we call the blues. The first of these concerts will feature the Robert Cray Band on Friday September 7th and Saturday September 8th at **Terry & Zeke's**. Tickets will be $4.00 and are available at T&Z's. The **Statesboro Blues Band** will be opening both shows both nights.

Terry & Zeke's advertisement, September 1984, The *Magazine*.

Only "Only's," they say

By Jeff Latawiec
September 1984 - The Magazine. Page 4

Don't say "the **Only's**," because as group member will stress, it is only Only's. Only's are three excellent musicians, with none of the lack of sound problems inherent in many rock trios. With any luck, it's only a matter of time until the greater masses– locally and elsewhere– begin to hear the different sound and reward them with some well-deserved recognition.

Sitting in the darkened interior of a near empty **Nino's** listening to Only's, I found myself thinking what a drag it is that the rest of Tucson still isn't hip to this band. It is a rare occurrence when a local band excites me to the point that I become utterly convinced they could, should, and are going to make it. Out of three more recent groups to stir such deep emotional conviction with me are the **Veins**, **Jonny Sevin** and **Green on Red**.

The band consists of **Jack 'Mack' Martinez** on bass guitar and lead vocals; **Johnny Ray**, drum kit; and guitarist **Jeb Lipson**. Each of them is a seasoned musical trooper. Now that they are armed and ready with Only's music, totally determined to win the war for rock and roll success. **Johnny Ray** has had a taste of that success when his old band, **Veins**, came close to signing a contract with a major label. Martinez fingers run nimbly through an intricate bass riff while he sways his lanky body back and forth in front of the mike when singing, and otherwise uses every bit of his left side of the stage to prance around. On the right, Lipson stands firmly planted. An intense look of concentration possesses his face.

Martinez composes Only's songs. They have plans for a second video. The group plays consistently at Nino's and **Characters**, usually Tuesday nights.

Only's photo, September 1984. *The Magazine.*

Tucson's specialty music stores

By Neil Costin
September 1984 - The Magazine. Page 6

One does not always find what is being sought after to satisfy musical tastes in the standard, large, corporate stores. Music heard on local community radio, or outside radio stations may be hard to find at the average music store. Try one of Tucson's "specialty shops" that carry specific records not found elsewhere.

AL BUMS, on 6th Street across from the UA stadium, is Tucson's oldest "used" record store. You name it, you could probably find it there. They carry used LP's, 12" singles and cassettes in almost every category. There are large soundtracks, classical, soul, jazz, gospel, comedy and compilation selections available. Behind the front counter, there lies an extensive group of collections, hard to find albums.

The **BLUES COMPANY**, on North Campbell by Grant, is the city's newest, yet most select used store. All products are sold in plastic covers. They not only offer blues, but also country blues, city blues, piano blues, Chicago blues and Delta blues. Also are comprehensive sections on Cajun Tex-Mex, Folk Music, Ragtime, Country and Jazz.

ROADS TO MOSCOW, on University Blvd., one block west of the UA, is an outgrowth of a store opened years ago in Tempe. Though basically a used store, it does feature some "unopened" releases. It not only has a large heavy metal section, but also a really interesting group of 12" and 7" imported singles to please any listener to new and different music.

OTIS RECORDS, on Grant Road between Stone and Miracle Mile, will also satisfy many fans of blues, country and bluegrass, as well as the general listener.

PDQ RECORDS, on the eastern end of Pima Street, is Tucson largest store, featuring used releases for all tastes. This is Tucson's biggest music store!

JEFF's CLASSICAL RECORD SHOPPE, on Speedway Blvd., west of Campbell Avenue, stocks not only, as the name implies, classical music, but also has Tucson's most comprehensive selection of motion picture soundtracks and Broadway musical cast recordings.

As its name indicates, **ONLY OLDIES**, on 22nd Street (formerly **Mad Daddy's**), only sells the older, used product. The vast majority of what is found there are releases from the 1950s and 1960s.

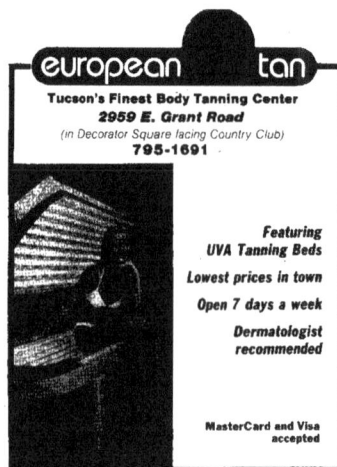

Roads to Moscow and European Tan advertisements, September 1985, The *Magazine*.

Hard production work pays off in vinyl

By Jeff Latawiec
October 1984 - The Magazine. Page 9

This is one trick disc. If you like straight ahead, well written and played hard rock and roll. The only negative thing I can say about this new solo EP by **Roc Lochner's** bass player **Rick Travis** is that only four songs are not long enough.

The EP is a totally local creation– from the homegrown musician himself, to the recording and production work both done at Tucson's **Sound Factory Recording Studio**.

It's obvious that this was no one-off, quick shot, deal. The end result is thoroughly professional; something that could only be achieved with careful planning and a lot of effort by Travis. He said the project has been in the works for over two years.

Before you even hear it, the record reaches out and grabs at you with its striking cover. The front picture is a shot of Travis holding a guitar embossed with a circular design that is continued on his shirt. The predominant motif for both guitar and Travis's clothing is black-white. It was a concept developed by Travis and works well.

Once you get inside the package, and slip the disc on your turntable, your ears can get in on the sensory enjoyment. All of the tunes were penned by Travis, who also plays all of the instruments– except on "You Can't Keepa Secret" (where he gets a little help from his brother **Craig)**. The other three songs are, "Down and Out," "Only Love Survives" and "The Gift." All of the songs are medium paced hard rockers. The vocals are strong and the music is tight.

It's easy to see why one of Tucson's premier rock bands, Roc Lochner, chose Travis as the new bassist. His originals, now part of RL's live set, fit perfectly with the bands' style.

Photo: Rick Travis performs with Roc Lochner. Photo by Jeff W. Smith. October 1984, The *Magazine*.

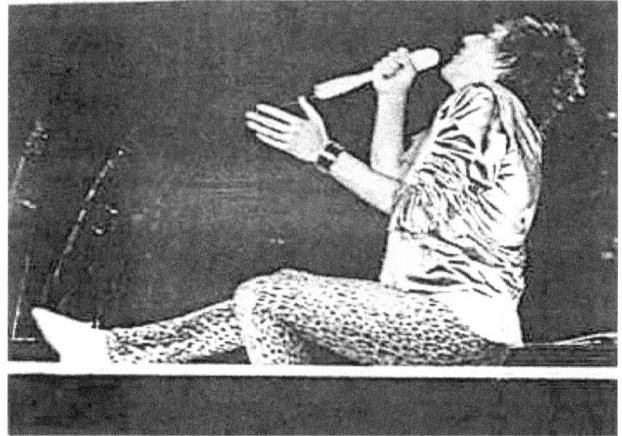

Rod rocks the TCC

Singing rock and roll for more than two decades, Rod Stewart has forged a distinct and enduring presence within the music he loves. On "Camouflage" his 17th album, he's still leading a musical charge that has made him known to millions for his trademark vocals, astute song craft and rollicking stage presence.

Stewart's first band found him sharing the stage with the young Rolling Stones, and in 1964, he joined legendary blues-rocker Long John Baldry's Hoochie Koochie Men. He also sang with Mick Fleetwood and Peter Green in the band Shotgun Express before they went on to found Fleetwood Mac. Rod Stewart appears on October 28 (1984) at the **TCC.**

Left Top: Ad display, *Magazine*, October 1984. Page 9.
Right Top: Rod Stewart up close at the Tucson Convention Center.

Left Bottom: Starship drummer stand before the show.
Right Bottom: Gracie Slick up close.

Concert photos by Robert Zucker, *Magazine*, 1984.

Starship with Gracie Slick in concert at the TCC.

TRANSATLANTIC

MARLI GRAS
TUCSON

98KUPP

FM

BACKSTAGE
ACCESS

GENERAL

The Rolling Stones

Stadium

DEVO WORLD TOUR
1981-82

AFTER SHOW

ile

GUEST PASS

DATE

SIGN.

ALL ACCESS

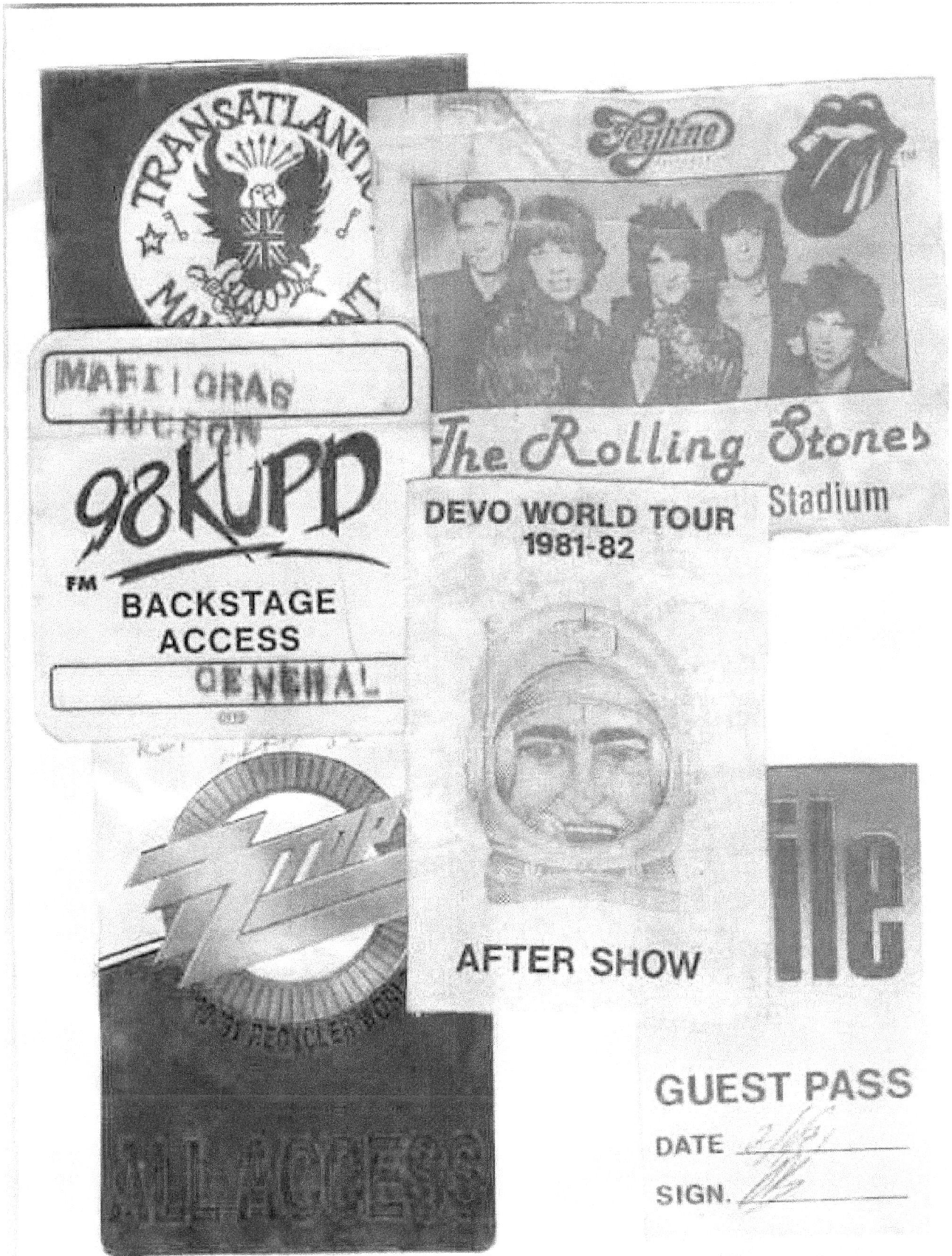

Samples of concert press passes from *Entertainment Magazine* archives.

Let's have the V-8's

By Cindy Aquillo & Peri Savery
October 1984 - The Magazine. Page 9

Seven months ago, a Tucson band called the **V-8's** was formed. They play straight-forward American pop and have been making the local club circuit. The band's members include **Keith Miracle** as lead vocalist and lead guitar; **Bruce Halper** on drums, background vocals, piano and synthesizer; **Steve Conklin** on bass guitar and background vocals. The group also has an additional sit-in member named **Russell Wells** who plays guitar. When Wells plays with the V-8's, they are known as the **4 Cylinders**. Everyone in the group writes music and lyrics. They have a unique style of music that cannot be compared to any other group.

"When we play, we try to create a party atmosphere," said one of the members. Presently, they are working on an album. A music video entitled "Making the Scene" is being edited. It will be cablecast on TV and a local music video program soon.

Where the Music Goes!

November 1984
Magazine

WHERE THE MUSIC GOES is a handy way happening music-wise in Arizona. Check th and display ads for more information.

If you know of a musical happening, send it to the *MAGAZINE* before November 21st.
Listings are subject to change

November 1984 Calendar of Events, The *Magazine*, Page 23.

October 1984: Local bands try to get a break

By Jeff Latawiec
October 1984 - The Magazine. Page 13

B y now, it should be no secret that I'm a fanatic when it comes to supporting local music, particularly bands adventurous enough to play originals. One thing I fail to understand is why local radio, especially our FM channels, don't do a whole lot more to offer that support.

A perfect example is the four-song solo EP by **Roc Lochner's** bassist **Rick Travis**. The recording quality is good, and all four songs lend themselves easily to the regular formats of both **KLPX** and **KWFM**. Copies were made available, so why aren't they played? Roc Lochner did a whole week at **Rockefeller's** in early September. Every night I was there, they packed it in. They have finished recording their mini-LP, and it's still scheduled for a release sometime around Thanksgiving. An interview will be in the next edition.

Two of the newer hard-metal bands in town are **We're Here** and **Neighbors**. We're Here threw a party in the boonies this summer – that was pretty trick. I don't know if anyone remembers a local band called **Hot Lucy** with a dynamic guitarist by the name of **John Molina**, He has resurfaced in a band called the **Neighbors** and sent me a demo copy, There is a nice melodic overtone to the hard rock backbone of the tunes. Check them out next time they play live.

Another demo I received was a four-song tape by **J.D. Rock**. Guitarist **John Desportes** described the group as more hard rock than heavy metal. Whatever you call it, and there are definitely two metal sounding cuts to me "Bottom Line" and "Rock Music." It really kicks.

Italian hardcore crew Raw Power are returning to the states November 1st. They will definitely be back here. I've heard rumors of an up-and-coming **KXCI** benefit with **U.P.S.**, **Mighty Sphincter** from Phoenix, **Progerian Youth** and **Our Neighbor's S*CK**.

Correction time: **Nick**'s new band is **Triantulon** and **AJ** plays guitar. They are doing a cover of the **Seed's** "Pushing Too Hard," and will be opening for T.S.O.L. (from LA) later this month in Phoenix at the Mason Jar. Didn't I say last month that former **Just Us** singer **Paneen** was leaving town? She is supposed to be coming back already,

Good and bad news dept.: The September 27th gig at **UA Cellar** with U.P.S., Progerian Youth, headliners **Die Kreuzen** went over really well. The band maintained control of the crowd, and when it was "mosh, mosh, mosh" on the dance floor it was still cool. There was no damage. The bands, along with some volunteers, cleaned up the place after the show. Why then is U.P.S. now banned from doing gigs anymore on the UA campus?

Later that same night, there was a party with the same bands at the **Chicken Coop**. It was a "human sauna" as one party-goer put it. But, the bands wailed. Die Kreuzen was described as real "party animals." They have a new album coming out called "Dirt and Decay." **Los Hamsters** are going to begin practice in early October. Phoenix rock-a-billy band Hellfire is playing at **Characters** October 5-6th.

In closing, I'd like to thank **Ray Ann** and **Kelly** at **Rocks** for their invaluable help the **Neighbors** and **J.D. Rock** for the demos; **Roc Lochner** and **Rick Travis** for their patience; **Tawny, Tom, Matt** and **Lydia** for their help; and **Laurie** for the best positive aid in awhile. Once again, to any land sharks out there ... absolutely no thanks.

Roc Lochner: Roc and roll

By Jeff Latawiec
November 1984 - The Magazine. Page 2

I t started on Tucson's eastside three years ago. There were rumors of a new band with an incredible young lead guitarist. Word of mouth carried the news. Every time these guys did a party, more and more people began to show up.

In the summer of 1984, one of Tucson's FM rock stations was looking for a local group with enough draw to pack'em in at a bash they sponsored at **Old Tucson**. **Los Lasers** were mentioned, but finally, this eastside band was chosen, despite some skepticism as to their popularity.

Two separate phenomena were in bloom, and clearly, illustrated on that summer party night. One of them, taking place worldwide, was a demonstration that hard rock is back in vogue, and on any given night a decent exponent of this genre can fill a place up with hard rocking, hard partying devotees.

The other phenomenon was a local one. For on that night a hometown band flexed their muscles and silenced the skeptics in a proof positive demonstration of their popularity.

That phenomenon is named **Roc Lochner**.

After three years of playing other peoples' music, the band is now secure enough with fan support to begin playing quite a few original tunes, songs that when I heard them I thought they came off much better than the cover material.

Roc Lochner is composed of five guys determined to make a living playing rock and roll. Unlike many youth of today, they appear to have the patience necessary to see it through. That incredible young guitarist that had folks talking even more than three years ago is **Robby Lochner**. His brother, **Charlie**, also plays axe in the group. **Ken Triphon** handles the vocals, **Troy Richards** is the drummer, and the bands' most recent member is bass player **Rick Travis** (see *The Magazine*, October 1984 for interview). I've talked with few bands that project such a positive attitude.

The band has just finished recording a six-song mini-LP locally, due for release in late November. In addition they have sent out demos to various record companies, receiving a reply from Atlantic Records who encouraged the group to keep sending in material. Until they get the proverbial big break, which they hope will be hastened by their up-coming record, they are content to stay in Tucson.

"We have family here, jobs here, and popularity," said Travis. "Our act can be polished up here."

"It might be easier to get a break here," added Rob. "There's a chance of getting swallowed up in a place like L.A."

Currently, they play 16 originals throughout their set, with three more tunes on the way. Everyone in the group writes for the band. Ken described their original sound as a cross between Aerosmith and ZZ Top. He stressed that it's the music that will talk for Roc Lochner more than anything else.

He said he doesn't think the band needs to rely on a certain look, such as everyone wearing studs or leather to create attention for themselves. "Let the music speak for itself." Right now, the band is "playing it by ear" as Rob puts it. They hope local radio will support their disc, give it regular airplay. But they aren't counting on it.

"At this point, we have to depend mostly just on ourselves," Travis said. "We have to treat every time we play as event."

It's exactly this kind of attitude that has placed them at the top of the heap in local music ... and will take them much further on. Anyone doubting their popularity has only to see them on one of their nights at Tucson's HR club, **Rockefeller's**, where even on weeknights they fill up the place. In assessing why they are so popular, Lochner's vocalist Ken said, "I pretty much feel it's the music."

BLASTERS photo by Bob Jankowski

November 1984 MAGAZINE

5

The Blasters
with the Resultz

Sunday, November 18
8:00 PM
Tickets: $6

Joe "King" Carrasco
and the Crowns
with special guest

Tuesday, November 20
8:00 PM
Tickets: $8

Europa Productions

both shows at

THE WILDCAT HOUSE

1801 N. Stone
622-1302

(Left) November 1984 cover photo of Roc Lochner Band. The *Magazine*. Page 5. Photo courtesy of Olan Mills Studios.
(Above) The Wildcat House advertisement for The Blasters and Joe "King" Carrasco concert, November 1984, The *Magazine*. Page 5.

Roads to Moscow hits the road; Embers smolders

By Jeff Latawiec
November 1984 - The Magazine. Page 9

Tucson's music world lost something very precious this past month. The city's only true alternative music store closed its door on Halloween Day (1984). From what I understand, **Roads to Moscow** owner **Steve** decided to shut down the Tucson outlet because it was never a moneymaking venture. We won't have to go quite as far as Russia to supply ourselves with the type of music Roads to Moscow made available, but for those into punk, hardcore, or European and obscure heavy metal, the acquisition of these vinyl tidbits will be more of a hassle.

I'd like to welcome **Lydia Young** to the *Magazine* staff. She will be doing a music column of her own, covering some of the areas I used to, thus giving me more time to devote my space to metal, local and otherwise.

The month of November seems like it will be getting off to a good musical start early. **Rockefeller's** is presenting a showcase with Jet recording artists Madam X. The band is fast gaining a powerful rep for themselves in the HM ranks, winning accolades from notables such as Priest singer Rob Halford, who said, "Here's one band to watch. Green Manaleishi is a hard thing to do, but these guys do it! It made me shiver."

Another longtime rock and roll institution also closed its doors this month. The **Embers** nightclub shut down forever, to be turned into a used car lot. Definitely, no bargain for local music.

A new hard rock band named **Aftermath** is now in existence, though I have yet to hear them. Another new group is **Blaze**, with **Ken** from **Speedway Domino's** on lead guitar. **J.D. Rock**, whose demo I praised last month, has undergone a line-up change with lead singers. The new warbler is **Alan Blankstrom.** They have expressed an interest in playing a party with **Roc Lochner**, so ... if anyone is interested in getting such an affair together contact me through the *Magazine*.

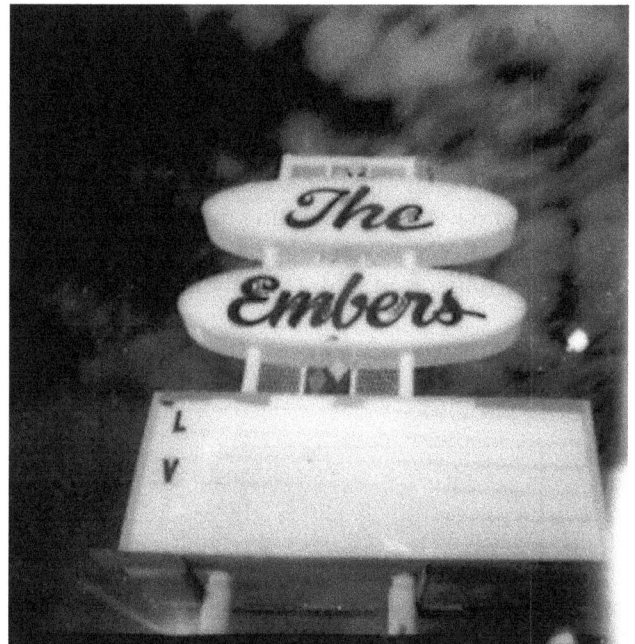

I ran into **Only's** guitarist **Jeb** recently, and he told me the band is doing an album. Their show with Romeo Void went over pretty decently, and a lot of people left after they played, not being able to take more than a few of RV's non-stage presence delivered songs.

I also saw former **Jonny Sevin** guitarist-singer **Mark Smythe** at a friends' house. He wouldn't say too much about some rumblings I heard putting them back into the studio soon. But, he didn't say no to them either.

(Top) The Embers nightclub (on Speedway) sign, *Entertainment Magazine* archives.
(Bottom) Blues Co. advertisement, November 1984, *The Magazine*.

The progressive music scene in Tucson

By Lydia L. Young
November 1984 - The Magazine. Page 7

There are not that many outlets for newer music in Tucson any more, but the local musicians keep the music flowing in and out of town. Against just about any odds, it seems the musicians still believe in themselves. They change, interact, and become mobile depending on what they need to continue.

On October 20th (1984), NBC filmed a made-for-TV movie at **Nino's** featuring a female band in L.A. called "Girls Club." Opening for local band **Street Pajama**, the event did not pull in much of a crowd and the filming was brief.

U.P.S. had an unusually busy October, despite heavy press attacks on their character, October 5th and 6th they opened for **Hellfire** at **Characters**– the first night drawing the most people. Word has it that Friday night Hellfire felt outplayed by U.P.S., so Saturday they practiced all day long only to play less well that night. They did get other attending musicians, including **Joe Dodge**, on stage for special spotlights (or help?).

On the 22nd, Characters drew over 200 people and was a night of surprises. U.P.S. opened with singer **Lenny** falling from the stage in dizziness, only to stand up with more energy and guitarist **Paul**'s parents attending to appreciate the new, to them, scene. The Screaming Sirens (from L.A,) were next; not too professional were these screeching cowgirls. Headlining was L.A.'s T.S.O.L. and the raw rock and roll energy we have come to expect from them was tighter and better than ever. Lead singer Joey has worked his Morrison-like style more into the true framework of the band.

October 26th was a busy night on **Congress Street**. **Cox Cable** and **TWIT** set up-a pre-Halloween costume party for videotaping. Once again, U.P.S. was in the forefront with a controlled riot in the street coming off amusingly well. The **Freds** played their rumored last gig at **Jack's Pub** down the street that night, also getting into the video. The club ended up with standing room only and a consistently filled dance floor. Good times were had by all.

After comments on the fragmentation of the Freds, singer-guitarist **Don Dalen** mentioned a new project called **Spontaneous Cheesemakers** involving himself, **Tony Dow**, **Chris Wagner**, and **David Slutes**. They are currently working on a tape, which from the songs I heard is highly experimental.

The **Giant Sandworms** have also been busy, recently playing a successful show at Madame Wong's in L.A. They will be returning to the coast in November, both for scheduled shows at the Music Machine and to record. **Howe Gelb** said the band has changed dramatically. **Scott Garber** is the only other original member, and they have a new material except for two songs. Howe's other band, **Blackie Ranchette**, has no immediate plans but might be in New York come January. The summer project of the **Salmon Brothers** has resurfaced with a new drummer. Their **UA Cellar** show the 25th was true to form and fun. They are working on new material and looking for dates.

Jeff Keenan of the **Phantom Limbs** said there is no new news about the band. They had a very successful show the 27th at **Characters** with **Stab in the Dark** and **Love Tractor**. The **Brain Dead/45 Grave** and **Meat Puppets** are confirmed at Characters as of press time. **Black Flag** is looking towards the **Chicken House** at 115 N. 2nd Avenue as a performance location. **Ipso Facto** is spreading its wings a bit with November gigs at the **UA Cellar**, **Granfalloon Saloon** and **Nino's**. Bassist **Joey** said they have plans to record in L.A. There is a new drummer, **Adrian Will**, in the **Resistors**. They have plans to do a video of "Downtown People" on their own and another with Cox Cable. At the moment, they are looking for a new saxophone or horn player.

Good-bye and good luck to local impresario **David Roy** who has moved to Phoenix to pursue new creative outlets. Local hardcore band **Just Us** is definitely defunct, and **Progerian Youth** is at least, on vacation.

Giant Sandworms reattack!

Giant Sandworms Scott Garber (l) and Howe Gelb (r). December 1984 *Magazine* cover photo by Lydia L. Young.

By Lydia L. Young
December 1984 - The Magazine. Page 2

Tucson's own **Giant Sandworms** have resurfaced forcefully with new music, new determination and new people. Talking recently with bassist **Scott Garber**, I received some information on the current machinations that are keeping the band alive.

Scott Garber of Giant Sandworms.
Entertainment Magazine archive photo by Lydia L. Young. December 1984.

With the loss of drummer **Billy Sed** and guitarist **Dave Seger** one would have expected the band to fragment. Instead, it seems to have strengthened them. "We were that much more determined to continue," Scott said.

A decision had been made when problems arose in May that should any single member leave, the band would no longer exist. Scott said, over a period of time he and **Howe Gelb** (guitars and vocals) decided they wanted to continue working together. There is a very good understanding and communication between us of what we are now trying to do."

The *what* is a more direct rock approach. "We've gone back to a lot of basics and are much more defined in terms of the material and it being more congruent song to song," Scott remarked.

Referring to the old problems of trying to put the finger on precisely what type of band the Giant Sandworms was, Scott said, "It sounds like one band now, not four or five."

A couple of different events led to the resurgence of the band as it is. Before fragmentation began, the new material had already been started. They were also already booked in Los Angeles when Billy left the band. Spurred on by a suggestion, Scott asked now ex-**Gentlemen After Dark** drummer **Winston** to play the gig and he said yes. They received very good response to their new material in L.A. "It gave us a lot of confidence," Scott confided.

Giant Sandworms photo by Lydia L. Young. December 1984.
Entertainment Magazine archives.

That prompted the **Sandworms** to go ahead with recording in L.A. Scott said he and Howe had been kicking the idea around for a while and the time seemed right. As to when the record will come out, he said, they would like to get it out as soon as possible. "We need a record bad."

At the moment, they are hoping for at least a press and distribution deal, but will do it themselves if necessary.

Tom Larkins (Soul Rebels) is drumming for them locally. Scott said they were all very pleased with the local response when they played at **Jack's Pub** on November 21st.

"I think we are hitting a different audience now. There were a lot of kids and some hardcore people there. I find it very encouraging."

Scott said the Giant Sandworms are just now getting mobile. They are working on more gigs in L.A. and hope to reach other areas as well. For now, he and Howe are concentrating on the songs and new direction. Look for them at Christmastime for their next local gig.

Progressive Music: Tucson keeps on rockin'

By Lydia Young
December 1984 - The Magazine. Page 9

Despite the cold weather that is descending upon Tucson, there was a great influx of bands in November, I cannot, being only human, make it to all the shows, but I do my best.

Joe "King" Carrasco and the Crowns appeared at the **Wildcat House** November 18th (1984) drawing not quite as large a crowd as a few months ago, but one just as lively. In spite of a bit of P.A. trouble, the music was powerful and accented by The King's anticipated acrobatics. Local blues-rock band **Mobile Cubes** opened the show with a mixture of originals and covers. Guitarist **Rueben Ruiz** said the band is expecting to play more frequently.

L Mondo Combo played at **Nino's** November 15th. Minus **Pat Murphy**, they sounded better than expected. Perhaps this was due to the celebration of their (and my) friend **Chris Schrager's** birthday.

Also, that night at **Jack's Pub** downtown was a **Razzmatazz** sponsored party complete with high fashion, photographers, wine, champagne and balloons, not to mention the sounds of Ipso Facto and the **V-8's**. I did not make it to Palace West for the Ramones and Black Flag that night in Phoenix, but I heard the show was tremendous. I also heard a rumor that **Hellfire** is breaking up.

The Monday night jams at **Terry & Zeke's Friendly Tavern** are drawing quite a crowd these days. I stopped in the other night and caught **Russell Wells** on guitar and **Liz** (ex-drummer for **Feline**), just to name a few.

Crosby, Stills and Nash was like a trip into my past the 14th at **UA McKale Center**. The band incorporated oldies with respective solo material and graced the stage with acoustic as well as electronic sound. The audience joined in on many songs, especially "Carry On," and "Teach Your Children." The old spirit is still there!

Charlie Musselwhite returns to Terry & Zeke's for two special performances on December 12th & 13th. He will be joined with Tucson's own **Statesboro Blues Band**.

Due to diversity of interests and too many obligations, **Bruce Halper** said the **V-8's** have officially broken up. They will still release their video "Making the Scene" as the V-8's. As of this moment, the **Freds** have reformed including ex-**V-8** bassist **Steve Conklin**. How permanent this will be is unverified. The **Meat Puppets** gig went on as scheduled at **Characters** November 10th. One of my longtime favorite Arizona bands was surprisingly mellow this time around and did not make me laugh as much as usual. Wasn't that their trademark?

The Ragged Bags Show seemed ill fated from the start. Not only did we get the name wrong for the last issue, but the band had bad driving weather, getting in too late to play at the **Chicken** House the 15th. They did play the next night at **Robert Laundryman's** house outside in the freezing cold to approximately ten people. What happened to all the support? They were great and despite everything, loved Tucson.

U.P.S. has unfortunately been out of the picture recently. Guitarist **Paul** broke his shoulder and will not be able to play for a while which prompted the lead singer to take a cross-country vacation. They hope to be playing again by the end of the year. The **Giant Sandworms** surprised themselves and the crowd at **Jack's Pub** on the 21st with their new sound (see interview, this edition).

What may be Tucson's only locally produced Christmas record this year is a new **Street Pajama** single– a fun little jazz/pop number called "Mrs. Claus Angst."

Rockefeller's Nightclub advertisement, December 1984, The *Magazine*.

Tucson metal isn't dead– yet.

By Jeff Latawiec
December 1984 - Magazine. Page 11

Madam X, the HM band set to play at **Rockefeller's** last month unfortunately cancelled. Consequently, we got Rail, a pretty good replacement. They sold out the first night and so were held over for another. The crowds really seem to dig them and guitarist/keyboard player **Andy Baldwin** took some time to do an interview.

But, he made one remark I definitely disagree with– that HM is on the wane. Well, maybe radio stations aren't smart enough to play more of it than they currently do. But all that says to me is that it's typical of some of the people in charge of the entertainment field. It doesn't mean jive at all.

There are some people who tried to say it was dying at the end of the 1970s. But the fans refuse to let it die. I personally believe that it is bigger than ever. As long as it can be put to such good uses as described above. I do not think anyone will write a successful epitaph. 'Nuff said.

We're Here also played a Sunday-Monday stint at The **Rock** in November, as well as a party late in the month.

Keep eyes open for info on a possible, benefit with **Roc Lochner** headlining, and groups like **JD Rock** and **Aftermath** also playing.

Only's are having some regional success with their locally made video "Do the Distance." It is getting regular rotation that means constant airplay in Denver on a show called "Tele-Tunes." They definitely have a record in the works but are keeping silent on the details. They are playing at **Jack's Pub** December 19th (1984).

Early in the month I saw local metalists **Storm Warning** at the **Tequila Mockingbird**. They were playing to an almost empty house. But, guitarist **Mike Jay** refused to let it dampen his spirits. He rocked his socks off, constantly in motion. He played some pretty trick leads, too.

"Rick Travis"

A 4-Song EP by
Roc Lochner
bass guitarist
Rick Travis

Available now at
Record Bar
Otis Records

for just $3.99

The group's original was good. But, I thought their cover material dragged a bit. The singer sounded good on the band's own tunes. **Jay** told me he wrote the originals. If so, the group **Blades** has lucked out because he has moved over to take up the guitar chores for them.

I'm sure everyone who is going already knows, but, just in case, don't forget the metal night **KLPX** is putting on at the **TCC** this month. Krokus is heading the bill **WASP**, a band I have heard a lot about, is going to play.

As usual, when Roc Lochner plays The Rock they pull in a pretty decent crowd (see Roc Lochner interview November 1984 edition, The *Magazine*), especially on off nights like Sunday and Monday when more than the usual amount of people for such nights will show up. Their drummer, **Troy** told me the mini-LP has been pushed back to a January release date.

That's all for now, folks. Keep head banging, especially to local sounds. Don't let anyone get you down. As usual, be aware of the sharks out there. I'm still recovering from a shark bite from last spring.

I mentioned a new band, **Aftermath**, in the last issue. Well, **Troy** and **Ray Ann** from Rockefeller's took me along one night to see them practice. On the way, Troy told me the band was really metal. "I mean super heavy metal," he stressed.

He wasn't kidding. They have to be, without a doubt, the heaviest band I have seen in Tucson. They are doing all originals. After hearing them I have high hopes for their future. Look for a feature on them soon.

They have a twin guitar attack with both guitars kicking butt. The singer, **Rich**, is a former guitar player from **Snowblind** and this is his first time handling lead vocals. He has a good voice and can hit the high notes with ease.

The songs are well written and fairly complex. Currently, they have about ten down tight. They plan to stick to doing only their own music, for which I admire them, and to make it financially possible most of the members have a full time job.

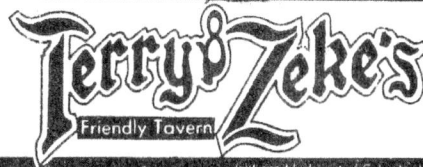

Rick Travis, Characters and Terry & Zeke's advertisements from *Magazine*, December 1984.

UPS: Useless Pieces of Shit

Lenny Mellow, lead singer, Useless Pieces of Shit (U.P.S.), April 21, 1984, "The Shit House," Tucson, AZ. Photos by Fonda. *Newsreal*, November 9-December 14, 1984. Page 8.

By Brian Schottlaender
November 11-December 9, 1983 –
Newsreal. Page 8

Newsreal: Tell me about the bands you guys were in before U.P.S.

Lenny Mellow: Okay. **Phil** (bass) and **Slug** (guitar) were in **Corporate Whores. Paul** (guitar) was in **Civil Death**, with me ... I played with a group called Excess Noise in Massachusetts. We only did one show and then we broke up. We had the bass player from (Boston's) The Freeze. (U.P.S: drummer, Doug, was previously with Michigan's Free Cheese.)

LM: There are so many different influences that we all have."

NSBL: What are some of your influences, musically?
LM: Musically?
NSBL: Who do you like? Let's put it that way.
LM: Bands I like? I like Neos, from Canada. I like some Finnish bands that I've heard. I like D.R.I. I like a lot of bands. I like a lot of American bands; there's tons of them.

NSBL: What about some of the other influences in the band? What is Slug into, for instance? He and Phil, I notice, are more into electronic sorts of stuff.
LM: They're into industrial music. Thrash music too: Finnish hard core, Italian hardcore ... Paul really– metal. He loves all kinds of music. He's really into Jimi Hendrix. He likes all kinds of stuff, really. He knows so much about so many different bands and records. He's like an encyclopedia. U.P.S. has ... all the people in our band have a lot of friends ... our scene is just all of us. We're just all friends. A lot of us hang out together.

NSBL: You guys are really active (though).
LM: It's really nice when people get their stuff together. I don't know. I don't see there being that much of a Tucson scene: really. I see some people doing some stuff.

NSBL: Don't you think it's gotten better in Tucson, or no?
LM: I think it's better because there's a lot more young kids that are getting involved. That's really good to see.

NSBL: What do you (especially) like that's going on in Tucson now?
LM: All the new bands starting. That's the thing I think is the best.

NSBL: What do you think Tucson needs the most?
LM: "What it needs most right now is an all-ages club with no alcohol. That would really help things the most. That would show who was really interested; who would go for the bands, not just go for the party of it all. 'Cause that's what it is a lot of times. It seems like it's a party."

NSBL: Tell me about the two aspects of 'Fuck Shit Up.'
LM: "Well, it's a song we wrote. It's about just how you can try so hard in life to feel good about yourself, to be, to make it through every day and do the right things. It seems like you're always fucking yourself; like you're your own worst enemy. I'm my own worst enemy. I get myself in more trouble ... That's what fucking shit up is all about. It's like every chance you get you just keep fucking blowing it. That's what it's about. But what has happened, since it is a kind of chant type song, a lot of people (mis)construe it as ... I think a lot of people think 'Fuck Shit Up' is about ... just fucking shit up! But that's fucking shit up too, you know what I mean?! I mean, you can take it wrong, and that's it - you've blown it again! You've really fucked shit up.

WREX Records and Nightclub advertisement, December 1985, *Magazine*.

189

Overview for '84:
Don't step on Tucson's blue suede shoes

By Anonymous Bluesmen
January 1985 – The Magazine. Page 8

A s 1984 passes on, it may be remembered, among other things, as the beginning of a blues renaissance in Tucson. In most cities, the popularity of aesthetic music varies, but generally maintains support and is accessible to its fans.

In the past, the low level of support of local music in Tucson has forced many of the arts underground (Hence, the **Subterranean Blues Band** of the early '80's). 1984 saw the surfacing of an enormous amount of blues support here.

The **Statesboro Blues Band** has reminded us through the past year (weekly at **Terry & Zeke's**– with some exceptional performances with the likes of Bo Diddley and Charlie Musslewhite), how exciting and soulful this music can be. Popularity and interest in the blues and R&B has grown considerably. The main beneficiary of this increased interest and support has been Tucson's blues loving public.

Over the past year, the Old Pueblo has seen more blues than in the preceding decade. The people at Terry & Zeke's Friendly Tavern have shown themselves to be enthusiastic proponents of the blues. Being one of the smallest venues east of Chicago has not hindered Terry in bringing some of the world's greatest living bluesmen to Tucson. The closeness to the artist creates an intimacy that enhances any performance there," The **Temple of Music and Art** has recently been the scene of equally top notch blues shows.

In September, the Robert Cray Band left its mark on Tucson. Cray, a relative newcomer to widespread popularity in his field, is a very upbeat performer and interesting R&B stylist. The band comes from the state of Washington, but bears the influences of Chicago, Texas and New Orleans. Cray has a sweet, soulful, yet powerful voice, and a captivatingly melodic style of guitar playing. The band played several blues classics, and many tunes from Cray's most recent "Bad Influences" album. The Robert Cray Band's sparse, funky arrangements are the epitome of the contemporary blues sound of the 80s.

Blues harpist James Cotton brought his sound to Tucson directly from the Long Beach Blues Festival. Many old fans were surprised by the modern, more hip sound of Cotton's rhythm section. Certainly quite different than that of the Muddy Waters Band, which Cotton played with for so many years. No surprise though, was the caliber of the music, and musicianship with which Cotton surrounds himself. His latest release is a high-energy project, "High Compression."

While Texas Bluesman Clarence "Gatemouth" Brown spent Thanksgiving week at T&Z's displayed a musical excellence that is admired in any genre, and his great band, Gate's Express, are in fact, very much at home in any musical arena. This six-piece band sounded like twelve (due to Gatemouth's arranging and guitar voicing). They played music ranging from Texas Swing thru Count Basie, the blues from up-tempo to low down. Not only is Brown a uniquely superb guitarist, he is equally talented on the violin. Long before he fiddled through a polka, some red hot zydeco, and Cajun music, and a beautifully pure, sweet country ballad I understood why Gatemouth Brown won the W.C. Handy award as the best blues instrumentalist of '84.

Two of blues' senior members, Willie Dixon and John Lee Hooker gave youthful performances at the Temple. Dixon, backed by the Chicago All Stars, set aside his walking cane and belted out many of the blues classics he penned. Willie's energetic and dexterous handling of his upright bass belied his 60 plus years.

Charlie Musslewhite, king of the blues harmonica, put on a stellar performance at Terry & Zeke's in December. Many longtime blues fans said that was the best they've heard Charlie play.

Musselwhite's trademark is the up tempo blues. He strolled up and down that blue avenue with the pace of a stock car. And when he slowed down, his playing was as soulful and low down as can be. As with Musselwhite's spring show, he was accompanied by the **Statesboro Blues Band**. The combination was ideal. The sensitivity for the music, and each other these musicians felt was quite evident. At times, Musslewhite and guitarist **Pat McAndrew** broke into riffs borrowed from the Benny Goodman Sextet. The bands strong rhythms and musical integrity made this a totally enjoyable concert.

The Statesboro Blues Band also played opening sets for the Robert Cray Band, James Cotton, and Gatemouth Brown. The SBB and **Denis Offret** led an evening of boogie and soul at the **Temple of Music and Art** New Years Eve. All looked very debonair in their new Powder blue tuxedos.

Other local bluesmen of considerable talent are solo performers Denis Offret and **Professor Paul**. Both men perform at Terry & Zeke's on the weekends from 7:00PM to 9:00PM.

The Professor plays Chicago style blues with great enthusiasm on Friday nights. Paul loaned his cherished 1912 upright piano to Albert Collins' pianist, and was invited to sit in with the band. They were joined later by **Los Lasers' Danny Cox** and Statesborito **George Howard**.

Dennis Offret has been gaining a reputation- as an authority on the blues as well as one of the southwest's finest country blues players. Offret played the opening sets for the Albert Collins show. Most of Offret's repertoire was up tempo traditional blues. He is a strong player, keeping rhythm with his thumb, while chording and playing the melody in the style developed in the Piedmont area of the south-central east coast. Denis' intensity may have caught some people off guard.

He playing was very soulful. He seemed to mean every note. Denis sees this recent period of increased interest in the blues as a historical period that will keep Tucsonan's in touch with the roots of American music.

Although he has played a number of clubs and types of music, Offret considers himself, and is proud to be, a bluesman. In part, because "...blues fans are great. They're most appreciative."

Radio has been terrific where blues and R&B are concerned. Community radio station **KXCI** (91.5 FM) airs **Harmonica Mike's** Traditional Blues Show on Saturdays at 11:00AM. **Terry O**'s Blues Show, Saturdays from 5:00 to 7:00PM, has become a Tucson favorite. Both men have done well interviewing, and spotlighting the music of artists to coincide with their Tucson appearances. Also on **KXCI**, **Kid Squid** and **Mr. FM** spin the most amazing assortment of our musical roots. Their time slot of 3:00PM to 5:00PM Saturday is a listening must. As well as Sunday mornings' Gospel Hour.

Those in the northern reaches of Pima County, and those with super-antenna can pick up KMCR (91.7 FM) and indulge all weekend in Phoenix's Public Radio. Saturday (evenings, 6:00PM to 9:00PM, is the new time slot for "Reggae Sound System/Rhythm International." This show spans reggae, African, blues, R&B, doo-wop, and soul music, and often plays unreleased or very rare recordings. Sunday brings the blues to KMCR. From the 9:00AM live recordings of the **Juneteenth Blues Festival**, to the locally produced Hollow Blues at 10:00AM, and the long running N.P.R. Hollow Blues one can perhaps divine the answer to the musical question, "How blue can you get?" The **KWFM** (92.9 FM) Sunday Night Jazz Show has been playing more blues than their normal fare lately.

Bill Pitts, host of **KUAT** (90.5FM) Just Jazz Show, Saturdays from 8:00 to 10:00PM, has on a couple of occasions invited **Denis Offret** to co-host his show. In these few spots, they've sampled all the contemporary blues artists. Those were absolutely terrific shows– as those of us who recorded them are often reminded.

1985: Entertaining Month by Month

January 1985: Sandworms become Sandwurms

By Lydia L. Young
January 1985 - The Magazine. Page 11

Note the change in spelling from **Giant Sandworms** to the **Giant Sandwurms**. According to **Howe Gelb** the change reflects the new concept direction of the band. At present, the Giant Sandwurms are still working on their new material and looking for a drummer. Gelb also said **Blackie Ranchette** has been approached to tour France. Nothing, however, has been finalized.

Al Perry and the Cattle began recording a six song EP at the **Sound Factory Recording Studio** on January 2nd. Perry said it should be released by February (1985). **Jeff Keenan** said the **Phantom Limbs** are scheduled to record a second record in San Francisco during February.

Tom Larkins has officially quit **Lance Kaufmann and the Soul Rebels**. He said he is moving to Santa Barbara, California to tour with **Chuck Wagon and the Wheels** for a few months.

David Roy, who recently moved to Phoenix, has put together a band including **Steven Davis** on bass, **David Golder** on guitar and **Barbara Cason** on drums. Assuming the name the **Numbskulls**, they will do writing and vocals for the glam-style band, reminiscent of The Stooges, The Heartbreakers and T. Rex.

Word from **Spontaneous Cheesemakers** is they have changed their name to **Road Furniture**. **Tony Dew** said they are constantly working on new songs and are planning to do a video in the very near future. Watch for them to be appearing anytime now.

Chuck Dukowski, ex-bassist for **Black Flag**, has formed a new band called **SWA**. They will open for **Minutemen** at **WREX** on January 19th. WREX recently opened at 1035 E. Broadway, just east of Park Avenue. The building combines a nightclub with an auditorium atmosphere, along with a record store. Co-managed by **Chris Olivas**, WREX plans to offer quality alternative (i.e. "not mainstream") entertainment for everybody. All ages are welcome.

Some new, young local talent, **Clayton Calhoon** and **Joe Perillo**, have formed a band, still without a name. They will appear at **Flowing Wells High School** January 15th.

Stab in the Dark is a great blues-rock band that is playing out all over town these days. The rhythm section is tight and strong providing a powerful base to the band. I caught them December 16th at **Characters** and enjoyed every minute. Not too many people turned out so the club closed early despite protests of its patrons. You will be pleasantly surprised by a sound not too prevalent in Tucson.

New Year's Eve found me experiencing a couple of exciting things. The **Freds** played at **Splinter Brothers Warehouse**, with **Chris Wagner** on synthesizer (his first time on stage). A sprinkling of **Road Furniture** popped up in their set a special surprise.

Phantom Limbs jamming'

Phantom Limbs photo, circa 1985, *Newsreal* archives.

Phantom Limbs also performed as tight and uplifting as always. The sound was surprisingly good, and I dare say, everyone enjoyed.

Later that night (morning), a jam happened at **Razzmatazz** that inspired **Tommy Mosh** (drummer of **Progerian Youth**), **Pat Murphy** (bass of **Los Lasers**), **Paul Young** (guitarist of **U.P.S.**), **Marx** (drums for Los Lasers), **Matt Griffin** (bass for **Los Hamsters**), **Danny Cox** (guitar, Los Lasers), **Chris Stagg** (vocals on **Wild Thing**), and **Russell Wells** (guitar and saxophone) among many others. The energy level was definitely high ... even in the early morning hours.

More Tucson clubs close, bands prepare LPs

By Jeff Latawiec
January 1985 - The Magazine. Page 16

Here we are in a new year. 1984 went out with a bang, as December's musical happenings were numerous. If things keep going like they did this past month, '85 will be a year hard rocking fans rave-it-up. The biggest event in the next few months will be the Iron Maiden concert at the TCC. Following that, probably sometime in March, there will be a benefit concert for The *Magazine*. Headlining that will be **Roc Lochner** and Tucson's heaviest metal conglomeration **Aftermath** has agreed to also play. Other groups are being arranged.

As 1984 closed, so did Tucson's number one hard rock venue, **Rockefeller's**, **Mark Newman** has taken over the old **Outlaw** (which has also closed), on West Lester, and renamed it the **Roxy** (The Outlaw moves into The **Rock's** old home). The Roxy will give local rock bands a larger place to play and continues to showcase up-and-coming bands.

As I'm talking about bars, that brings to mind another change that began with the New Year. Unfortunately, the drinking reverted back to age 21. I agree that the past years have seen an increase in problems related to alcohol such as drunk driving. But, isn't it better to have people drinking in a controlled environment than running around the streets? Why make criminals out of kids who are going to drink regardless? Also, It's damned hard to take away a freedom once granted. This Victorian type law is sure to hurt local bar owners, and in a time when money is tight for everyone. What is being played up as responsible government, for all the above reasons, I don't think is at all.

Okay, now for some music news. **Roc Lochner** was at the forefront of local music again. During the early part of the month, they played an open-house type party at **Splinter Brothers Warehouse**. The place was packed, and Roc Lochner did the whole show by themselves. They played the songs from their upcoming LP, due out this month. I've never seen them rock better.

I ran into local guitar hero **Mark Smythe** again recently. He confirmed that he does have recording plans, although nothing to do with his ex-band **Jonny Sevin**, as incorrectly mentioned in November's column. They are gone forever.

Naked Prey may be signed

Another Tucson band seems near to the vinyl dream. I've heard rumors lately that **Naked Prey** may be signed, if not already, with Slash Records in L.A. Hope so.

The group's mentor, **Van**, has been a mainstay or the local music scene for a long time. He was drummer for onto of the city's first generation of punk bands, the **Serfers**, who have since gone on to a good measure of success as **Green on Red** in L.A.'s neo-psychedelic movement.

Naked Prey is an originals' band, with Van doing the songwriting. The few times I've seen them I liked the sounds, which hit me as being almost Cream-like (from their Disraeli Gears days), but with a modern, new music flavor. Go see them yourself to get a good idea.

Los Lasers stopped waiting

Los Lasers, cover of January 1985, the *Magazine*. Photo by Tim Fuller.

By Lydia L. Young
January 1985 - The Magazine. Page 2

I f I say **Los Lasers** debut album "Waiting for Bardot" is like a book, it might be read as a simile to a play "Waiting for Godot" by Samuel Beckett. I do feel the album is like a book, but for the simple reason that it is complete; it has a beginning, and ending, stories and a well designed cover. After writing, playing and performing for over five years, with only a few changes in line-up, Los Lasers have presented us with an album that expresses who they are.

This blend gives their originals a punchy, danceable sound that also edges into their cover material. Their music is unmistakably theirs and "Waiting for Bardot" does them beautiful justice.

Each song has its own sound and statement. Side one consists of a more diverse line-up of songs, while side two pushes the well-known Los Lasers edge. **George Hawke** who composed all of the songs, said they want to build on the album. "It's already helped us and we haven't even started shopping around." He stressed that they would like a contract, but for now it is a tool to get bookings out or Tucson and wider exposure.

The title song, "Waiting for Bardot," is laced with late '70s mellowness, though the expert guitar work of **Danny Cox** makes it a quick, fast paced tune. "Drive Time" is a clear rock and roll/roll blues song, full of the energy and enthusiasm the band expresses on stage. **Randy Lopez** on tenor sax accentuates the slow, hushed mood of "too many nights in my Cadillac." Los Lasers rhythm section is a powerful force with **Marx B. Loeb III** on drums and percussion, and **Pat Murphy** on bass.

Especially on "Hole in Her Handbag," the percussion intro carries the entire song in which the fresh Los Lasers edge comes through. One of the most outstanding songs on the LP, "(Everyone's In Love With) Stephanie," is straightforward rock and roll, heavily reminiscent of the Byrds and Beatles of the '60s.

"Waiting for Bardot" is a refreshing album. Mixed and recorded here in Tucson at the **Sound Factory Recording Studio**, the quality of the record exhibits professionalism and hard work it took. The vocals are well balanced with the music, each trading spotlights, but neither overpowering the other.

Hawke stressed the album is definitely a beginning rather than an end. "We will keep playing and do some recording in the next few months," Hawke remarks.

Birkenstock and Blues Co. advertisements, January 1985, The *Magazine*.

It's the Aftermath that'll get you

By Jeff Latawiec
January 1985 - The Magazine. Page 2

Aftermath ... defined as "the result or consequence of something destructive"– like after an atomic bomb has been dropped. Aftermath ... it is also the name chosen by a local band consisting of five guys who are totally immersed in heavy metal.

"We play a party and three days later, people's ears are still ringing. That's the 'aftermath.' They'll remember us by that," says the band's bass player, **Joe Nutt**.

Standing in the band's small practice room, listening to them run through their repertoire, one is immediately impressed by their sound. It ranks with the best in their chosen genre. The music is a virtual assault of the senses, overpowering and forcing the listener to notice and digest it.

Their is an air of professionalism about their presentation and sound that is surprising considering the current line-up (which they firmly state is the final and definitive). They've only been together about three months as Aftermath, when drummer **Rich Von Glahn** had joined.

Aftermath shows no signs of sloppiness or loose edges usually associated with a newer group bound and determined to play their own music- and just their own music.

Besides their polished and aggressive sound, the other thing that makes this band stand out from the crowd is that commitment to original music.

Of Aftermath's two guitarists, **Cliff Finney**, sums it up: "Our attitude towards our Instruments is just too radical to be playing Top 40 copy tunes." So far, the band has 13 tunes. Some titles include, "Pandemonium," about "just crazy chaosness," "Killing Time," their opening song, "Hit Man" and "Never Gonna Wake Up" about getting killed in a car crash.

"I relate it to the guy in Hanoi Rocks," said lead singer **Richard Shaka**, referring to the recent and tragic accidents in which drummer for Hanoi Rock was killed when Motley Crue singer Vince Neil wrecked his car after getting too loaded.

"Hear the sirens calling for you. Twisted metal, yes, it's true.

All the times you think you learn. But it's too late, you'll never learn."

Instead of relying on one or two basic riffs, their songs are intricate compositions highlighted by the twin-guitar attack of **Finney** and fellow axe-man **Brian Stowe**.

The two trade off leads during the instrumental breaks of their tunes, providing two different solo styles in each song, as well as a constant rhythm guitar to compliment Nutt and von Glahn's solid backing.

Former guitarist-turned-singer Shakas voice is unique in a way. He has a clear, easily heard voice, not yet all "thrashed out" as the band put it. And, defying the current trend, he is not a Rob Halford rip-off not sounding like anybody but himself.

In fact, the first experience Shaka had with the group was during a gig at **Rockefeller's** last April when the then-singer for the band walked off the stage in the middle of a set. Richard helped out on a few tunes he knew the lyrics to. But, according to the band, all that went on before is nothing. To them, Aftermath is a new project, and they are totally devoted to it. "It's really new to us, but it's progressing," says Finney.

Aftermath has been around for about three years in various forms. Cliff and Joe always remaining together all along. There was a period when they only played instrumentals because of trouble finding a permanent vocalist. They have not yet debuted any of their originals, preferring to hone themselves to the sharpest edge possible before playing to an audience. They have agreed to join other local bands in a benefit concert for the *Magazine* this spring.

"It's not easy doing it their way. Most band members have full-time jobs to support themselves while working on the Aftermath Sound.

"We don't want to fall into the bar circuit," says Finney. "That's not to say they don't want to play for local fans, if they want to do it in their own manner."

"We'll play bars, but with another original band," Shaka added. When asked why they chose to play HM, and how they felt about the recent statement by a member of Rali, who says metal music is dying– the band was very definite.

"Why Heavy Metal?" quipped Finney. "I like the challenge I get from playing it. Anything else bores me."

"It's better than not playing something that's true to your heart," Shaka remarked. And, as it its dying, Nutt has this to say, "No way, I think it's more on an uprise. What's going to happen is with the 14 and 15 year-olds that like it now– they're going to grow up and still like it."

Tucson has a class act with Aftermath. With recording plans set for 1985, and their upcoming live debut, local metal freaks can get set for a treat.

"We're just going to put it on the line and hope it works," Finney concluded.

Aftermath photo by Shawn Siqueros. Entertainment Magazine archives.

February 1985: Tucson musicians rock WREX

By Lydia L. Young
February 1985 - The Magazine. Page 9

Before I go on, I want to apologize for not making it to too many shows lately. I was working heavily on a major article for this issue, which could not be finished without being fair to everyone. While taking pictures at a show, I was standing on a chair that decided to jump from under me. Of course, I did not want to hurt the camera. So, I landed full force on my hip causing a painful, but temporary, partial paralysis and numbness on the right side of my body. All in a days work. And, still, there is much to be said.

WREX had an unusual line-up January 9th (1985). Stark Raving Mad from New York cancelled, but two of Tucson's own played. **Los Hamsters** opened with the energy and excitement of a rock and roll show. The band was tight, playing mostly originals reminiscent of the '60s and '70s and a few covers such as "Little Red Riding Hood" and "Sister Susie's Turn to Throw the Bomb." Los Hamsters is a great band, inspiring amusement and dancing. Their rapport with the audience was fantastic. The diversity in fashion added to the fun. **Linda**, whose fingers flew on lead guitar, brought the '50s to mind. **Matt**, on a bouncy bass dressed in all red, flashed '60s. And vocalist **Splatt**, writhing on the stage, was definitely '70s hard-core punk. **Julia**'s sticks were a strong backbone to the band– much more noticeable in her talent than hidden behind the drums. An encore was inevitable.

The second band to play that night was **What Went Wrong** I could ask the same question. The guitarist was hot, but the rest of the band gave the impression that they could care less. That rubbed off on me.

Italy's Raw Power band heard last summer is definitely hitting the U.S. in March. They will be touring with Breakout in California. It is possible that **U.P.S.** will do the south and Midwestern dates with them. **Brian Bromberg** [45] has returned to the local scene. I caught him briefly at **Jack's Pub** January 17th but look forward to hearing more.

Chances burned to the ground

Chances Night Club, 6542 E. Tanque Verde Road, was condemned hours after an arson fire ripped through the building Thursday, January 11, 1985. The bar opened in November 1978.

Chances Night Club, *Entertainment Magazine* archive photo.

---

[45] **Brian Bromberg** was born in Tucson, Arizona on December 5, 1960. (brianbromberg.com)

T&Z to serve drinks, Chances bites the dust, Roxy and DanceTrax rises

By Lydia L. Young
February 1985 - The Magazine. Page 9

The new **Roxy** is a beautiful, roomy club, with a great stage and sound system, I saw **Concourse** on January 5th (1985) and was not impressed by their unoriginality and same old cover material. Let's hope for some good shows. **Chances** burned to the ground, reportedly by an arsonist, in January.

Speaking of new clubs, another all ages club opened on North Oracle called **DanceTrax**. They will feature recorded music.

Dance Attack is a multi-colored show synched up to the music flash on screens as the "O Team" DJ's spin a wide variety of music. It happens at **WREX** Friday, February 8th from 9:00PM to 2:00AM. Be there for "the "Midnight Break off" when breakdancers take to the floor.

Terry & Zeke's now has their liquor license, says **Terry Glassman**. That means they now serve well, call and mixed drinks in addition to a wide selection of beers, wine and champagnes. I ran into an unusual contrast of attitudes at Terry & Zeke's Monday Night Jams. Everyone had a good time on January 14th. There were so many changes in musicians I could hardly keep track. Everyone was encouraged to join in. The following Monday I went down and the musicians on stage refused to let anyone else play. I got the blues.

The **Flipper Show** at **Characters** January 24th apparently was not heavily attended. The next day, Terry Glassman said, Characters has been temporarily closed for renovations. That makes two bars lost. And, oh, no, a third.

Tucson bands rock the clubs

I was definitely impressed with the **Speedways** at **Twin Peaks** on January 12th (1985) Their music is basically old rock and roll covers, but they are tight and talented.

U.P.S. is auditioning serious drummers. **Paul** said the band wants to record and get ready to go on the road. There was a party January 12th that brought a new local band out of the desert. The band, **River Roses** consists of **Chris Seldom** (rhythm guitar and vocals), **Gene** (lead guitar), **Kate** (bass and vocals) and **Rob** (drummer). They were without a drummer, so **Julia** (drummer for **Los Hamsters**) sat in. River Roses is a band worth hearing. They do almost all originals with a couple of Velvet Underground covers. Sort of a new version of folk/rock, Los Hamsters also played the party– fine tuning themselves for the major gig at WREX.

Liz Youngren (ex-drummer for **Feline**), who can be seen rather regularly jamming at Terry & Zeke's, said she is keeping her beat in shape and looking to audition for a serious band.

Mark Smythe said he is currently writing new material with plans of going into the studio to record a few originals. One of those will be "Stride by Stride," co-written with **Van Christian** that was performed at the **Virgin Vinyl Christmas Concert**. Mark said he is already shopping his songs in the L.A. area. **Road Furniture** has been working very hard lately. They have finished a personal video called "Road Furniture" which will be aired on **TWIT**, January 31st between 9:30PM and midnight on public access channel 37. **Tony Dow** said the band will play live on February 1st and work on another video with **Cox Cable**. Dow added, Road Furniture had-been polishing their originals in preparation of doing professional quality video on February 9th (1985).

January 11th was an eventful night at WREX. **The Cattle** opened, with, I was told, one of their best sets including three new songs (see interview, this edition). **Naked Prey** played second to approximately 150 people. Many sources reported that **Van Christian** instigated violence and a general negativity over the whole show, singling out people in the audience with a deliberate attempt to cause fighting. **Charlie Pickett and the Eggs** played next and tried their best to turn the negativity around. They played a very good set.

Jeff Keenan of **Phantom Limbs** said they are auditioning drummers. Because of this disruption, they have moved their San Francisco recording date to March. **Al Perry** said the new album will be in approximately six to eight weeks.

The band IF... (l-r) Will Chapman, Darrel Mayers, Spanna and Dan Hill. Photo by Simon Alev © 1985.
Entertainment Magazine archive.

There is a new experimental rock and roll band in Tucson called **If**. Members include ex-**Hi Top Stink's** main men **Danny Hill** (arctic guitar), and **Spanna** (guitar and percussion), Also there is **Heidi Hegwer** (drums) and **Darrel Mayers** (bass). All members of If do vocals.

Ipso Facto has been having some very successful weekends at **Nino's**. **Joey** (bassist) said they are trying to put another tape out, preferably live, Also, he said, **Ipso Facto** is planning some gigs outdoors in the near future.

Lots of **Los Lasers** action. Bassist **Pat Murphy** quit the band January 12th. Pat said he will be trying to get a band together in March or April. Also, drummer **Marx B. Loeb III** is leaving March 2nd. He said he is planning on starting another rock and roll oriented band. **George Hawke** said they have hired a new bassist named **Jim Miller** and have not given up on Los Lasers.

The **Resistors** are going into the studio to record a demo and to shop around. Word is that their original sax player, **Murphy**, has returned. The band is working on new songs and doing some heavy rehearsing. They won't be playing for a while.

I did not see the show, but I heard **Chuck Dukowski's** (ex-**Black Flag**) new band **SWA**, played WREX on January 19th and was discordant, slow and metalish with no real direction. The **Minutemen**, however were said to have played their best Tucson performance ever. They did two full encores to about 300 people.

The Outlaw changes

By Fonda, February 1985, The Magazine. Page 18

Country music enthusiasts have surely noticed a big change with the moving of the **Outlaw** to 5822 E. Speedway. Fortunately, they will still offer live music.

Terry & Zeke's Friendly Tavern advertisement, February 1985, The *Magazine*.

February 1985

SUNDAY	MONDAY	TUESDAY	WEDNESDAY	THURSDAY	FRIDAY	SATURDAY
					1	2
					Thrills Galore	
3 Thrills Galore	4	5	6	7	8	9
				Thrills Galore		
10 Thrills Galore	11	12	13	14	15	16
				Outrage *(from Portland, Ore.)*		
17 Outrage	18	19	20	21	22	23
				Little Sister		
24 Little Sister	25	26	27	28	1 March	2
				Little Sister		

Vertical column labels: CLOSED TO ADD THE FINAL TOUCHES (Monday) · KWFM ROCK 'N ROLL PARTY WITH CHRIS RYAN AND THE PARTY ANIMALS (Tuesday)

TUESDAYS	**WEDNESDAYS**	**THURSDAYS**
KWFM ROCK N' ROLL PARTY	LADIE'S NIGHT	PARTY NIGHT
92¢ Well, Wine, Bottle Beer	Ladie's No Cover & 75¢ Well and Wine	for Everybody
$1.50 Pitchers	Men Get 50¢ Drafts	$1.00 Well and Wine

THE *Roxy* Nightclub

144 W. Lester
622-6363

Roxy Nightclub advertisement, February 1985, *The Magazine*.

March 1985: Local music lights up Spring Fling

By Lydia L. Young
March 1985 - The Magazine. Page 3

The Lone Ranger (Clayton Moore) will ride into the Old Pueblo March 28-31 (1985) to host the **University of Arizona Spring Fling**. It promises to be a fun-filled four days. Besides the traditional rides, food booths and games, the music line-up is a "gonga!" thanks to **Stacey Simms**, entertainment director of Spring Fling. The auditory senses should gear up for what could turn out to be a truly euphoric experience.

The first night of festivities on March 28th features **Friendly Warning** and **If**. The March 29th schedule includes **The Outcrowd**, **Buddy System**, **Mobile Cubes** and a surprise performance.

Split Decision cranks things up March 30th along with the **Saddle City Band**, **Rainer & Das Combo**, **Only's** and **Gentlemen After Dark**. That same day, the Lone Ranger is scheduled to emcee an awards ceremony at 6:00PM. An hour later, a dance contest breaks out. Lots of prizes are up for grabs.

The last day of Spring Fling on March 31st has **Long Island Sound** performing with **Street Pajama** and **Brian Bromberg** throughout the day. Check the centerfold calendar for times of each performance. Shows are included in the price of admission.

Al Bums advertisement, *The Magazine*, March 1985. Page 4.

Spring sprouts local music news

By Lydia L. Young
March 9, 1985 - The Magazine. Page 9

According to **Jeff Keenan** of **Phantom Limbs**, **Howe Salmon** (the **Dogs** and previously with the Limbs) is going to be drumming for the band when they do their recording in San Francisco (date still tentative). A giant sorry for missing the show with Rank & File, which I heard was excellent. A pound of cheese to Jeff Keenan.

On February 3rd (1985) **Manifest Destiny** played **WREX**. With only a few days notice **Los Hamsters** opened and **Matt Griffin** (bass) said they were not quite ready. **Manifest Destiny**, a mid-tempo original hardcore band was reportedly decent. I was told that the sound system was not working well and there are hopes the band will return for a fairer review.

Sharon O'Brian and camera took on the night of February 8th for me. The Dance Attack (break dancing) at WREX was especially enjoyable. Also fun was **Jack's Pub** that night featuring the band **If** with a circus theme. Unfortunately, the camera was not working properly and the pictures did not come out well. Nevertheless, I thank Sharon for her determination.

River Roses played energetically at the **UA Cellar** during "Eat to the Beat" February 13th. I hope to hear more of their thought-provoking, inventive music. Not too many people showed up for the Toxic Reasons show on Valentine's Day at **WREX**.

Word is the band was very tight and their message came across clearly… to inform people to be aware of controls put on us. The international mixture (one American, one Canadian and two Englishmen) blended well to bring forth different viewpoints. The opening band **What Went Wrong** managed to get themselves kicked off stage due to disorganization and a laissez-faire attitude (thank you for the fan mail).

Al Perry said the new **Cattle** album should be out soon. Current plans are for a record release party at **Tequila Mockingbird** on March 23rd.

I spoke to Mauro Codeluppi (vocalist) of the Italian band Raw Power who said the band will be flying into Canada on March 22nd. The tour actually begins April 1st. For the first two months (at least), Breakout will be opening for them, after which **U.P.S.** is expected to join them. Their new LP, recorded on their last American tour, will be out in two weeks.

Mark Smythe (ex-**Isaiah**, **Pills** and **Jonny Sevin**) has been working hard on his own material lately. He was in the studio last week, backed by **Only's** to tape a song co-written with **Van Christian**, "Stride by Stride." The sound is one the heavy metal side, but the Mark Smythe emotion and dance attraction is evident.

Smythe describes his new direction as "compulsive, gut rock and roll." He has plans to spend as much time in the studio as possible, in order to put his material in shoppable form. Smythe said he is more interested in playing guitar for a band than leading one. He also has something up his sleeve, but is not talking.

I saw the **Veg-a-matix** at **WREX** February 19th as was very impressed. Their music is fast paced, rock and roll rooted with pop overtones. The professionalism of the band was brilliantly evident on stage in the way the member's complimented each other. Soon after the show, **Hope Gorecki** (vocalist) contacted me with news the band had changed its name to **Enola Gay and the Tokyo Bombers**. The weekend of the 23rd the band spent working in the studio. They feel very happy with their progress and experimentation.

Last heard of as the **Giant Sandworms (Giant Sandwurms)**, **Howe Gelb** and **Scott Garber** have moved to Los Angeles and are recording as **Giant Sand**. Garber said the name was changed to end the affiliation with the movie, So far, he said, they have had good response to the change. For the moment, Garber said, "No comment about the record."

February 20th at **Tequila Mockingbird** was a bit surprising. The **Johnies** opened and were described as a garage band performing mostly covers ranging from Nancy Sinatra's "Boots" to "Sister Ray" by the Velvet Underground. Their set was loose, but fun. Most of the crowd left after the Johnies and The **Cattle** had a good, but short set, due to equipment being knocked over.

Jack Martinez of **Only's** said the band is about three quarters done with recording. "We are trying to get a real good piece of recording and it's going great." Martinez added that they have imported a professional producer, Doug Williams, from Los Angeles. He also stressed the band is not pressing an album.

Pandemonium seemed to be the order of the evening at WREX. February 24th. Some fights broke out. There was destruction to the club and cars were vandalized. The bands, however, were great. **T.S.O.L.** was tighter and more professional than ever. Their heart and soul were bared as they played. There was a bit of jamming with T.S.O.L. and **M.I.A.** at the end of the show that was both unusual and pleasant.

DanceTrax advertisement, March 1985, The *Magazine*. Page 5.

The heavy metal edge; Roc Lochner new release

By Jeff Latawiec
March 1985 - The Magazine. Page 11

With the close of this month, we are getting near the release of **Roc Lochner's** long awaited mini-LP. They filled in the waiting time by playing the **Roxy**, and a gig at the **University of Arizona Ballroom**. They also managed to get out and see some music by other bands. Most of the group was present Friday the 22nd (1985) for **Aftermath**'s gig at **WREX**.

That was one good show, despite being plagued with a late start (**Aftermath** didn't go on until after 1:00AM) and some sound problems. They were hot, tight, and all the other, adjectives you use to describe a band you like. They have trimmed down to a four-piece, since one of the guitarists is no longer with them. But **Cliff** handled all the guitar chores with no problems. A lot of that is due to **Joe Nutt's** incredibly good bass playing. Along with Rick's drumming, the space behind the lead solos is amply filled. This is singer **Richard's** first time as lead vocalist for any band. But he looked as if he's been doing it always Friday night. That means he was good.

We're Here and a band composed of **University of Arizona** students called **Believer** also played the same show. WH has also shaved down to a four-piece, getting rid of their lead vocalist. As mentioned last month, they have gone original and they seemed to please quite a few folk with their new style. I didn't arrive in time to see Believer, unfortunately, but I heard they did a lot of metal covers; and seemed to get a decent audience response.

The Magazine Concert Update: We finally located a site to put on the planned benefit concert. The people from WREX, mainly **Chris, Joe** and **Daryl** have made arrangements to use their hall for the show. The next step is finding a date when all the groups can play. Anyhow, it's going to happen. I hope tons of people come so that the *Mag* can become an ever better independent publication.

I was out looking at records the other day and I saw some discs made by local groups in the bins. It's really nice to be browsing through the slabs and be hit with a name like **Naked Prey**, who had just released their first album. Hope to see more of the same. As usual, the people I owe thanx to are legion. But, I'd like to single out Joe Nutt, **Raeanne, Tawny**, my brother and **Tommy**, and finally, **R.Z.**

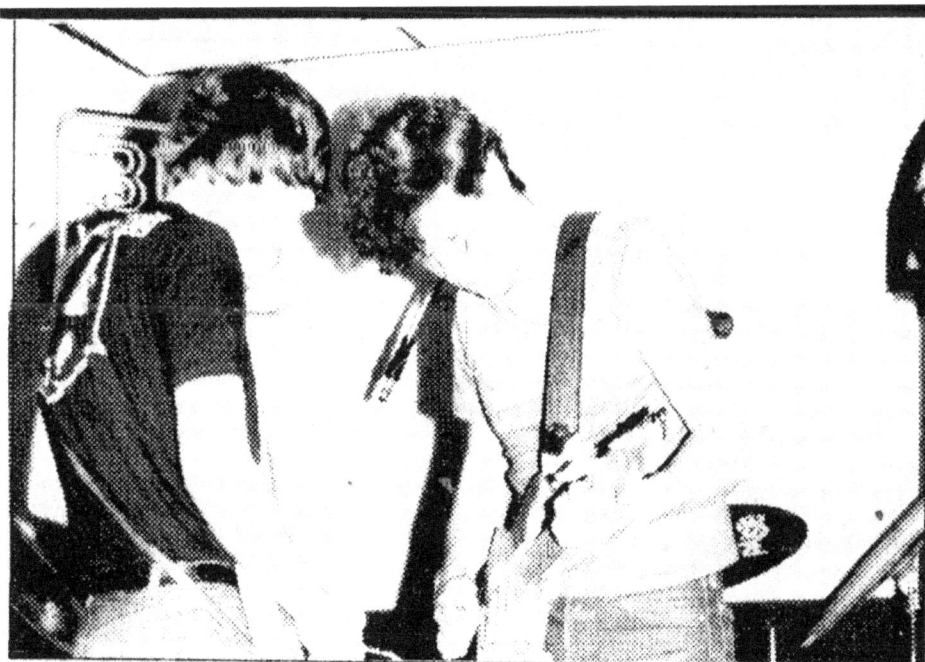

Kevin Daley and Al Perry jamming at Terry & Zeke's. Photo by Fonda. March 1985, *Entertainment Magazine*. Page 11.

HMS in performance, September 1985. Photo by Robert Schotland. The *Magazine* archives.

WREX advertisement, *The Magazine*, March 1985. Page 21.

Etude prepares video

"Etude" members (l-r) Larry Munguia, Tomas Gonzalez and Thom Bissey in between audio and videotaping. *Magazine* Photo by Stephanie Samoy.

By S. Castillo Samoy
March 1985 - The Magazine. Page 23

A sound is blaring from the small color TV set at Channel 37's downtown headquarters. The vocals crying through the glass screen are singing, "It's tuff, so tuff. Get tuff, it's tuff," while guitars are screaming with a vengeance.

Faces of emaciated Children from the Third World and South America flash across the screen. Mid-Eastern soldiers with severed limbs show the grimness of war through their pained facial expressions.

When the song is over and the pictures fade, a rousing cheer spreads within the cramped room. **Etude**, a Tucson-based rock trio, has successfully premiered its first video, "Tuff," on the "Tucson Air Show."

Etude, a term used in classical music that means a composition intended mainly for the practice of technique, accurately describes the activities of this three-man band.

Guitarist/vocalist **Tomas Gonzales**, 27; bassist/vocalist **Thom Bissey**, 25; and drummer **Larry Munguia**, 28, are always working on their craft as musicians, whether as a unit or on separate projects.

Gonzales, a book clerk by day, spends his free hours writing tunes for Etude (he penned "Tuff"), working on videos, searching for other musicians to jam with, and is currently fielding an idea for a Tucson-based demo-recording studio.

Bissey, the band's "Renaissance Man" who hails from Chicago, is a classical/jazz trained musician who is also a photographer, theater actor and potter.

The bearded Munguia, who went to **Salpointe High School** with Gonzales and is now self-employed as a parking lot sweeper, says, "I would like to just be able to play music for a living and not have to worry about a so-called job." Motown and the jazz influence of Miles Davis is the Bissey factor, the heavy metal of Led Zeppelin and Keith Moon fanaticism is Munguia's contribution, and the Beatles influence comes from Gonzales' background.

One homogenous thought among the three men: "Tucson needs more places for live music– live, original music," Bissey says. "Original!" shouts Munguia in the background. "Here, here," Gonzales reaffirms, "Second that original music." Amen!

New radio station on cable TV

March 1985 - The Magazine. Page 28

KBLE-FM, Tucson's first cable radio station will go on line in early March (1985). Locally owned and operated, KBLE-FM will be available to basic subscribers of **Cox Cable** through the audio portion of a yet to be assigned channel.

For a nominal monthly fee of approximately two dollars, KBLE-FM will be receivable through the subscribers' FM stereo via a cable hook-up.

Because KBLE-FM is broadcast over a closed-circuit medium, its signal suffers none of the atmospheric or multi-path interferences of other FM stations.

Playing a new and distinctive dance format, KBLE-FM will offer listeners an alternative to contemporary music currently offered in Tucson.

KABLE-FM advertisement, March 1985, *Magazine.*

Rock Videos: Fad or Culture Shock?

By David Moskowitz
March 1985 – The Magazine. Page 7

Are rock videos a slowly dying fad? Are rock videos stagnant and all basically the same with a few alterations and slight additions between the majority of them? The quality of the videos do not stand up to the quality of the music," says **Pima Community College** (PCC) music major **Frank Sorrenti** as he so aptly puts it.

Dennis H. Leibowitz, an analyst with Donaldson, Lufkin & Jenrette says, "Anything that gets this much attention still has the smell of a fad. We are just going to-have to wait and see."

It is estimated that at least 1,200 music videos were made in the United States and Europe in 1983, double the number made in 1982, according to an article in the *New York Times*. MTV (Music Television, a 24 hour cable music channel that reaches 22 million households), reports that production of videos recently reached a steady pace of 35 per week and that figure continues to grow. MTV has been an important tool to promote record sales and helps give bands more exposure.

Sales and rentals of videocassettes totaled $1 billion in 1983. Four percent of that went to music videos, according to F. Eberstadt & Company, which compiles such statistics. The statistical research firm added that music videos are expected to rise to 25 percent of a $5 billion market by 1988.

The networks, cable channels and independent stations have rushed to offer music video programs. Today, there are more than 200 of them on the air and still growing.

Hollywood studios have already produced a steady stream of music video films, such as "Flashdance," "Footloose" and "Purple Rain," to name a few, and most with record and videocassette releases in mind.

It is reported that record companies have increased their rate for the cost of videos. They now pay anywhere from $40,000 to $60,000 for each, and sometimes, even more. But, they are also asking for more complex, dazzling, expensive and aesthetic productions.

"There is a great future (for rock videos)," says **Carl Blanton**, president and owner of **High Risk Venture Productions**, a local company that makes and produces videos through the **Tucson Community Cable Corporation**. "Young people," he added, "are brought up with the television and the visual medium and expect to see something visually stimulating. Music videos are immediate and a good, short, concise way to be presented."

"People are also going to want to see the people (performers) they like on the screen whom they would not normally otherwise see and maybe only once a year in a concert," says **Mike Dicambio**, a music major at PCC. Dicambio also proclaims, "As long as rock and roll is around, videos are here to stay! Pop music is constantly changing and videos are going to have to keep pace."

But, most record companies continue to regard videos as an expensive form of promotion. They also continue to resist the attempts of video producers to lift production fees. "The amount of money needed to make a video is rising and getting too costly," adds Sorrenti. Analysts say that they are unsure of the stability for the long-term profitability of the video music rage.

"The market hasn't defined itself yet," states Dr. **Clifford Brock**, chairperson of journalism and media technology at PCC. "People have an expectation of seeing things instantly. The delivery of traditional information is blending, shifting and changing rapidly. The media will shift according to market needs. With technology, the quality of production is getting better."

Despite the enormous demand for the music video, the product has just not become profitable. The problem is that money is not yet rolling in music videos. They are getting increasing play on cable and broadcast television. The pulsating "music video look" is spreading into films, commercials and fashion for which it could very well be considered a style setter for streetwear, thus 'fashion music.' Cassettes of music videos are expected to playa growing role in the blossoming home video cassette market.

The history of music videos dates back to the late 1970's in London where it was originally financed, in part, by rock groups looking for new ways to present their songs, Today, the major release of a record is often accompanied by a music video.

"In its importance, the rock video clip is comparable to the development of the 45-RPM single," says Bob Krasnow, the chairman of Elektra-Asylum Records. That's pretty obvious. Just look at the video jukebox at **Golf 'n Things**.

"The videos that are the most interesting are the ones that are innovative, creative, imaginative and have originality," says PCC music instructor Dr. **Larry Solomon**, Namely, some examples are; computer designed graphics, videos for educational purposes to stimulate the brain, different music genres such as baroque, classical, romantic, contemporary, country, blues, etc., etc., captions for learning impaired, store merchandise catalogs on video (although quite costly) with music, and the ideas go on.

One thing for sure is that break dancers and dancers in general are enjoying increased employment. Blanton would "like to seem more people who have not made it in videos. There's a lot of talent that have not met the right people." Anyone who would like to contact Blanton should call the **Tucson Community Cable Corporation**.

Wooden Nickel advertisement, March 1985, The *Magazine*. Page 26.

Do people interpret videos differently than when the song is played? Will one lack imagination by watching the video instead of listening to the song? Blanton answers, "Listening gives you the opportunity to create your own visuals and use your own imagination. With video, you are just accepting somebody else's visualization of the music. (For students) it would stimulate them to see things that they would never have thought of, and makes them create things building on that idea (in a video)."

In studying cycle changes of music through the course of history, Dr. Solomon predicts that "the genre of rock music, itself, will eventually fade away, but the rock phenomenon will be remembered during the twentieth century period."

But, one question arises. Does profitability and quantity necessarily mean quality in videos?

Connie Breeze: Breezin' down life's highway

By Casey
March 1985 - Magazine. Page 31

What does Tucson's **Oasis Television** channel have in common with MTV? **Connie Breeze**! After leaving her job as News Director at 13-**KHYT**, Connie followed her media instincts deeper into television.

Her recent endeavors included a public service taping for the Cerebral Palsy Foundation, "I did the PSA and then went on my merry way." Connie's eyes sparkle with her story.

"Somewhere between Christmas and New Year's I was in the Oasis studio. We were fixing up some things and someone had flipped on MTV. I heard Martha Quinn say "We'll be right back after this." Then, I heard, "Hi, this is Connie Breeze ...""

"The Cerebral Palsy Foundation PSA was done through **TWIT** and was set up by **Dave Bukunus** and **Darwin Hall**. We had a great crew. Let's see, there was **Joseph Boudreaux**, **Lisa Horner** and **Randy Hartis**." And Connie.

Connie Breeze Photo by Richard Kepharp, Los Angeles

Connie is a fresh breeze of media energy from Grand Blanc, Michigan, a suburb of Detroit. Motown. "I love funk," she says as she sets her coffee mug down. She looked around the restaurant, as if searching for a band and a dance floor. "I like to dance a lot," she adds as she swings back to the table.

She danced her way through high school. A few years later, she was armed with a degree from Michigan State University.

Connie first came to Tucson in January 1981 to apply for a job at KHYT. She didn't get the job. Months later, she was in California when she bumped into KHYT's program director. He offered her the job and she literally jumped on the plane with only the clothes on her back.

Connie drank the last of her coffee and then she took a minute to reflect on radio and television before heading for the studio, "In radio you can fool people easier. You can give them an impression that may not be true. Television is much more exhausting because you have to keep your face on."

She bounces into the studio with a "hi, everybody" that somehow seemed to charge the atmosphere. As she waits for her cue to go on camera, Connie remarks, "I decided when I was five that I wanted to be a TV star. I've always been a dreamer, a fantasize."

The dream comes true for Connie as she goes live on TWIT and hosts the "Tucson Air Show" rock videos.

Connie also works on the Cultural News Program and helps teenagers who produce **Cablewaves**. She is also helping to set up an Explorer's Scout Post in conjunction with Cablewaves. The twenty-four year old former

Explorer Scout comments, "Exploring molded my life. It taught me to exist in a cooed environment with energy, enthusiasm and excitement. It takes a lot of energy to get involved in as many things as Connie tackles. But that is the way she likes it. I'm not really happy until I'm almost at overload- when I'm doing too much."

After she set in the studio, she comments on the origins of her involvement with television. "I got into the whole thing by chance. Last June, Dave Bukunus called the station looking for another person who had expressed interest in hosting TWIT for one evening. That person was out of town and I landed the spot. Then I became a regular."

Connie smiles as we leave the studio.

"The most incredible things happen when you know what you want and you bop along life's highway."

Life's highway twists away from the glamour of the television studio and into the Tucson Mountains. A crispish tinge of winter envelope's Connie as she trudges through the desert. Her thoughts turn away from media, as she focuses on her inner self and relationships.

"I have an interesting birth sign– the cusp of Sagittarius and Capricorn. You're polite enough to ask someone to move out of the way, and when they don't you run them over."

"I don't need someone to entertain me. I can do that myself." She pauses to look out over the desert from Gate's Pass. "Men think they can't make me happy because I'm so multi-faceted. That's not true at all."

What is true that Connie Breeze will follow life's highway– to wherever it may lead.

Midnight Star with Special Guests Shalamar and Klymaxx advertisement, The *Magazine*, March 1985. Photo by Marc Hauser/1984

Tucson's Reggae History

By Neal Ullestad
March 15-April 12, 1985 - Newsreal

The rhythms and beat of reggae are seductive pleasures. Swaying and skanking to the heartbeat of the reggae sound, we hear sensitive love songs and astute social commentary. Roots music has been more than an exotic Jamaican import for some time now. And here in Southern Arizona we have our own history of reggae– got live if you want it.

Live reggae in Tucson got its first big boost when Steel Pulse, Britain's premiere Rasta reggae band, performed on the U of A campus early in 1981, hosted by **Rising Star Productions**. Tucson's own **Upsetters**, a lively two-tone band, sprang earlier from the fertile desert soil in the fall of 1980.

Our first local reggae outfit eventually spawned the Anglo-reggae **Uptones** whose local mini-EP from **Westwood Recording Studio** featured "Africa is at War" and "One Free New World," as well as the energetic cross-over of **Moses Smith**'s **Ninth Street Checkers**. These early homegrown reggae experiments were great fun, and serious as well.

Peter Tosh, one of the original Wailers, was the next international performer to play the U of A. The enthusiastic audience transformed the staid auditorium into one big party. Legalize it, eh? From the deep roots that were sunk by such prominent world-class musicians as Tosh and Steel Pulse, a rash of bands emerged to jolt Tucson's reggae scene. Through various transformations, the rootsier **Tin Roof** (which emerged in April, 1981), the **Moor Rockers** (a communal Rastafarian experience) and then Burning Bush played at the **Copper Star Café** and the popular little club at 1122 N. Stone Avenue and Speedway.

Stars and **Smokey's Nightclub** regularly booked reggae: the Uptones following their trip back East; Kansas City's Blue Riddim Band; Chicago's Armagedeon, Burning Bush, and Shagnatty from Phoenix. Shagnatty's potent mixture of musicians – men and women; West Indian, Canadian and Southwestern– generated the distinctive sound captured on their LP Rejoicing (Jah Works/AUAround Records). Now based in L.A., Shagnatty will soon release a new album with assistance from Arizona musicians.

Once again, the UofA with community radio this time, hosted international talent with the first Tucson appearance of the Itals vocal trio backed by Jamaican rhythm masters the Roots Radics. And the cultural exchange of reggae sounds was fostered with Tucson's own **Louis Virie Blanche** performing in the Jamaican SunSplash. Tucson's Reggae Splash, multimedia presentations brought together by **Ras John** at the **Splinter Brothers Warehouse**. **Sisters Warehouse**, featured movies of Caribbean Life, Linton Kwesi Johnson's Dread Beat And Blood, as well as video of the legendary Bob Marley. The Twinkle Brothers, direct from Jamaica, contributed the live music.

In May of 1984, Steel Pulse returned to Tucson. Their well-crafted sound and visual antics stimulated the integrated audience– red, black, brown and white, young and old, gay and straight. And, the band once again featured their riveting attack against the "Ku Klux Klan" as their first encore. Then, in July the **Meditations** performed their more spiritual repertoire at Quijotoa backed by the **Papago O'Odham Reggae Rockers** on the same weekend that the Itals again featured their subtle harmonies and critical vision of the brutal system (out deh), this time backed by **Jah's Children**. This "Summer Reggae Festival" presented, in addition to the headliners, Phoenix's own Sons of the Captivity (formerly Driftwood) and the newly emergent talent of **Neon Prophet** at the **El Casino Ballroom** (which boasts the finest hardwood dance floor in Southern Arizona).

Springing from the fluid local scene, **Neon Prophet** brought together newcomers and seasoned musicians to play roots reggae plus funk, country, rock and jazz. The **Sons of Captivity**, whose deep roots feature talented Black and Pima and Mestizo Indian musicians, captivated reggae fans with their haunting riddims.

Later, in September, **Moha** also played the **El Casino Ballroom**. Finally, to cap a "dread-full" year **Eek-a-mouse** brought his distinctive, vocal stylings, social conscience, sly word play and outrageous stage show to the **Temple of Music and Art** for a **KXCI** community radio fundraiser in mid-October. Jahmalla, New York's hottest reggae roots band (with a sought-after album of their own), backed the Mouse, and Neon Prophet opened in top form. Two nights of posing, reasoning and dancing cemented KXCI's pivotal role in the local reggae scene.

1985 got off to a flying start locally. The early February valley snow drove reggae fans indoors at the **S B&S Warehouse** for hot apple cider and **Galaxy 500** (reggae/rock). Brian and Neon Prophet are at **Brooklyn's** for the **Wah-Deh Connection**. Then, for Bob Marley's birthday, Los Angeles' Creation Rebels (with an Anglo woman vocalist on keyboards and former members of the Rastastafarians and Twinkle Bros.) and the Sons of Captivity played Brooklyn's. This club promises to feature reggae regularly with shows booked for Arizona talent throughout March.

New Bands Heat Things Up

In this year of "pop" reggae, kicked off by MTV's New Year's Eve exposure of UB40 and General Public; two local bands may help bring reggae into Tucson's mainstream. **Brain Damage** and the **Wah-Deh Connection** appear to be sinking some solid roots here with their distinctive styles, unlike more transient talent who've moved on from Tucson's relatively "unprofitable" scene.

On February 22^(nd) (1985), the hottest new club in town to feature reggae, new wave (tinged with blues & country) and soul– **Brooklyn's Nightclub** chances nightclub at 2436 N. Stone– brought together these two local acts to get people on their feet, dancing and sweating. **Smokey Covington** has drawn enthusiastic crowds to enjoy well-respected, established groups and exciting new ones in the comfortable, mid-size club just north of Grant. The venture seems to be paying off.

Brain Damage Orchestra

Brain Damage Orchestra, 1986. *Entertainment Magazine* archives.

Brain Damage is the perfect vehicle for introducing reggae to a new audience. Similar in key ways to Dave Wakeling and Ranking Roger's General Public and San Diego's Untouchables, the Brain Damage 7-piece orchestra offers a dynamic and eclectic fusion of pop, rock, reggae, blues, country, soul and ska. The sound features enough familiar things to catch the ear, and enough exotica to challenge and entertain.

With eight solid originals (soon to be available on tape) that touch on love and fun, as well as the pillage of the desert and the hard lives we live today, and with worthy covers of Blues classics and early rock & soul hits; this is a band to watch. Their distinctiveness rests on the interwoven harmonica and saxophones, but each of these women and men put in a solid performance. (As with any young band, and **Stephan George** not withstanding, the vocals can certainly use some work.) With more substance than Culture Club and as much fun as Madness, Brian Damage sets the mood to party.

Wah-Deh Connection

The **Wah-Deh Connection** is a rootsier reggae band. But, the night the two bands shared the stage at **Brooklyn's**, Wah-Deh played, in addition to well-crafted originals, an inspiring cover of Hendrix's "Wind cries Mary" and a deep roots version of "Johnnie B. Goode" that could put Peter Tosh on guard.

Kinee Wade's gentle "Falling In Love With You" is a sensitive song that epitomizes the sensual and sexual power of reggae music. The band tends toward the militant style (so much the better these days) inspired by Linton Kwesi Johnson and the youthful Jimmy Cliff. In my mind, Kinee shares the title of hardest working drummer in Tucson with **George Howard** of the **Statesboro Blues Band**. With trumpet and keyboards to flesh out the strong percussion, guitar and bass; this band is hot, especially **Dubwise**.

Though the **Wah-Deh Connection** developed from a split from **Neon Prophet** - Tucson's oldest currently working reggae band; the fact that local reggae is experiencing a new wave of popularity should mean there's room for everyone to meet the new demand. (The biggest disappointment for me was the break-up of the tight three-part harmonies of Kinee, **David Dean** and **Joseph Jarman**).

Tucson reggae clubs

Today, Tucson clubs have changed with personnel changes altering the make-up of different groups; but reggae is definitely experiencing a surge in popularity and availability locally. Our own bands are being booked, not only at the clubs above, but also at **Nino's** on North First Avenue, **Terry & Zeke's**, **Tequila Mockingbird**, **Café Olé**, **Jack's Pub** downtown, **Gentle Ben's** on N. Tyndall just south of University Blvd., the **Food Circus** and the **Elk's Club** on S. Meyer. So there's no excuse not to dance to the sensual reggae beat.

The fact that all the local reggae-based bands are forging ahead with new combinations and ideas, instead of relying on old standards (Neon Prophet is previewing a tape of six originals), means there's a new vitality in the Tucson scene. Watch for more exciting things to come!

Fred Espinoza: Lights, Camera... Stress

By David Moskowitz
April 1985 - Entertainment Magazine. Page 7

The word "tour" somehow always sparks up ones eyes with magic and gives the feeling of "being on the inside" and having a sense of importance and authority. But that is just only one side of the public perception of "going on tour," as production manager for the promoter, and sometimes promoter himself, **Fred Espinosa** explained before last month's Midnight Star, Shalamar and Klymaxx show.

"The reality," he said, "is traveling on one of the band's tour buses and sometimes winding up on the floor (due to sliding or falling out of the bunk) when you fall asleep."

He also added that "there is a large distance between the places where the band plays" and can become quite a long and tiresome trip. Although the buses are quite comfortable, they even have a "recording studio in the back of the bus," which is becoming more common with bands touring– along with the usual color TV's, VCR's, phones and bars.

"In the east, the cities are much closer together, making traveling there a lot less lengthy. The road crew could travel by plane, but that would be too costly for both the band and their recording company to pick up the tab. On special occasions, they do.

Espinosa has traveled with the Midnight Star Planetary Invasion Tour to a couple of cities including Albuquerque, New Mexico, Phoenix, as well as nationally. He explained that "some of the other dates are someone else's gig," meaning that another promoter in that area will take over.

Mondays
FOXFIRE
(rock)

Tuesdays
NADINE & THE MOPHONICS
(orig. rock, rhythm & blues)

Wednesdays
LADIE'S NIGHT
with Male Dancers

Thursdays
BLUE WAVE
(blues)

Sundays
SIR REGINALD
(funk/soul)

FRIDAYS & SATURDAYS
Fri/Apr 5: *WAH-DEH CONNECTION (reggae)*
and *NEON PROPHET (reggae)*
Sat/Apr 6: *NEON PROPHET*
Fri/Apr 12: *PYRAMID (funk/soul)*
Sat/Apr 13: *PYRAMID*
Fri/Apr 19: *NEON PROPHET*
Sat/Apr 20: *BRAIN DAMAGE (rock reggae)*
Fri/Apr 26: *WAH-DE H CONNECTION*
Sat/Apr 27: *PARTY MUSIC*

BROOKLYN'S
2437 N. STONE
791-7542

Brooklyn's advertisement, The *Entertainment Magazine*, April 1986.

Espinosa, a native Tucsonan, has worked for the past ten years doing production with different bands. His company is called **Creative Entertainment**. Another promoter and a Tucson native, says Espinosa, "**Roger Leon** gave me my start position as a stage manager six years ago."

He explained some of the characteristics of someone wanting to go into the field, as "a musician who'll find that there is more money in it (promoting). It strikes you as glamorous at first, but then you find that it's just a job. It's very challenging," he added, but emphasized very strongly "that there is a monumental amount of stress involved, and a lot of ends to connect."

He advises those wanting to get into the business to "start out on the local scene by working in clubs with bands." The promoter has to make sure, and oversees, that everything goes as smoothly as possible (which is a very rare instance) and that all schedules are met on time. With all the money that is involved in a show, one must have to think quickly in emergency situations.

Espinosa reminisces back to the beginnings of Creative Entertainment, "When we started doing R&B concerts, people had told us not to do it and that it would never work. They also said that we would never be able to give away tickets!" He added, "The people in the industry told us that this would never work in the southwest. And then we hit hard with five shows that were very successful. Then, other people decided to do the same thing, but it didn't work out for them." Creative Entertainment organizes shows that are considered "family entertainment."

"We like working with this type of show (Midnight Star) because they bring in a very intelligent, well-mannered crowd, that really knows how to enjoy themselves, Unlike the metal shows, our audiences do not damage chairs, break windows, assault each other, or the acts (such as throwing articles toward the stage)."

"There's something wonderful about bringing a show of this caliber to Tucson and watching 9,000 people thoroughly enjoy themselves. It's a very satisfying experience."

Espinosa sums up his unique profession this way; "It's a great job for a person who has never had a nervous breakdown, and that always wanted one."

Backstage at a concert is not as much fun as the people in front of the stage might think." Photo by Seymour Butz. Pima County Fairgrounds. *Entertainment Magazine*, 1985.

April 1985: *Magazine* is now *Entertainment Magazine*

After publishing since 1982 as The *Magazine*, the monthly publication changes its name to the ***Entertainment Magazine***. The *Entertainment Magazine* is a "sister" publication of the youth-oriented tabloid ***Tucson Teen***, published through **Southwest Alternatives Institute, Inc.**, by **Robert E. Zucker**. Each month, 20,000 free copies are distributed into all Tucson **Circle K Stores**, hundreds of local businesses, the **University of Arizona** and **Pima Community College** campuses, all **Tucson** and **Pima County Public Libraries** and City and County Recreation Centers. The first April 1985 edition featured the **Michael Landon Tennis Tournament**.

Photo: cover of the April 1985 edition of the *Entertainment Magazine*.

Saddle City Band stars with Michael Landon

The **Saddle City Band** will again be appearing on NBC's highly rated and very successful TV series "Highway to Heaven," starring Michael Landon and Victor French.

The band appeared in the premiere 2-hour episode which aired last fall, as well as the "Highway to Heaven," "Song of the Wild West" episode which co-starred Ronee Blakley.

The summer repeats are beginning and the Saddle City Band will again be seen on those two episodes The "Song of the Wild West" will air again April 3, 1985 on NBC (**KVOA** Channel 4) in Tucson.

The Saddle City Band (April, 1984) is **Rick Nuttall** on guitars and vocals; **Mike Sullivan** on guitars and vocals; **Duncan Stitt**, keyboards and vocals; **Gordon Lynde**, bass and vocals and the newest member **Mike Holloway** on drums and vocals. The band has writing and rehearsing new material for their new album and made several concert appearances at **Old Tucson**, UA **Spring Fling**, **Pima County Fair** and the **Outlaw Nightclub**. On May 6th the Saddle City Band appears in concert with country legend Merle Haggard for one show in Tucson.

The Saddle City Band with Michel Landon (center). From right to left: Mike Sullivan, Mike Holloway, Landon, Rick Nuttall and Bill Cashman, the band's producer. Photo courtesy of Art Attack Records, March 1985.
Entertainment Magazine archives.

April 1985: Tucson's got all the jazz!

By S. Castillo Samoy
April 1985 - Entertainment Magazine. Page 9

Spring is here and Tucson's jazz and blues scene continues to offer some choice pickings. Places about town that you can frequent include: **Terry & Zeke's**, **Brooklyn's**, **Keaton's**, **Poco Loco Bar & Grill**, **Temple of Music and Art**, **Jack's Pub**, **Café Olé**, **Cushing Street Bar & Restaurant**, **Gus & Andy's Steakhouse** and on and on...

Along with Albuquerque, N.M., San Diego and Houston, Tucson lays claims to two jazz supported groups; **Eneke**, the 35-member "guardian angel of avant-garde" and the **Tucson Jazz Society**. The Old Pueblo also has the **Tucson Blues Society**, which is here "to educate and promote an awareness of blues music and culture in Tucson" (their motto).

Loser's Club debuts

April 1985 - Entertainment Magazine. Page 6

Four veterans of the local music scene have combined to form Tucson's newest and most exciting band in some time. **Chris Burroughs**, whose **Nationals** played here two years, has returned from Los Angeles to join former **Los Lasers** members **Marx Loeb** and bassist **Pat Murphy** and **Stab In The Dark** guitarist **Rick Kirkpatrick**. Loeb, who played drums with the Lasers for six years, just recently left that band, as did Murphy, whose other local credits include The **Soul Rebels**, **Wellington White** and **Arizona**. The **Losers Club** will play all originals written and sung by Burroughs, Kirkpatrick and Murphy and will debut the middle of this month, playing most of Tucson's rock and roll clubs before disbanding in June.

Terry & Zeke's (4376 E. Speedway) and Tequila Mockingbird (3601 E. Broadway) advertisements,
The *Entertainment Magazine*, April 1986.

Nadine & the MoPhonics: Singing for success

Nadine & the MoPhonics (l-r) Dan Sorenson, Cathy Zavala, Lisa McCallion, Bob Casler, Neil McCallion and Nancy McCallion. September 1986. *Entertainment Magazine* archives.

By S. Castillo Samoy
April 1985- Entertainment Magazine. Page 11

Nadine and the MoPhonics is the name of one particular Tucson rock and roll rhythm and blues band. But you won't find a Nadine among the bunch. And, you won't find a MoPhonic either.

"We decided we weren't gonna tell people why we call ourselves that. It's policy," lead guitarist, sometime "grunter," **Dan E. Sorenson** says.

But, he makes an exception this once and explains the origin of the band's name. "We actually used to have a bass player who was a speech teacher." Oh.

Nadine and the MoPhonics actually have had several bass players and a few drummers before settling down with their present line-up. Lead vocalist **Nancy McCallion**, age 22, co-founded the band with her partner rhythm guitarist, vocalist **Cathy A. Zavala**, also 22.

"We met in a guitar class at **Pima College**," McCallion says. "We knew each other because we had a mutual friend, and this mutual friend talked about the fact that Cathy played, wrote songs and stuff, and I guess…and then we met and listened to each others songs."

The rest of the line-up includes Sorenson, 35; bassist/vocalist **Cathy M. Davidson**, 24; and drummer **Bob G. Casler**, 32.

The band released a cassette tape last year entitled, appropriately enough, "Nadine and the MoPhonics," which includes six original songs by McCallion, and, or by Zavala. "We do our own songs much better than somebody else's. If you write it... " McCallion says. "It's you," Zavala interjects.

The band also needed the tape to sell themselves to club owners for prospective gigs. "It's pretty hard to work in certain clubs," McCallion says. "I guess we don't fit into their type," Sorenson says. "We don't have green hair," Casler adds.

But, if Nadine and the MoPhonics get their way one year from now, "I'm hoping we'll have a really good following ... and playing as much as we want." McCallion says. "Five years, from now I hope I'm not here anymore. I hope to be farther along."

Zavala's wish is fairly simple. "I want a nice car."

"Well, I want a big house," McCallion says.

"Oh, I want a house, too," Zavala adds.

Nadine and the MoPhonics

Nadine and the MoPhonics. Photo by Tim Fuller. *Entertainment Magazine* archives.

Local scene bursts with spring

The Johnies warm up the crowd at The Cattle's record release party. Photo by Lydia L. Young. *Entertainment Magazine*, April 1985. Page 18.

By Lydia L. Young
April 1985 - Entertainment Magazine.
Page 18

With spring finally upon the Old Pueblo and in my step, I seem to be making up for lost time and catching a variety of new and old local talent. Much has been happening.

During "Eat to the Beat" in the **UA Cellar** on February 28th (1985) the debut of **Affirmative** was a fresh surprise. The band includes **Tim Saunders** (vocals, guitar, keys), **P. Joseph Peters** (drums), **Jan Marie** (bass), **Graydon Lindskold** (guitar), and **Chris Wheatley** (keys) with originals and covers in the techno-pop vein. There was quite a turn out for the show and the band hopes to be playing more often.

Jack Martinez of **Only's** said they are planning on doing more video work. "We are moving in a forwardly manner and want to do some touring," he said.

Impressive at **Jack's Pub** on March 15th were **Giant Sand**, now residing in L.A. The dance floor was jumping and the evening ended only after **Hector** and **Van Christian** (**Naked Prey**) were asked to join in. **Scott Garber** (bass) said everything is going fine in their new home. We await the record.

Word is out that **Chris Holliman** of **River Roses** (ex-**Seldoms**) wants to do a live tape. I was told the concept would be a "garage Woodstock." The line-up so far includes River Roses, the **Johnies**, the **Dogs** and **Los Hamsters** (see article this month). The **Wah-Deh Connection** brought some pleasant reggae sounds into **Brooklyn's**. The band has a subtly complex style that makes the spirit move within.

I saw **Los Lasers** at **Nino's** March 22nd and despite upset in band members, their music was prime. Local stick wizard **Tom Larkins** (**Chuck Wagon and the Wheels, Blackie Ranchette, Chris Burroughs and the Nationals** to name a few) is drumming with Los Lasers through May. Larkins said he is then returning to California to drum with **Giant Sand**. **Danny Cox** (guitar) said he has a couple of projects he is interested in, but as yet has made no decisions.

A big surprise this month was The **Cattle**'s Record Release Party at **Tequila Mockingbird**, March 23rd. **Fish Karma** opened the evening on a humorous note. His self-proclaimed "novelty songs" were often straightforward fun poking at current issues, local musicians (in particular) and himself. The **Johnies** who performed second with their unusual pop-country-blues music brought the crowd to the dance floor. Lead singer, **Dorian Cacavas**, was stunningly charismatic the band was slick and energetic.

The **Cattle** experienced some equipment and sound problems, but were enthusiastic and giving towards the audience. Joining The Cattle was **Jeff Keenan** (**Phantom Limbs**) who played his heart out. It was quite a party with wall-to-wall people webbed into the excitement! I applaud the public's large scale appearance.

Unfortunately, the album never made it out of Nashville to The Cattle in time, so the real(ease) party is yet to come.

I happened to run into **Road Furniture** (see last edition interview) just after they had edited their videotapes. **Don Dalen** (bass) said some comments had been made so they decided to clean it up a bit. By the time this issue hits town, they will have begun work on a 16-track recording of two new songs, "Sometimes I Ask Why" and "Vinnie." **Bruce Halper** has been replaced on drums by **Tom Dow**, **Tony Dow's** (guitar) brother.

Enola Gay and the Tokyo Bombers (once the **Veg-a-matix**) are going to be playing out quite a lot this month. They have just finished recording a self-titled tape. **Hope Gorecki** (vocalist) said the band is involved in a benefit for Multiple Sclerosis scheduled for May.

Stab in the Dark

Stab in the Dark, undated.
Entertainment Magazine archives

Bruce has returned to **Stab in the Dark**. He said he felt it was time to pursue other projects as well. With the help of **Mike Reinhart**, he is currently working on a solo EP of all original dance music.

Bruce said Stab in the Dark is making some changes in personnel and material. They are scheduled to play with **Scott Goddard** in L.A. during the summer. Bruce is also planning to do a one-man-club-act here, calling himself **Lounge Lizard**. "It is going to be a really tacky show," he said.

Ticket buying: made easier

April 1985 - Entertainment Magazine. Page 10

The **Tucson Community Center** has installed a computerized ticket system. Through an agreement with **Diamond's Box Office**, the TCC can now offer improved service. It will now be possible for patrons to purchase tickets at Diamond's department stores at **Park Mall** and the **Tucson Mall** between 10:00AM and 9:00PM Monday through Friday and 10:00AM to 6:00PM on Saturdays.

Every patron will have the same selection of ticket location at the same time. The computer outlets will have access to all available tickets regardless of location. TCC outlets at **El Con Mall** and the TCC Main Box Office have the capability to sell tickets to all events on Diamond's system. This includes most events in Phoenix and at **McKale Center**.

There is a 65¢ per ticket service charge added to all tickets purchased at the Diamonds stores. Tickets purchased at the Main Box Office and El Con will have a 65¢ per ticket service for events other than those held at the Center. Tickets can still be purchased on the TCC Charge system or charge tickets on MasterCard or Visa for $1 transaction fee per order only for events at the TCC.

Wah-Deh Connection: Reggae Connection

April 1985 - Entertainment Magazine. Page 12

The **Wah-Deh Connection** has quickly established itself on the Tucson reggae scene and now plans to spend the spring getting as much exposure as possible. They perform regularly at **Brooklyn's**. They also appear at the 4th Avenue Street Fair and **Nino's**. Guitarist **David Farzalo** is back after two weeks in the east. In his absence, the band was filled out by **Azie Ali** and **Steve Dubwise** on guitar and occasionally **Vinnie-I**, formerly of the **Sons of Captivity** on vocals.

"It's nice to be a rhythm section that can adapt itself to different situations," says **Kinee Wade** (drums and vocals). "We have a good dub sound that comes from our bass player **Jamie Cirritto**. He's a good dub rapper. He got his experience in New York with people like Winston Grinnin and Banky Banx. Drum and bass cooperation is essential in dub." Floating above the rhythm is the trumpet sound of Craig Dye of Pittsburg. It adds another dimension to the sound and his keyboard helps fatten the dub.

Kinee says, "There's a rumor that I'm going to rejoin **Neon Prophet**," a band that Wade started last spring. "That's not the truth. I would welcome their singers however if we do go through personnel changes. Jamie and I plan to stick together. The Wah-Deh Connection is here to stay.

Blues Company and Dead End Record Stores advertisements, April 1985, *Entertainment Magazine*.

WREX closes, but the beat goes on

By Jeff Latawiec
April 1985 - Entertainment Magazine. Page 19

The month got off to a rousing start with the March 10th (1985) Iron Maiden-W.A.S.P. concert. Then there was the St. Pat's Day gig at the **Roxy Nightclub** with **Aftermath** and **Roc Lochner**. But after that, hard music fans had to go out of town to find any satisfying musical happenings. Phoenix hosted what sounded to be one killer of a metal feast, with Metallica, Armored Saint and fresh from the night before in Tucson, W.A.S.P.

Unfortunately for local music, especially the punk and metal bands and fans, the just-months old **WREX** nightclub has already closed down. Too many rumors to sort out the facts. But **Chris**, from WREX, will still be involved in promoting shows. He is scheduled to have a hardcore gig at his house.

Locally: There's been some studio work by Tucson bands during the past several months. We can look forward to checking out some home town vinyl soon which ... (hint, hint!)… our last true blue rock radio, **KLPX**, will give some airplay– not on just once a week shows.

I talked with one of the members of Roc Lochner about their forthcoming mini-LP. It seems they had some problems with the final mix, some things they weren't satisfied with. Anyway they took it out to California to try to find someone to get it right. Hooray! They did and final work is being done. I'm happy because my favorite Lochner tune, "I Need to Know," is included on this record.

Another local band that graces the space of my column regularly is also working on getting a slab of plastic out. Aftermath went into the studio last month to do on EP. I was lucky enough to hear it before the final mix. There will be four songs, and it should prick some ears when heard. They have a unique style of metal, something hard to do nowadays. The EP will give metal fans something new to devour, plus represent them to the record companies.

I recently talked with **Joe**, their bassist, and he was not at all happy about the lack of places for original bands to play. In fact, he was quite succinct about his feelings, especially with the WREX going under. Something to the effect of "this town stinks as far as local music goes." Anyhow, the recording is done. All they have to do is finish the art for the cover.

RAW POWER
From Italy

1985 NORTH AMERICAN TOUR
APRIL 20 IN TUCSON
(CALL WREX RECORDS FOR INFO)
APRIL 21
STRUTS CLUB IN PHOENIX

TOXIC SHOCK
Box 242, Pamona, CA., 91769
(714) 620-6265
NEW ALBUM: "Screams from the Guitar"
Available at WREX Records
1035 E. Broadway. 624-6282

Message Spot: I am going to check out a band called **Exodus** at the **UA Cellar** April 3rd. I've heard they are a metal-oriented bunch, so it could be fun. Congrats to **Naked Prey** on their fine LP, and a special compadre's embrazo to ex-compatriot **Sam Blake**. You did it, Buddy.

So goes another month. Maybe, April will see the opening of another venue to showcase local talent. As always, thanks to the musicians the most. Next, thanks to those who support them, may there be many more of you, especially, at the shows. You don't have to be afraid to come out and see your local HM bands.

Toxic Shock advertisement, *Entertainment Magazine*, April 1985. Page 14.

Los Hamsters?! You got it!

Los Hamsters (clockwise) from top: Julia Meuller, Matt Griffin, Linda Andes and Peter Catalanotte. Photo by Fonda, *Entertainment Magazine*, April 1985. Page 19.

By Lydia L. Young
April 1985 - Entertainment
Magazine. Page 19

You might ask what kind of name is **Los Hamsters** for a band? It is the brainchild of 25-year-old **Matt Griffin** (ex-**Conflict, MPS Chunks, Corporate Whores**) who calls himself "a bit strange." Therefore, the band is not of the to-be-expected type.

In April 1984, Griffin began trying to build a band. "All the music I had been playing before had been experimental music or hardcore and I wanted to try something different, but at the same time keep the energy that hardcore has going," he said.

Griffin went through quite a few 'bands' before the current line-up was found. In the fall of '84, he hooked up with **Linda Andes**, who, although she had no musical training, was very enthusiastic about Griffin's ideas. He helped her learn to play thee guitar and the energy to play grew. She introduced **Julia Mueller** (drums) and **Peter "Splat" Catalanotte** (vocals) to Griffin, and the band was complete. The first song learned was always asked for "Little Red Riding Hood." Los Hamsters first live performance was in November 1984.

Mueller had some doubts in the beginning. "It's getting better now. But, I was so scared the first time we played," she said. The audiences are always enthusiastic, which helps. Los Hamsters have captivating stage presence. Musically, they are impressively talented, energy bouncing off the band and to the audience and back to the stage.

"It is as important to think about how you look and what you do on stage as to listen to the music," Griffin said, "It is always important to look good ... or at least Interesting." Most of the original music is composed by Griffin, but Mueller had contributed a song. They want to expand their original list. They are not sure what to call their music– trash-pop, garage punk and jazz-fusion were all offered. Griffin said loosely, "We are part of the new Tucson garage band movement."

May 1985: Local progressive music hops

By Lydia L. Young
May 1985 - Entertainment Magazine. Page 9

Arizona's own **Meat Puppets** have just released a new album on **SST Records** called "Up in the Sun." This is their third album and represents the much slower, country based sound the band gave us last time they played Tucson. They were formed in Phoenix in 1980. The band includes both **Chris Kirkwood** on guitar, **Kirkwood** on bass and **Derrick Bostrom** on drums.

The Resistors, photo by Rick Aldridge. July 1985, The *Entertainment Magazine.*

The **Resistors** are getting ready to enter the studio, as well, with additional musical input from **Street Pajama's Lamont** and **Bruce Tost** of **Statesboro Blues Band**.

I caught an energetic show at **Jack's Pub** April 13th (1985) featuring **Los Hamsters** and **Road Furniture**. Los Hamsters were fun, as usual, but exuded a bit more polish and confidence.

Road Furniture kept the already mobile crowd on the dance floor with their characteristic synth-pop fusion. **Chris Waggoner** (keyboards/vocals) stole the show with almost the only noticeable enthusiasm. The rose petals he tossed to the audience were a nice touch. I just heard Los Hamsters are planning a 16-track recording in June. They have already done some taping.

Stab in the Dark has brought in **Curt Sample** as their new guitarist and is moving ahead with plans.

Recently, quiet **U.P.S.** is going through some personnel changes. Lead guitarist **Paul** has left the band to pursue other projects. We will have to see what other changes have been made when they play this month.

Enola Gay and the Tokyo Bombers have split up. Singer **Hope** said she plans to keep the name and branch off with a different sound. She said the rest of the band will continue under another name. There is never a dull moment with this group.

General Delivery: Delivering since 1985

By John Thompson [46]
May 1991 – Entertainment Magazine. Page 18

Take five guys with a combined musical experience of over 120 years. Throw in a Hammond B-3 organ, a tenor sax, a tight rhythm section and five vocal parts. Now, add in a repertoire that prowls through the last forty years of rock and R&B. What do you get? Well, not your average oldies band. That's for sure. You get **General Delivery**, an association of five of Tucson's veteran musicians who each bring something a little different to the band's musical style.

General Delivery members (l-r) Shep Cooke, Richard Gomez, Skip MacWilliams, Clay Brown and Richard Tompkins. May 1991, *Entertainment Magazine.* Page 18.

Richard Gomez, a Tucson native who's been playing professionally since the sixties, plays keyboards and pitches in on vocals.

With a Fender Rhodes perched precariously on top of his venerable old Hammond B-3 organ, Gomez injects the band's music with funk, humor and soul. Blessed with a raspy yowl of a voice, he takes the lead on rhythm and blues classics of Fats Domino, the Coasters, Rufus Thomas and Lee Dorsey.

Then there's **Shep Cooke** on bass and vocals. If you have followed Shep's career over the last 25 years as one of Tucson's most accomplished folk singers and songwriters, you might not recognize him when he leads General Delivery through a revved-up take of the Rolling Stones "Satisfaction" or a simmering version of Peggy Lee's "Fever."

Missouri native **Richard Tompkins** brings yet another perspective to the band. Claiming to come from a "country/heavy metal" background, his sincere vocal delivery and creative lead and rhythm guitar work carry the band through the blues of BB King, the backwoods rock of ZZ Top and the country soul of Bob Dylan and Neil Young.

Saxophonist **Clay Brown** contributes tenor sax fills and solos, while drummer **Skip MacWilliams** drives the rhythm. Brown is a veteran of many local bands including **Bob Meighan** and the **Shake**, and has performed with world-renowned jazz musicians Airto Moreira and Flora Purim.

---

[46] **John Thompson** is a local songwriter who digs the desert.

General Delivery performs at Granfalloon Saloon. *Entertainment Magazine* archives.

General Delivery's roots go back to 1985 when Tompkins, new to Tucson, hooked up with **Skip MacWilliams**, previously the drummer for the **Backstreet Boogie Band**. Brown and Gomez came on board with another bass player and General Delivery was formed, playing the local club circuit through the late eighties until breaking up in 1990. MacWilliam's career dates back to a performance at the inauguration of President John F. Kennedy as a drummer in the Leonard Hall Naval Academy Band.

After playing in various other Tucson bands, Gomez and MacWilliams joined with long-time Tucson musician **Shep Cooke** to form at trio called the **Class of '64**, Soon after, Tompkins and Brown returned to the line-up and, early this year, General Delivery was re-born.

With five versatile, experienced performers in the band, who's in charge? "Well, says Richard Gomez, "that's what's nice about this ballad. Every one of us plays a different kind of music. All the leads have a whole different thing, but we blend together."

And when the band modulates into a jazz workout in the middle of "Do You Love Me (Now That I Can Dance)," you understand what one listener meant when he told Skip MacWilliams, "Man, when you guys play these songs, it sounds like you wrote them!"

The band members' camaraderie and mutual respect are evident in their performance. Lead vocals and instrumental breaks are passed around comfortably, and a loose humor and easy rapport with the audience keep the mood light. The band is not averse to taking a little creative license with classic songs, such as the appearance of a Great White shark in Cooke's version of "Under the Boardwalk."

General Delivery will be mixing it up and shaking it down at several local clubs during May, including a stint at **Generations** on May 16th, 17th and 18th (1991).

Tucson is jazzin' it up!

By S. Castillo Samoy
May 1985 - Entertainment Magazine. Page 11

Could it be? Tucson appears to be saturated with jazz ... but one can never get enough. Be prepared to spend a Sunday in the park with Tito Puente and his All-Star Sextet at the **Reid Park Bandshell** on May 5th (1985) or more affectionately known as Cinco de Mayo. The Latin jazz fiesta starts at 3:00PM and **KUAT-AM** 1550 will broadcast live this musical event.

While the topic of radio is at hand, here's a friendly reminder that jazz flows through the airwaves every Sunday, 7:00PM to midnight, on **KWFM**'s Jazz Show with host **Chris Ryan** and **KXCI** plays jazz every Tuesday night.

Now, a note on one local band, the **Black Sun Ensemble**. Guitarist **Jesus A. Acedo**, 22, and drummer **John Brett**, 25, along with their former bassist **Michael Glidewell**, released a demo tape recorded at the **Sound Factory Recording Studio**. Their first album on **Pyknotic Records** will be out in June, with a second album to follow in late summer.

Acedo, who produced the tape, says the band's music "is not progressive music," and that he hopes people won't think he's "trying to be John McLaughlin Jr." Take a listen.

The **Statesboro Blues Band** has entered the studio to record. A tape will be available in the near future with several of their original tunes and "derangements" of other people's material.

(Above) Reid Park Bandshell during a 1980s outdoor concert. Photo by Robert Zucker.
(Below) Moon Paraphernalia and *Entertainment Magazine* advertisements, *Entertainment Magazine*, May 1985.

Roadrunner: Making music country-style

By Fonda
May 1985 - Entertainment Magazine. Page 20

Although Tucson is "in the heart of the West" every now and then most of us get caught up in the city and forget what a beautiful area we live in. I've found a place surrounded by saguaros where one can escape to a great meal and some down home country music.

The drive down Ajo Road is a relaxing one on the way to the **Roadrunner Restaurant & Lounge** at 5975 W. Western Way Circle. The Roadrunner began as a small family owned deli. Soon business was increasing and they began serving liquor last October, then expanded into a full service restaurant. About that time, **Jim Ingleman** (the owner's son) came down from Oregon to help out for a while. Ingleman added fresh seafood flown in from Oregon to the expanded menu. Today, they offer breakfast, lunch and dinner all at moderate prices.

When Ingleman was not in the restaurant, he was getting to know the neighborhood. It was in a nearby saloon that he found **Jack Marksberry** playing guitar on a barstool. Marksberry moved out to Tucson only five years ago from Owensboro, Kentucky to concentrate on his songwriting.

Marksberry soon found himself doing an acoustical act at the Roadrunner two nights a week. Six weeks later, the response was so great that Ingelman asked **John Preston**, a one-time Tennessee farmer who once played with **John E. Mann**, to join his act. In the meantime, the folk at the Roadrunner had installed a brand new P.A. system as well as different lighting to accommodate the band. After only a few weeks with the expanded act, Ingelman was forced to add a second full service bar for his growing clientele.

"This is our first try at something like this," says Ingleman. "We are really happy about the tremendous and steady response we've had to the band." Plans are already being made to build a stage and expand the dance floor. Named for the peak behind the Roadrunner, the **Catback Mountain Band** are finally complete with the addition of drummer **Jim Miller**. It's obvious they will be entertaining us for some time to come. They have a fresh sound featuring a variety of danceable tunes. Best of all, they do several original songs. One called "Tucson Home" has already become a favorite among the regulars.

Roadrunner Lounge advertisement, May 1985, The *Entertainment Magazine*.

The Cattle are now on vinyl

By Fonda
May 1985 - Entertainment Magazine. Page 18

I t has finally arrived in record stores all across Arizona- the long awaited debut album by local trio The **Cattle**. Led by guitarist **Al Perry**, the Cattle have previously released two cassettes. This is their first vinyl product and it is a good one.

The Cattle starring Al Perry, Dave Roads and Julia Mueller. Addled Recording, 1989. *Entertainment Magazine* archive.

"Cattle Crossing" captures all the energy and power of The Cattle's live performances.

The album contains a balanced mix of material including several instrumental tracks. All but one of the songs is original, the exception being **Fish Karma's** "Die Like A Dog."

Perry's guitar playing on this album proves he's heavily influenced by guitar greats like Link Wray, and by traditional blues. There is no real category to put The Cattle into, although this album has blues favor, it contains plenty of garage style and even a little thrash.

The addition of engineer **Steve English's** pedal steel guitar on 4WORV gives it a splash of country sound as does co-producer **Jeff Keenan's** fiddle playing. The meshing of all these factors and influences make "Cattle Crossing" a fresh, well-done album that shows off some of the best talent this region has to offer.

Birkenstock advertisement, The *Entertainment Magazine*, June 1985.

June 1985: Jack's, Rockefeller's gone, Circus on

By Lydia L. Young
June 1985 - Entertainment Magazine. Page 11

Once again summer is here in Tucson. There is also a lot of music around. Things seem to be picking up with the heat– and some things seem to be cooling off. Local musicians are still hitting the studios. Apologies for the rumor about **Only's** last month. Thanks to drummer **Johnny Ray**, it is clear that the band is still going to Los Angeles to record. As the list of bands grow so does the anticipation for their work.

Jack's Pub, one of my favorite clubs, has closed its doors to live music. I am sorry about this as I feel it was a great outlet for the bands and a good place for shows. But, this is not the first club to close, nor will it be the last, I am sure. The spirit of music keeps alive.

There is a new music venue, too. Not new to Tucson, though. The **Food Circus** has started putting on shows. So far, all concerned seemed pleased.

Rockefeller's also closed down.

The May 15th (1985) appearance of **U.P.S.** was a true hardcore experience. Since guitarist **Paul Young** left the band there have been no real changes in its format.

Paul, however, has started a new band called **Bloodspasm**, yet to play live, but smacking distinctly of the rock-hardcore energy. Other band members include **Mike Gonnan** (guitar), **Eric Snyder** (bass), **Tommy O** (drums) and **Bob McKinley** (vocals). They are working on an original song list at the present.

The Tuesday night gigs of **Rainer** at **Terry & Zeke's** seem to be going the way of the jam. Good times are had by all as musicians eagerly join the stage.

Not surprisingly, the following of **The Losers Club** seems to be getting more diverse. They reach a new audience every time they play. Yet, the dancing and appreciation is always exuberant.

Road Furniture opened for **Tupelo Chain Sex** at Nino's May 19th for the 11th Anniversary of the *Newsreal*. Everyone had only good things to say.

It seems **Stab in the Dark** won't be opening for **Scott Goddard** this summer in L.A. **Bruce Halper**, drummer, said the band has changed Its plans and will be playing in Tucson more regularly.

The Fanatiks: They're ironically fanatic

By Connie Breeze
June 1985 - Entertainment Magazine.

The **Fanatiks**, the newest rage on Tucson's exploding music scene, was founded a few months ago by **Rob Paulis**, one of four average guys... sort of! Rob is 20 years old, half of which he's spent playing guitar. The electric violin is another story. **Rick**, Rob's brother-in-law recalls, "I remember only a year, ago Robbie picked up that old fiddle. It laid around the house untouched for years. A week later, he was playing unbelievable things. The brown-haired, brown-eyed Rob says, "I took some of my songs and ideas to **Steve Mersky** and we collaborated. That was the beginning of the Fanatiks.

Steve Mersky, the oldest and most experienced member of the group, is 28. He's a respected keyboardist with eight years on the music scene that is displayed in his free-flow playing. Steve and Rob saw their dreams materialize with the addition of **Dave Nahan** to the group. Dave, like Rob, is a **University of Arizona** student. A distant glance at the 23 year-old-red-haired bass player from the entrance **Nino's** brings to mind the insatiable desire to say "Opie!" That is, until Dave starts dancing.

The Fanatiks. Photography by Déjà vu Photography. *Entertainment Magazine*, June 1985. Page 10.

"Sometimes we live on candy bars, you know." He turns quickly, stops and says, "Everyone had a really good time tonight!

Playing to an enthusiastic weekend crowd is a bit easier than playing hour 20 of a Muscular Dystrophy Dance-a-Thon. That task was led by **Pat Darnell**– the 23 year-old business major who made it his business to inspire a gymnasium of dedicated volunteers to dance.

The whole band relaxes and reflects upon dreams they share in what Rob's father fondly remembers to be his woodworking shop. Now fully remodeled and padded for sound, the Fanatiks enjoy in their familiar room. They chuckle at being asked once more. "How do you describe your music?" Dave and Rob collaborate. "It's jazz-rock fusion with a progressive European edge." It all comes together through complicated individual playing that settles and bonds in all of the right places.

The Fanatiks took advantage of a great opportunity by making a video with **Carl Blanton**, producer of the **Tucson Community Air Show**. Their song "International Language" is a favorite on Channel 37.

The Fanatiks played The Brewery in Bisbee and appeared on Channel 37 in May. On June 1st they perform at Nino's with the **Outcrowd**. They named their group "The Fanatiks" because of their fanatical love of music. But, the way they touch the soul is best described in their song about music itself– "International Language," the language of the world.

Not just another Buddy System

By David Moskowitz
June 1985 - Entertainment Magazine. Page 10

What's a **Buddy System**, you ask? And, how do you get one? "We don't have any buddies. We're not part of the system!" **Michael Edward**, lead guitarist for the Buddy System, jokingly answers after their recent gig at **Nino's** in May. With a reply like that, you would come to think that the band doesn't have any fans. This is just the antithesis. Their following is large and their audience is one of the most attractive that I found a local band to have.

"Hard-edged, thrash pop" is how spokes musician and throatist **Brad Brooks** describes their own original brand of music. Other Buddy System members include **Rock Dotson** (drums), **Mark Anderson** (rhythm guitar) and **Greg (Geddy Lee) Minter** (bass). Quite a lively, aerobic ensemble. Join the system and approach the buddies around town.

Other summer music

By Neil Costin
June 1985 - Entertainment Magazine. Page 10

The **Mobile Cubes** have been recording three originals and have shot a video for "Good, Clean Fun." They report that Chrysalis Records A&R Dept. is interested and wants to hear more material. Upstairs at the Temple is just that. The room "upstairs" at the **Temple of Music and Art** is a club-like atmosphere that begins this month presenting local acts in a new setting. This month includes **Nadine & the MoPhonics**, **Sidewinders** and **If**. From about 8:00PM to 1:00AM every Friday night & Saturday night patrons will get their hand stamped at the door and then be free to come and go as they please.

Adam Graham: The other half of O'Leary

By P.L. Wylie
June 1985 – Entertainment Magazine. Page 2 & 23

Comedy is getting a face lift in Tucson and one of the contributors to that is **Adam Graham**. He Is the writer/producer/director behind the **Graham and O'Leary Comedy Show** which now consists of **Peter O'Leary** and Graham.

Adam Graham, June 1985. *Entertainment Magazine*. Page 23.

Graham originally came from Chicago where he used to go to the Second City Club that highlights sketches formed from improvs. He came to Tucson because he likes the weather and the laidback lifestyle here.

Graham attended the **University of Arizona** Drama Department, majoring in Drama Theory. There was a group of students in the Drama Dept. (now called Studio Series) that was freer and did not use stylized acting methods. While he was involved with this group, he discovered his ability to improvise and that he had a feeling for comedy timing.

However, he considered himself mainly an actor, and has appeared in many local productions, most recently as the waiter in **ATC**'s "Death of a Salesman" and the **Stray Theatre's** production of "Cloud Nine." For this part he studied four-year-olds in the malls until he got their mannerisms down pat. He did (and still does) enjoy acting, but finds it a narrow route.

He neither wants to be known as an in actor nor a comedian– but as a "professional performer."

What propelled him into professional comedy was an overall lack of opportunity in Tucson in the acting field. His partner, Peter O'Leary (who also is trained as an actor), and himself were in a **Comedia del Arte** group, and they found themselves doing "Second City" improvs with others in the group. From there, they decided to concentrate on comedy.

Graham says it is incredibly difficult to change from one field to another. For instance, an audience at a play is respectfully silent. Many actors and actresses get uptight if someone in the audience rattles their program. To switch to standup comedy was a culture shock, as hecklers are part of the package. He said that at the beginning there were a couple of incidents that threw him. But now he looks for hecklers and incorporates them into the act. If there are no hecklers, he has some techniques to get the audience involved the act. After seeing their act, this reporter can attest that Graham is good at improving off as the heckler/comic exchanges.

Graham and O'Leary started with the **Public Access Channel** on **Cox Cable** and then appeared at **Characters** in April 1984. After Characters closed, they appeared at **Tequila Mockingbird**, **Voila**, and now often appear as headliners at the **Comedy Zone** on Friday and Saturday nights for two shows. The response has been very good.

He said a description of the Graham and O'Leary Comedy Show would be "cerebral" with a lot of soul, and low

comedy with a whimsical point of view. Their comedy routines is topical with references to many local people we see on the tube– **Jim Click**, **Madeline Garish**, **Mayor Law Murphy**, **Wally Seitz**, **Bob Beaudry** and **Lee Levitz**.

When asked why he thinks it is difficult for comedy to get a toehold in Tucson, he said that we get into the "mañana mentality" and maybe don't want to go out to check the shows. Also, people in other sections of the country go to a comedy show expecting to laugh. Here, some audiences have the attitude, "O.K., so now make me laugh." However, as the population increases, this will no doubt change, he said, and also, there are several very good local comedians that will develop a following. He also thinks the media is comedy's best friend.

This summer, the team plans on giving Los Angeles a whirl. They will appear at the Comedy Showcase there. The procedure is three minutes on amateur night; then Master of Ceremonies for amateur night, and if the audience still likes you, a fifteen-minute stint on the weekend show.

Graham is also an accomplished guitarist, and barters with guitar lessons. He said he loves comedy work. The lows are lower than acting, but the highs are also higher.

The future of Graham and O'Leary Comedy Show in five years? Graham envisions film work in comedy, but said that his definition of success us making a living at what you love and are good at.

With that definition, I would say that Adam Graham is already a success.

The **Arizona Theatre Company**'s production "The Robber Bridegroom" by Eurora Weuty played until May 19th. This was a foot stomping bluegrass musical, with imaginative dance scenes. The performers were in constant motion on the stage. This was ATC's last production until fall, but they are going to feature "Summer on Stage" which are classes for adults and young people beginning June 17th.

A great place to always have a good time is the **Gaslight Theatre**, 7000 E. Tanque Verde. Their last production of "Calamity Jane" gave everyone a chance to hiss at the villains. Their next production is "Scooter Wens, Boy Detective, And The Secret of Skull Cove!!" This sounds like a fun evening. It runs through July 13th. There is always a packed house (P.S. They serve free popcorn!).

Aces high on the go

By Jeff Latawiec
June 1985 - Entertainment Magazine. Page 12

With the closing of **Rockefeller's**, the east side was left with one less venue. The **Tequila Mockingbird** has been picking up slack by booking some hard rock. For instance, the 28th and 29th of June (1985), **We're Here** is scheduled. They will split the night with a new band called **Aces High**.

I went to the AH party the other night and thoroughly enjoyed It. I was especially knocked out by the lead work of guitarist **Mike Turner**. That cat smoked on some of his breaks. The amazing thing is, Turner is only 18 years old and is already so good. It kind of parallels another local guitarist by the name of **Robby Lochner**.

The kind of material they play is aptly described by the band as "danceable metal" like Ratt and the Scorpions. Once people get to know them, they will start Injecting their own stuff that they said would be in the Maiden/Queen mold.

The other band members are **Rick Boss** on voice, guitarist **Steve Hatala**, bassist **Mark Marschinke**, and drummer **Tim Reed**, the "silent one."

For only being together a short while, they sounded quite good. They have a beginning band's positive attitude, which I hope they maintain. See them at the Mockingbird.

Aces High has been together a little over a month. So far, they have about twenty tunes down. Currently, they are concentrating on learning covers, and will move on to originals when they have more material and more exposure.

On the local vinyl front: I talked with **Rick Travis**, Lochner's bassist. He told me the band is really happy about the record and the way it turned out. They will get their copies this month and from there it should be about four weeks before it arrives in the stores.

I've heard the only thing holding up **Aftermath**'s recently recorded EP is a hassle with the cover. As I've already said, if you like total heavy metal, you will like this record. I did when I heard it, and being lucky enough to possess a rough demo, I play it a lot.

Losers Club gain a winning reputation

By Lydia L. Young
June 1985 - Entertainment Magazine. Page 12

The **Losers Club** might have started out as a joke, but the seriousness of the music and members is something Tucson is lucky to have. The band has been playing town now for two months and they have been taken to many a music lover's heart.

The band plays a base of rock and roll originals influenced by the various backgrounds of its members. There is a blues sound, country, pop, and funk that appeals to almost anyone who listens. It has been a long time since I have seen so many people making a point of catching a show.

Originally, after formation, The Losers Club was supposed to disband in June. Things have changed a bit and the band will possibly be playing into July. Don't be fooled, however, because the members do have other obligations that they intend to honor and the Club is not here to stay.

Guitarist **Chris Burroughs**, previously with the **Nationals**, was in town from Los Angeles and called **Marx Loeb** (ex-**Los Lasers** drummer) one night and said, "Why don't we get a band together and call it the Losers Club?" Within a couple of days, bassist **Pat Murphy** (Los Lasers) and guitarist **Rick Kirkpatrick (Stab in the Dark)** has joined in the club and the music was born.

The band looks at their formation as a way to have fun, a learning experience and an outlet for their creativity. Songwriting is done by Burroughs, Murphy and Kirkpatrick, who also does vocals. They are all pleased with the results. Burroughs is decidedly going back to California, so that adds to the limited existence. But, he stresses, "We always felt even a really good band has a limited time.

"Because it is a collective, we're all contributing to the sound of the band," agreed Kirkpatrick. Burroughs said he feels comfortable and that impression might stem from the fact that he wrote the majority of their current 24 songs.

All members of The Losers Club are enjoying the band in all ways. They give many reasons for their current success including the compatibility of the members, new and different musical experience, learning from each other, a lighthearted approach, the time limit, the public's desire for something inconstant, and of course, their manager **Steve Rabinowitz**.

There are no plans for The Losers Club after July. Each member is already working in new directions. Do catch the band.

The Losers Club certainly aren't losers anymore.

Tucson has the comedy fever!

By P.L. Wylie
June 1985 - Entertainment Magazine. Page 22

Tucson is getting on the map for comedy and two nationally known comics have appeared in the Old Pueblo recently.

At **Karmel's Comedy Zone** (Broadway and Country Club) on May 17th & 18th (1985) appeared Claire Berger from Los Angeles with local comedian **Gary Hood** as host. Berger has appeared at such well-known places as The Comedy Store and The Improv in LA, and Dangerfield's in New York.

Another national figure to appear here May 7th at the UA campus was Larry "Bud" Melman, [47] for two shows. All of your insomniacs out there who watch the late night David Letterman show on TV know about Larry "Bud." He appears regularly. A native of Brooklyn, Melman is now a cult-figure, especially with the college crowd. His act is from his TV skits, but he did feature "Toast on a Stick" routine. He even threw some samples to the audience. He told this reporter that he had just come from "dead-Phoenix" and was "glad to be in live Tucson."

Every Thursday night, Karmel's Comedy Zone continues their open mike program for standup comics. Anyone wanting to appear should call **Marc Levinson** before 8:30 Thursday nights. At **Tequila Mockingbird** in **El Con Mall** on Tuesday nights beginning at 9:00PM continues the "father" of the open mike program for comics. This was the original forum for comics trying to get started locally.

This reporter talked to **John Forler**, a comic with The **Comedy Corner** show in the **UA Student Union Cellar** during the school year. This group of seven men and three women perform skits. Miller Lite is their sponsor with shows to start again in the fall. During the summer, Forler and two others have put together a musical comedy band called **Dave**.

Upcoming in comedy: Gallagher is expected at the **TCC** on July 17th. A "tentative" date for George Carlin is July at the TCC. Dan Horn, Michael Bailey and Graham & O'Leary will perform this month at The **Comedy Zone** with **Mike Sterner**, a former UA Drama student.

Tucson comedienne Sharon Hodges standing in front of Tequila Mockingbird during a Tuesday "Comedy Nite."
Photo by Daniel Sprouse, *Entertainment Magazine* archives.

---

[47] **Larry "Bud" Melman**'s real name was Calvert DeForest. He passed away March 19, 2007.

Diverse talents mold Sidewinders

The Sidewinders perform at Tequila Mockingbird in June 1985. Pictured from left to right: David Moskowitz (guitar), Dave Andrea Curtis (vocals), Dave Slutes (vocals) and Rich Hopkins (rhythm guitar). In the background, is Mike Monke (drums) and Ron Zaestury (bass). Photo by Fonda.

By Fonda
July 1985 - Entertainment
Magazine. Page 8

In recent months Tucson has experienced a massive growth trend in local music. It seems as though more new bands are appearing every week. Many of these bands contain several familiar faces.

But, there is one group that seems to have come from out of nowhere onto the nightclub stages of Tucson. That group is the **Sidewinders**. This band is certainly a collection of "fresh faces" in the local scene.

The band was born from "evolution" starting with **Richard Hopkins** (who was then playing acoustic guitar), drummer **Mike Monke** and **Andrea Hopkins** as a vocalist.

These three used various means to find the rest of the band and eventually wound up recruiting **David Moskowitz** (one of Rich's co-workers and a reporter for the *Entertainment Magazine*) to play lead guitar. **Ron Zaestury** was chosen to play bass. A week before their first appearance, they added **David Slutes** to their vocal line-up.

One thing is certain about this band is the members have extremely diverse backgrounds ranging from techno-pop, country, early rock, to folk (in fact, this is the first time Rich has played electric guitar). The individuality of the band members leads to some interesting original tunes. Most of the music is written be the entire band. Rich often comes up with the basic rhythms and everyone goes on from there.

The Sidewinders look back to the rock sounds of the '60s and '70s for much of their influence thereby disregarding the "new wave" sounds of synthesizers and other electronic gear that covers the Top 40 these days. Their sound is a mix of smooth guitar riffs and unique vocals with a raw sound that gets back to the basics of rock. Their stage show is fun and energetic. It band is currently doing about 90% original tunes with a few well chosen rearranged covers.

In the two months the band has played they have already built a sizeable following. They plan to begin playing out of town, possibly the San Francisco area, as early as September. They have also enjoyed some airplay on both community and commercial radio stations. They hope to go into the studio from some serious recording by the end of the summer.

July 1985: Tucson musicians beat the heat

By Lydia L. Young
July 1985 - Entertainment Magazine. Page 9

I don't think anyone would argue that summer was in full swing during June. Although we may all have been dreaming of lazy afternoons in the sun or shade, this has been a busy music month. My pick for the best show was easily Canned Heat at **Terry & Zeke's** on June 26th (1985). The show had people rocking from the ceiling to the classic boogie sounds of the band. Canned Heat will be recording soon, but don't miss their return in August.

The **Temple of Music and Art** is offering weekend music, at times better than anyone else in town. **Road Furniture** had a hard time playing to a half dozen people with the energy so minimal. And we know how fun they can be when they want to. The band said Los Angeles is in their thoughts as a new home.

More blues in the news at **Terry & Zeke's**. John Hammond put on a stunning performance June 30th. Hammond's heart and soul were bared on stage through harmonica, guitar and voice: Look forward to John Cale, August 15th and ex-Gun Cluber, Goeffrey Lee Pierce, on September 11th. Owner **Terry Glassman** said both these shows are confirmed. The **Black Angus** on East Broadway is featuring something new. Every other Wednesday night they hold a contest featuring lip-synching to videos or records with cash prizes for the winner.

No more Los Hamsters

There was a party on June 8th (1985) featuring three local bands. The **Vegas Kids** opened in "full dress," causing quite a commotion. **Los Hamsters** put on an energetic set and the **Johnies** finished up without a bang. **Jeff Keenan** of my favorite **Phantom Limbs** exuberantly told me that everything is finally set for recording in San Francisco. I have missed the Limbs about town, but look forward to their return.

Our own Los Hamsters are calling it quits. They have a few scheduled shows they will be playing, but the band has already branched into new areas. "Flying Fingers" **Linda Andes** (guitar) is leading **Ortho 28** and has already headlined at **Nino's**. Ortho 28 seemed a bit nervous, but in time will probably wail. Los Hamster bassist **Matt Griffin**, formed a new band, **P.S. Bingo**. They were favorably received at **Nino's** June 24th.

Locals in the studios

By Neil Costin
July 1985 - Entertainment Magazine. Page 9

Local businessperson **Joel Rancehausen** is doing a little moon lighting lately in the music world. The result is a new tape that includes a song called "Hero." Rancehausen, who runs the 22nd Street location of **Pizza Pub**, has a voice that's been described like that as Bob Seeger.

There's a new band in town called **Your Gain** that features ex-members of **Conflict**, **LFB & The Apocalypse Horns**, **Chromatics** and numerous others. Sounds like a big band. Of special interest is a new cassette by composer vocalist/guitarist/etc., and former member of **Etude**, **Tomas Gonzales**. On what one might call a mini-cassette, Gonzales has written, sang, and played most of the instruments on a five selection tape collectively titled, "Short Stories: The Heart Never Learns."

New on current and past *Entertainment Magazine* staff members: **Vicki Borton**, vocalist with the **Speedways**; **David Moskowitz**, guitarist in the **Sidewinders**; and **Gerard Shoemaker** is in a new band called **Dress Code**.

HMS hums

HMS from left to right Mark Mellinger (bass), Jeff Booth (drummer) and John Venet (guitarist). June 1985. *Entertainment Magazine* archive.

A must see local band for this month is **HMS**, although, according to the group drummer, it's anyone's guess what the letters stand for.

Jeff Booth says, and believe it if you will, so far the group has come up with about 53 variations of what the letters could stand for. I like (and this is one of their examples) ham, mustard and Swiss.

This band's fine music has '60s written all over it (the era of the music– not the senior years). Within two sets one only hears one cover– Wilson Pickett's "Midnight Hour." It's done in their own select style.

Country rumbles: Bar hoppin' and Saddle City Stompin'

By Fonda
July 1985 - Entertainment Magazine. Page 11

Well, summer is in full swing. But, it's just too hot! So, I found a way to beat the heat. Stay inside under the cooler all day so you can hit the town on those warm summer nights. The summer has given me a chance to make it out to some of my favorite local clubs and catch some great country music and fun.

Not long ago, I headed out to the **Roadrunner** to catch the **Catback Mountain Band**. The place was really packed. Those boys are sure building a big following and they deserve it. The band sounded great and had the dance floor filled.

Another pleasant way to spend a summer evening is by driving out to **Lil Abner's Steak House** for dinner and the music of **Dean Armstrong**. He is somewhat of a local legend, as well as one of my very favorites. His trio performs plenty of classic country tunes and makes it worth the drive.

I finally got around to visiting the new location of the **New Outlaw**. The **Saddle City Band** is now serving as the house band and I must admit they really sounded good. They have added several diverse cover tunes to their sets, making them appearing to a broad audience.

The New Outlaw is in many ways a pleasant change. This club is a good place for those who like to dance and listen to the band. The atmosphere is far more pleasant than the old location. It has more of an intimate feel.

Next on the list is the **Maverick** where **John E. Mann** heads the house band. The crowd there is mellow and there is plenty of room to stomp your feet and plenty of good music.

Well, that was enough running around for now. If you know of any clubs or bands you would like to be featured, let me know. Til next month, keep cool!

Comedy: Fun times on Tucson's stages

By P.L. Wylie
July 1985 - Entertainment Magazine. Page 18

Tucson's own comedy duo "**Mols and Suzs**," consisting of **Molly McKasson** and **Susan Claussen**, will appear in July at the Doubletree Inn. Dates are July 12-14th and July 19-21st (1985) all at 8:00PM. **KUAT** is sponsoring a contest and the winner will appear on stage with **Mols and Suzs** at the July 20th show. The **Doubletree** also has a dinner and show package. Call the **Invisible Theatre** for reservations.

"We have a good deal for them," says **Mike Suarez**, manager of **Tequila Mockingbird**, for the comics who appear at their Tuesday night open mike program. Anyone who appears will receive $10.00 plus a gift certificate for food or drink from the Bird. Besides, you get to make people laugh.

The second annual **Arizona Summer Arts Festival**, an oasis of cultural and entertainment events at the University of Arizona, began June 3rd and will continue through August 10th. The theatre production In July will be "I Do! I Do!" opening on July 4th and running through July 13th. Then, on July 18th begins "The Sunshine Boys," a Neil Simon comedy that was also a movie. This runs through July 27th.

The **Tucson Film Commission**, in conjunction with the **UA Centennial Committee**, is sponsoring a 10-week film series of movies shot in Southern Arizona, which began in June. All films are shown at the **Gallagher Theatre** on UA campus Friday and Saturday nights at 7:30PM. If you are into Arizona background, these should be a must. See the events section for listings

KVOI-AM 690 and Master Promotions advertisement for the Petra concert, July 1985, *Entertainment Magazine*. Page 20.

Gary Hood: Local comedian
keeps his lines hot and his delivery cool

By P. L. Wylie
July 1985 – Entertainment Magazine. Page 19

"I'm just an ordinary guy," says Gary Hood one of Tucson's most active comedians. In this reporter's estimation, Hood gives new meaning to the phrase "renaissance man." Hood, not content with a job during the day in advertising and marketing, at plays various clubs as a comedian host. He is also a photographer working with 3-D pieces and built some of the furniture in his home.

Gary Hood, July 1985, *Entertainment Magazine*. Page 19

To talk with Gary Hood is to find oneself bombarded with funny observations on everything from the state of the world to Tucson's architecture. Hood says, "The only thing that will top growth in Tucson will be if we ever have a stucco shortage."

When this reporter asked Hood if he was always funny, he said, "It doesn't funny to me I just have always had a strange view of life."

Gary Hood moved here about five years ago from Los Angeles by way of Ohio, Texas and "all over the U.S."

In L.A., Hood worked in advertising, handling some big name accounts, among them Safeway and UTA French Airlines, wrote dialogue for TV shows and comedy routines for Fraiser Smith.

Hood came from a large family in Chicago, with an extended family of ever-changing relatives and friends called "Aunt" or "Uncle" always in residence. One uncle was a performer and his father was a musician, so he was brought up around entertainers. "We always had a large boisterous house and you bad to be a wise acre if you wanted to get your piece of the action," he said.

He wanted to be the TV weatherman when he was little. Due to his father's work, they moved around to different places and he had to adapt to changing situations. "I always saw the nutty or wacky side of things," says Hood. However, Hood does have a serious side and is quite knowledgeable about social issues. When this reporter asked him about his deep feelings on these matters and how he could reconcile it with comedy, Hood says he feels that some forms of comedy address all these issues.

"Some of the comics do talk about social problems, and it relieves the tension we have about these matters," he says.

Hood always wanted to be in the theatre. His "Uncle Rudy" acted in shows produced at the Desilu Studios in

L.A., and got him jobs there as an extra on several productions. "That seemed like fun, hut there was also a lot of hassles about getting parts and having the right costume," says Hood.

In college, he was originally a Psychology major with a Broadcasting minor, but dropped that for a while, and was immediately drafted during the Viet Nam War. Hood said, "in the '70s when I got out of the service, I could not sit still– I was a nervous wreck and I had not even been in the jungle shooting anyone."

Eventually, he went to work for a radio station in Palmdale, Lancaster. "I also worked in Blythe, California, plus at Palmdale– all the real international party spots," says Hood. Following that, he worked at a Spanish speaking radio station where he read the news in Spanish phonetically until someone figured out he only knew enough Spanish "to get slapped," Hood recalls. After those forays, he went into advertising and then turned into writing for TV shows.

When Hood came to Tucson there were several comedy teams working here. Most of them have now gone on to other cities. Someone introduced him to **Nick Sievert** of the then local comedy team of **Bob and Bob**. For awhile, Hood wrote jokes for their show or gave them ideas for skits. Nick told him he should perform. At first, he didn't want to, because, Hood says, "When I came here comedians were performing like seals– just getting something thrown their way like a T-shirt or a free record, to perform. I credit Nick Sievert with convincing the club owners that comedians were worth as much as the bands with blue hair that were playing at their clubs."

Hood thinks that Tucson has an inferiority complex about its hometown performers. He thinks people here feel if you are from Tucson you can't be as good as someone from somewhere else, even Phoenix.

He says people still ask him, "Why did you leave L.A. if you want to be a comedian?" But, Hood replies, "There must be some tradition of good, excellent performers here. Why do you have to leave from where you live to be a good performer?" Hood said that even though Tucson is a relatively small town, it still has its own **Museum of Art**, **Arizona Theatre Company** and the **Arizona Opera Company.** When asked what he would like to see developed locally for comedy, he said he and some other comics have discussed starting a Tucson comedian's guild, which would establish a list of performers and also what amount would be standard fair payment for their services. He and some other local comics are also trying to put together a comics talk show.

Gary writes 100% of his material. **Elliott Glicksman** (the other half of the Bob and Bob team who now performs solo) helps with some of his material. **Peter O'Leary** and **Adam Graham** of the "Graham and O'Leary Comedy Show" offer suggestions about skits at times.

Hood thinks that in comedy "you should be able to inform, challenge, bring up topics and discuss things with the audience." His material comes to him while he is working on ad copy, at meetings, watching TV or doing other things. "At the end of the week, I have a paper bag full of scraps of paper containing jokes and ideas, which I then try to figure out." He also gets a lot of his material from newspaper articles, especially the scandal sheets.

Hood is married and said his wife understands his "need to perform on stage."

Gary Hood has a smooth on-stage presence. When asked if hecklers ever get to him he said, "It's disappointing, but most are just interacting." When asked what bothers him on stage, "So far nothing," he says, "But maybe two weeks from now this will change. Going on stage is a real high."

What does the future hold for Gary Hood? "I would like Tucson as a base, and occasionally go back to L.A. to perform." He is also trying to develop a gallery here for his photographic 3-D pieces and finish work on his movie scripts. Hood doesn't want to narrow himself into any category. He doesn't mind if you call him an advertising man, a marketing man, a comedian or a furniture builder.

One thing for sure, Hood is a very funny man.

August 1985: Summer hot rocks fever

By Lydia L. Young
August 1985 - Entertainment Magazine. Page 11

A highlight for the month of July was the Benefit for Nicaragua at **Splinter Brothers Warehouse** on the 19th (1985). The turnout was almost unbelievable. The cause, however, a worthy one. Bands included **Blue Wave**, **Al Perry and the Cattle** and the outstanding **If**. The sound equaled the audience energy (or vice-versa) even when the PA blew during If's closing set. Congratulations to **Danny Hill** (lead guitarist) for keeping the crowd moving while the problem was being resolved.

Back in town and performing for the first time in three months were the phantastic **Phantom Limbs**!!! Their new material is as captivating and danceable as I would expect from the Limbs. Despite the bad sound, July 27th at **Nino's** was a great show. I caught a semi-local band, **Visitor** at **Tequila Mockingbird** July 6th that rocked with surprising talent. There were just a few people in the club, but the band was energetic, offering a variety of originals and covers. Visitor is currently playing six weeks in Sierra Vista. If they come back to Tucson, they are definitely worth seeing.

Mobile Cubes

The Mobile Cubes (l-r) standing Rueben Ruiz, guitar; Doug Wilson, drums; Rob Donath, bass guitar. Seated (l-r) Tom Privett, keyboards; and Jim Gasper, vocals. David Bean Photography.

The **Mobile Cubes** are putting the finishing touches on five new originals at Winstel Studios. The songs are being recorded at their own **Winstel Studios**.

One song, "Tennessee Man," has a video script in the works.

The video of "Good Clean Fun," which generated some interest at Chrysalis Records will air in August on cable channel 37's music show, "The Air Show."

Road Furniture may hit the road

R oad Furniture may not be with us much longer. They opened the Limbs show at **Nino's** July 26th (1985) and have one other date. But, lead guitarist **Tony Dow** said that the band will dissolve thereafter. Dow plans on collaborating with the illustrious **Mark Smythe** (**Jonny Sevin**, the **Pills**, **Isaiah**) that is an exciting thought in itself. Good luck!!

Street Pajama (from left to right) Jeff Masterson, Lamont Arthur, Merle Harmon, Mike King and Jerome Kimsey.
Entertainment Magazine, August 1985, Page 7. © Balfour Walker, 1985.

Street Pajama: On the Road Again

By Neil Costin and Angie Lumia
August 1985 - Entertainment Magazine. Page 7

Just when one had given up on the next **Street Pajama** release finally coming out on vinyl, it appears. The end of July (1985) saw the release of "Beast de Resistance," the new Street Pajama album (though with five songs one could justifiably call it an EP).

Tucson's Street Pajama members are **Merle Harmon**, **Mike King** (Mikey, of late), **Jerome Kimsey** on drums, **Lamont Arthur** on keyboards (a man not related to Prince) and bassist **Jeff Materson**.

With the sound behind bands today being so important, credit needs go to Scott Brand for engineering it on stage, and **Roger King** in the studio. Sister **Charlee Harmon** stands in as background vocalist, as does **Kaline Smith**, close friend to bassist Masterson. Street Pajama keeps it all in the family. The album was recorded at **Westwood Recording Studio's** fine set.

"The owners are old friends of ours," said Mikey King. "They gave us an offer. We wanted to get back with old friends, and work with them again."

The record has been in the works for the past couple of years. "It's more of a financial thing that held the EP back than an artistic problem," said King.

Street Pajama hopes the EP will be signed by a label with some money behind it to fund releases outside of Tucson.

What you will find on the disc is the same smooth, soothing, melodic sound that Street Pajama audiences have come to know and love for so many years. Titles that include "Livin' at the Deja View," and "I'd Rather Smoke Butts Than Kiss Them" are sure to attract any curious listener.

Only Merle Harmon can make the words "I hate you" sound really nice– close to complimentary.

"Livin' at the Deja View" and "I'd Rather..." are titles from out of the mind of lyricist Mike King. King writes the words and Harmon puts them to music, collaborating on both.

The fact that "the mixing took longer than recording" is what held up the release of the disc, according to vocalist Harmon.

Harmon's voice could probably fall into any style she wants to sing. A talent able to change styles is rare and gives the music variety.

Street Pajama is also an interesting band to watch. Band members throw their personality out to the audience. Harmon seems to love being on stage.

Although Street Pajama may be Tucson's longest lasting and most stable band, they do not plan to stay here forever, Harmon tells us that plans are in the works to return to Phoenix soon, followed by a trek "over to California." This includes a stop in San Diego and then to points north.

One way to express ones appreciation of this piece of vinyl would be to stop is at **Harpo's** and tell waitress **Charlee Harmon**, one back up vocalist on "Beast de Resistance."

Entertainment Magazine August 1985 edition cover photo, of Merle Harmon. © Balfour Walker.

Tucson radio offers alternatives

August 10-September 14, 1984 – Newsreal. Page 10

> *This is Radio Clash/on pirate satellite orbiting your living room/cashing in on the Bill of Rights ...*
> *This is Radio Clash/using aural ammunition/Can we get the world to listen?*
> *– "Radio Clash" - Strummer/Jones/ Headon/Simonon (CBX/Epic, 1981)*

W e've come a long way from the days when the Clash lashed out in protest against the state of radio in 1981. Today, John Cougar Mellencamp certainly isn't singing about Tucson's radio airwaves. Lately people have been celebrating a newfound diversity on the radio dial here in Tucson, a pleasant relief from the refrain that authority always wins.

> *I fight authority / authority always wins.*
> *– "The Authority Song" John Cougar Mellencamp (Riva/Polygram, 1984)*

Success has been ours to hear on the FM dial for over six months at 91.7 with **KXCI** and for nearly 2½ years at 96 Rock Sunday nights with the **KLPX Virgin Vinyl** show. And while there are real differences between these two aural blows against the corporate music empire, together KXCI and Virgin Vinyl represent something far more than radio alternatives as they open the airwaves to new, local and "non-commercial" music.

These audio emissions symbolize a dramatic extension of democracy in our lives. This surely compares in many ways to the nurturing of social harmony in this area provided by Tucson Meet Yourself, the cultural bazaar that has become as thrilling an open air event as Cinco de Mayo and JuneTeenth Blues Festival celebrations.

For those who still have turned their dial to 91.7 (98.7 on cable), or to 96 FM Sunday nights, here's something to entice you. KXCI is a community radio, a multicultural mix of sounds and information that spans the musical spectrum and relies on donations, memberships, underwriting and volunteers to stay on the air. The distinctive music mix, from 7:00AM to 6:00PM on weekdays, is a mingling of jazz, rock, blues and soul, Latin salsa, ethnic, folk and reggae.

There's meditation and women's music, and rockabilly, zydeco, polkas, and Mexican ballads, next to Dylan, Springsteen, the Beatles, Holly Near and Rita Marley, from Hendrix and Dire Straits, to Grace Jones, Lori Anderson and Bette Midler, from Gil-Scott Heron to Mango Santamaria, and even X. The word is diversity. It's a breath of fresh air in the predominantly stale radio programming arena.

The specialty shows on KXCI is where the community aspect really shines– there's something for almost everyone. And since we needn't rely on KXCI for all our listening pleasure, if the hardcore rock show, or reggae, blues or German music isn't your bag, then tune in at a different time for the gospel show, or political issue music, progressive rock, Latin music, the women's show or the Big Band sound.

The key to specialty listening is the Calendar in the Audio File program guide– free to all contributing members. Informed listening becomes a rewarding experience.

Chuck Graham: Sorry Dave, Chuck was first

By Tina Alvarez
August 9, 1985 – Newsreal. Page 3

It was bound to happen sooner or later– the **Chuck Graham** look is in vogue and is being transmitted via mass communications. For those of you who don't know, or have missed him at rock events, Chuck Graham is Tucson's illustrious, humorous and ever-jaded music critic for the *Tucson Citizen*.

Many of us are familiar with seeing Chuck at concerts and clubs, decked out in his standard fare of faded Levi's, a rock t-shirt and of course, his famous flasher trench coat. Don't forget the beard and disheveled hair (as of late though, Chuck got himself a nifty haircut and even trimmed up his beard).

So now, after years of incessantly harassing Comrade Graham on his hair, his clothes, his reviews, his recorded messages on the phone and God knows whatever else, it turns out that he is a fashion classic. He knew all along what he was doing, stuck with it ... and I think that's rather scary. What's more frustrating is that it irks me to think all my friendly comments and good pieces of advice have gone to waste ("Hey, did you just get down from the mountain?" "Chuck, you need a haircut." "With that trench coat someone might think I'm hanging out with a flasher.")

Let me talk about "The Look" itself. The Chuck Graham Look is basically one you don't necessarily want to be seen associating with, but of course, with someone of Chuck Graham's status you have to bend the rules. The Look, which you may have noticed but have not been able to place, is very much the rage at Greyhound bus depots, parks, and soup kitchens, not to mention plasma centers and, of course, on reputable rock writers.

One of the main supporters of the Chuck Graham Look is Eurythmic Dave Stewart. World beware.

This occurring phenomenon didn't hit me all at once. It took me a while to figure out what was gnawing at the back of my mind, but it dawned on me when I was watching the Eurythmics' video "Would I Lie To You?" (for the thousandth time) that Dave Stewart is capitalizing on the Chuck Graham Look. Check this out: he has the same hairstyle as Chuck, he has a beard like Chuck and his levis are just as faded as Chuck's. Although he doesn't wear it in the video, Dave Stewart also owns a trench coat.

It looks pretty suspicious to me.

Not only that, I'm sure Dave Stewart was influenced by Chuck long before this video. Before Chuck got his new, suave "do" – when his hair was long and it looked like it needed something done to it – Dave Stewart also let his locks be mangy. And that sly little copycat sheared his head after Chuck did. I think this admiration thing is going a little too far.

And what's the most terrible thing about this is the fact Chuck is not going to get any credit. Everyone's going to think Dave Stewart started this mode of dress just because he's a popular musician, he's on MTV, in magazines and on the regular television programs like "Entertainment Tonight." Chuck, on the other hand, is stuck in Tucson. He lurks in corners casing out acts. He's very modest and doesn't strut his look around. And what credit is he getting for this I ask you?

If I were Chuck Graham, I'd be pissed.

Chuck has spent many a year honing his look. It's his. Who'd want it? From the looks of it– everybody. True, imitation may be the sincerest form of flattery, but let the right person be flattered. So I consider it my mission this month to let the world know that Chuck was the first and not Dave Stewart. Holy hell, every time you turn around someone in some band is trying to look like Chuck Graham.

Another thing that has me worried is that my friend has sold out. Yes, I hate to admit it, but I will anyway. Perhaps not intentionally, he has joined the ranks of major trendsetters. Chuck Graham now has the potential to be a household world. He's right up there with the likes of Madonna, Cyndi Lauper, Michael Jackson and Boy George.

But, I'll still be his friend. And when this comes out in print I'm going to be the first person to have my copy autographed.

An old trench coat won't ever let you down, huh Chuck?

Virgin Vinyl advertisement, August 9-September 15, 1985, *Newsreal.* Page 16.

Black Sun shines through

By S. Castillo Samoy
August 1985 - Entertainment Magazine. Page 10

I t's always difficult for a local band to get started, commit and carry on. Let's face it. Tucson does not have the "buck support" that bands need to play their music full time. And, if your music does not fall into a definite commercial-appeal category, it's going to be rougher. It's a wonder the **Black Sun Ensemble** has put out its debut album on **Pyknotic Records**, with plans for a second album release in late summer.

Black Sun Ensemble, May 1987.
Entertainment Magazine archives.

The self-entitled album, which was produced by the band and engineered by **Steve English** (who has worked with **Nadine & the MoPhonics**) has twelve cuts that are definitely non-commercial. The thrust of the album (all instrumental) is the guitar work of **Jesus Acedo**, the band's guitarist and songwriter.

With the back up of drummer **John Brett** and former Black Sun bassist **Michael Glidewell**, Acedo fingers some interesting, off the wall noises– kind of like a psychedelic orchestration of Eastern music.

With song titles like "Red Ocean," "Ruby Eyes of China" and "A Chunk of Mandolin Love" the Black Sun Ensemble serves up a truly different, but tasty, platter. For a sampling, "The Black Sun Ensemble" can be purchased at **Dead End Records**, **Discount Records** and **Al Bums**.

Montreal is a rare Tucson breed

By Angie Lumia
August 1985 - Entertainment Magazine. Page 10

M ontreal's selection of cover tunes and beautifully poetic original lyrics make this local Tucson band different from any other. It's rare today to find a rock group that does songs from old rock bands, like Led Zeppelin, Pink Floyd, Rush and Jethro Tull, along with songs from current super groups as U2, Duran Duran and Billy Idol.

Guitarist and vocalist **Ed Edelbrock** writes most of the original material. The way his lyrics flow makes him unquestionable a natural songwriter. Montreal has a progressive sound that has a lot of its rhythm influence in Rush. Drummer **Tony Edelbrock's** style has a definite touch from drummer **Neil Peart**.

"While Paul tried to get the right synth sound," says Ed, "someone came over to me and said, 'You guys sound real tight; how long have you been together?' I answered, 'This is your band, members, the first time all three of us have and any tidbits you played together.' It was then that we would like readers to knew we were a band."

Montreal recently released a six-song cassette titled "Lost Over Seas." It includes all original material. The performance dates, tape can be purchased at the **Sound Factory Recording Studios** and at **KXCI** radio station for $5.00.

Nadine adds mo'Phonics

By Neil Costin
August 1985 -
Entertainment Magazine.
Page 10

Nadine & the MoPhonics perform. 1985, *Entertainment Magazine* archives.

Nadine & the **MoPhonics** just lost a member, replaced that player and added one more.

They now are a six-member unit. Keyboard player (a new sound for the group) **Neil McCallion** was recently recruited, along with wife, **Lisa**, as new bassist.

Both McCallion's are former members of the **Lincoln Street Bullies**, as well as having been in Bad Element, who are now the major force behind Nadine.

The rest of the band is made up of **Cathy Zavala**, lead vocals and rhythm guitar; **Dan Sorenson**, lead guitar and background vocals and **Bob Casler**, drums.

A combination demo and four-song tape has just been completed for local release.

The new band premieres on August 23rd (1985) at **Jeff's Pub** but will have a tape release (as opposed to a record release) party the first weekend in September at **Gentle Bens**, 841 N. Tyndall Avenue, with tapes to be won by audience members.

The band is shopping around with representatives for the Pointer Sisters, Tina Turner and other artists in hopes to get them to cover some of the MoPhonic's songs.

Tucson comedy clubs headlines Tucson's best

By P.L. Wylie
August 1985 - Entertainment Magazine. Page 18

A number of well know local comics put on a benefit show at **Cheers** on July 28th (1985) for a benefit of **Open End Halfway House** for battered women and children. Great idea for a worthy cause– and opportunity to see some funny acts. It was a show based on the "Tonight Show" format.

Tequila Mockingbird was the scene of the above group of comics performing their preview routine for the benefit on July 16th. It was a great crowd pleaser. The Bird is really trying to develop local comedians. If you want to give it a shot, come down to a Tuesday show. You receive a fee and a gift certificate for appearing. Call host **Gary Hood** at the Bird before 9:00PM to get your name on the roster.

A nationally known comic is planning to appear here in October. Actor and comedian Dom DeLuise will perform October 26th at the **Doubletree Inn** Grand Ballroom in the Annual Benefit for the Foundation for St. Joseph's Hospital.

The **Black Angus** on East Broadway is featuring something new. On every other Wednesday night they hold a contest featuring lip-synching to videos or records, with cash prizes for the winner. Some comedy routines are featured. Check in advance to see their weekly feature.

The **Comedy Zone** continues to feature outstanding comedians. On weekends is always a headliner and guest host. They also sponsor a contest of comedians on Wednesday nights, with the winner appearing at the Comedy Store in L.A.

Gary Hood (see interview July edition) tells me that 11 local working comics are forming a **Tucson Comics Association** to give comics guidelines regarding salaries and working conditions.

On the drama scene, the **Gaslight Theatre** is continuing with their high standard of old-fashioned melodrama. "The Sheik" will play through September 14th. Written and directed by **Peter Van Slyke**, with musical direction by **Dan Steenken**. The "olio" presented after the show (a set of songs and dances with a theme– this time "By the Sea") is worth the price of admission alone. Before the show, you can feast on a family style dinner at the restaurant adjacent to the theatre. Call for reservations. **Armen Dirtadian** stars as the Sheik.

The **Arizona Historical Society**, 949 E. 2nd Street, will screen its Old Time Western Series at 7:30PM through August 21st. All silent films are accompanied by local pianist **Emilo Osta**.

Tucson needs a little magic. Now, we have it with **Howard "The Magi" Morgan** table hopping at **Carlos Murphy's** on Friday and Saturday nights, 6:00PM to 9:00PM. Morgan does great card tricks and magic. He recently moved here from Los Angeles and will be expanding to other clubs during the week.

Armen Dirtadian, cover photo, *Entertainment Magazine*, September 1985. Photo by Galvin Larson.

Armen Dirtadian: A golfer in sheik's clothing

By P.L. Wylie
September 1985 - Entertainment Magazine. Page 19

Recipe: Take the **Tucson City Amateur Golf Champion**, mix with two-time winner of **Pima County Golf Amateur Championship** contest, stir in a big helping of acting/musical talent (exhibited in starring roles Including the recent **Arizona Theatre Company's** production of "A Funny Thing Happened on the Way to the Forum," add a dash of 6'-3" tall dark good looks, bake in the love of Tucson by a native. The resulting dish is The Gaslight's current leading man in their production of "The Sheik," **Armen Dirtadian**.

"The Sheik" is a melodrama playing through September 14th (1985) with Dirtadian performing a very romantic lead. The tendency in a melodrama is to play for laughs. But, Dirtadian plays "The Sheik" very straight and very believable. "I think every actor must act the part as though he really is that person," Dirtadian says, "or how that person would act. That is how I see it. If I were "The Sheik" and saw this girl and believed she was the most beautiful girl in my life, I would give up my kingdom for her. That is how I play it." Dirtadian thinks in "The Sheik" he has one of the best first entrances he has ever had. This is one of **Peter Van Slyke**'s best scripts (Van Slyke is the writer/director). Dirtadian said he had a fever and was very sick the first week of the run of the show but went on anyway. This reporter saw the show the first week and can attest that Dirtadian gave a great performance.

Dirtadian is a low-key actor/singer. When he took acting lessons in high school he was very shy and inhibited about going on stage. Also, he says, "I thought actors and actresses were weird people." He won poetry reading contests in junior high, was on the speech team in high school and was a speech major at the **University of Arizona**.

Not only a musician and actor, Dirtadian has been a teacher of Physical Education and Music/Drama at **Holiday Intermediate School** in Tucson for the past nine years. During the 1977 school year there, the school librarian told him about auditions being held at Salpointe High School for their production of "Fiddler on the Roof" and suggested he try out. He had not performed on stage since his high school acting lessons. He went to the audition "just for something to do," Dirtadian says. To his surprise he got the lead part. The play sold out every night, and from there he branched out.

Dirtadian progressed to many productions at **SALOC** (**Southern Arizona Light Opera Company**), appearances at The **Playbox Theatre**, the lead in "Simon Peter" for the past several years, the aforementioned Arizona Theatre Company's production of "A Funny Thing Happened on the Way to the Forum" and for the past three years various performances at The **Gaslight Theatre**. Between plays he has performed as a nightclub singer at The **Tender Trap** concentrating on jazz and standards. He recently completed a stint in SALOC's production of "Fiddler on the Roof" with a New York director. He is now taking a six-month hiatus from school teaching to further his musical and to appear at The Gaslight.

Dirtadian started at The Gaslight three years ago in a play entitled "The Pirate King" playing the Pirate. He followed this with the lead in Gaslight's "Zorro." In their production of "Shootout at Black Canyon City" he played his first bad guy role. "It's much better playing the bad guy than the good guy, because it is a lot easier"

After "Shootout," The Gaslight decided to produce "The Sheik" and hired Dirtadian to play the lead role. "Every actor and actress here at The Gaslight has worked on the legitimate stage, and it is a pleasure to work with professionals the caliber of the performers here," Dirtadian remarks.

Dirtadian has taken acting lessons at **Arizona Theatre Company**'s Encompass program, but feels he has learned a lot through experience. "I have seen people take acting lessons and then don't perform," Dirtadian said. "You should take acting lessons in order to act, but I have seen others getting tied up in the theory of acting. What they should be doing is getting hard knocks on the stage along with their lessons. There is no substitute for experience. You get on the stage and you give the audience the best you can and you learn from that."

Dirtadian's hobby is golf. He plays mostly in the summer. Even after winning several prestigious golfing awards, he has recently started taking golfing lessons from a local professional golfer. He says he now doesn't have to spend as much time on the fundamentals and is playing very well.

When questioned about which he prefers– acting, singing, golfing or teaching, Dirtadian said, "I'm not the kind of a person to prefer one over the other. I'm kind of hexed – I have to do them all or I can't be happy."

Dirtadian is a native Tucsonan, the oldest of three children. His sister, brother and parents all live in Tucson and none of them are interested in acting, but they all play golf. "Who knows where I got this interest in performing–maybe being the oldest child, the way I got attention was through acting," states Dirtadian. He is married, and says that his wife is not interested in acting "at all" but does come to see him perform.

Dirtadian says that he is staying in Tucson. "I love Tucson, and I am not wiling to give up maybe 10-15 years of my life to live in a big city to make it big in the entertainment business. That is what it takes. But, I think have a lot to offer Tucson with my teaching and performing. I intend to stay here. I really want to thank the people here for supporting me. They seem to like my work and I enjoy performing for them."

When asked why he thinks Tucsonans sometimes don't appreciate local talent, Dirtadian says, "Tucsonans cannot understand how anyone that is good can stay in Tucson. I think the mystique is that if someone is from L.A. or New York or Chicago, the audience automatically thinks that person is really very good. I have worked with people from those places, and I think we have just as good talents here. Just because you are from a big city doesn't necessarily mean you are good. However, I think people here feel this way about everything, not just acting; because a lot of people still think of Tucson as a cow town. If you really want to make it big financially in the entertainment fields you have to be willing to give up a big portion of your life and go to a city like L.A. or New York, because that is where everything is. And, I am not willing to pay that price."

This reporter believes that a lot of people in Tucson are glad Armen Dirtadian has decided to stay with us in this "cow town" and continue his enjoyable performing for us.

Tequila Mockingbird and Déjà vu Nightclub advertisements, August 1985, *Entertainment Magazine*.

Howard Morgan: Not just slight of the hand

By P. L. Wylie
September 1985 - Entertainment Magazine. Page 18

Tucson's latest addition to the entertainment scene is a very talented magician by the name of **Howard Morgan**. Currently he is entertaining dinner guests at **Carlos Murphy's** Restaurant on Friday, Saturday and Sunday evenings from 6:00PM to 9:00PM, with tableside enticing magic and card tricks. This reporter talked to Morgan at length on a recent Friday after his stint at Carlos Murphy's.

Howard Morgan photo, *Entertainment Magazine*, September 1985, page 18. Photo © Jeff Carter.

Morgan is a product of a varied background. His parents were missionaries in Latin America and he speaks Spanish fluently. He has been doing magic tricks since he was six years old. Morgan moved to Los Angeles in 1979 and had a successful career there. He has an impressive scrapbook detailing the same.

In January of this year (1985) Morgan visited Tucson. Morgan says, "I fell in love with the laid back lifestyle here. Also, I like the Latin environment."

This past July, Morgan pulled up stakes in L.A. and moved to Tucson permanently. He had a corporation in L.A called Magi Productions that produced all types of magic shows and parties, including theme parties. Especially popular was the "Sherlock Holmes Party" where guests were given a fictitious murder to solve, and then clues were left in various rooms for them to discover. Morgan is continuing **Magi Productions** in Tucson.

Morgan has done a lot of volunteer work putting on magic shows for the disabled. He was on the Governor's Committee for the Disabled in Florida. "I have also enjoyed working with the Boy Scouts and United Way, helping with und raising and other programs" he says.

Morgan plans to still do some shows in Los Angeles. However, he now considers Tucson his home and is planning to concentrate here on his work at clubs, appearances at school assemblies, private parties, conventions (here and in Phoenix) and with rock groups.

"Being able to understand how magic works and what makes people believe things that aren't true is the same as believing in mind control– it is the same principle. But this is a benign form of mind control," Morgan confides.

October 1985: Hot blues cool jazz

By S. Castillo Samoy
October 1985 - Entertainment Magazine. Page 15

The witching month of October is here and with its arrival comes some good-time jazz and blues. **Terry & Zeke's**, Tucson's Mecca of live shows, brought us Los Angeles recording artist The Frankie S. Band on October 3rd (1985) The **Mighty Flyers** perform on October 7th and the price of admission is $6.00 or $7.00.

Don't stop yet. San Francisco's Blues Survivors make a Tucson stop on October 8th. You can see them at Terry & Zeke's. The **Tucson Blues Society** is responsible for this cornucopia of concerts. **Gentle Ben's** also plays host to **Brian Bromberg**, October 2nd and 7th and the Jazz Terrorism on October 10th. The **Black Sun Ensemble** head west some time this month. **Jesus Acedo**, the band's founder, said Los Angeles looks enticing. The departure of the Black Sun Ensemble coincides with the release of its second album.

Ronnie Mack: Pickin' in the autumn

By Ronnie Mack
October 1985 - Entertainment Magazine. Page 13

I would like to introduce myself. Most know me as **Ronnie Mack**, though my given name is **Ronald McBride**. I am one of those natives of Arizona, born in Douglas. I was reared on a ranch of sorts, and from one mining town to another, although mainly in Florence. I've been playing music of all kinds since I was eight.

The **Southern Arizona Entertainment Association** (SAEA) has just elected new officers for 1986. They are: **Wanda Jean Mirand**, President, (formerly with **Radio Flyer** as their bass player), **Dyan McBride**, now 1st Vice President, (formerly the Secretary), **Connie Bailey**, 2nd Vice President, (of **Connie and the Bandits**) and **Diana Rey** is now Secretary. You will see her and Dyan around town with **Annie Ball**, filming Tucson talent for local cable television.

The **Southern Arizona Fiddler's Association** is sponsoring the 1st annual Old Time Fiddler Contest on October 5th and 6th. It will be held at the **Fire Fighters Hall**, 2264 E. Benson Highway.

Ronnie Mack photo,
Entertainment Magazine, January 1986.

265

Bands around town during fall '85

By Angie Lumia
October 1985 - Entertainment Magazine. Page 19

Nadine & MoPhonics

September 21st (1985) was a busy day for **Nadine & the MoPhonics.** In the afternoon they played at the Oktoberfest celebration. That evening they played for the Anti-Apartheid Benefit. Local record stores are carrying the new MoPhonics tape. They recorded the tape at the **Sound Factory Recording Studio**. The tape has been getting some airplay, mostly on **KXCI**. "**Virgin Vinyl**" also played a couple of their songs.

HMS

HMS is releasing their second audiocassette in early October. Their first, "Never Shoe A Dead Horse," released in February 1985, received favorable reviews from *Newsreal*. It and airs on **KXCI**-FM, **KLPX**-FM and "**Virgin Vinyl**" show. The tape will consist of six new original songs and was recorded at the Sound Factory in August. The yet untitled tape will be exclusively available at **Al Bums** record store and all HMS gigs. Also scheduled for release in October is the first video venture by HMS. The video is to the song "Ridin My Palomino" which was a clear favorite of the people at our shows and is the cut most often played on KLPX and KXCI. The video is being shot on 16mm black and white film by **Booth/Baker Productions** who also directed and co-wrote it with HMS. "Ridin My Palomino," the video, will be, like the song, a satirical look at "country-punk."

The Press

Former *Entertainment Magazine* and *Tucson Teen* writer, **David** ("Key Nerd" in the movie, "Revenge of the Nerds," and former guitarist in the **Sidewinders**) **Moskowitz,** is currently working on a three-song EP with producer/engineer **Roger (Street Pajama, Fanatiks) King** taped at Westwood Recording Studio. The name of the band is The **Press**. It is also the title of the album. Musicians included are drummer **Shawn** (formerly with the **Registers** - now the **Beets**) **Burch**, bassist **Dave** (New "Praise the Lord" Joy) **Cannal**, vocalist keyboardist piano **Bonnie (Easy But Not Cheap,** the **Flames** and **Breathless**), **Bonnie Essig** and **Phil Quintanilla** on sax, flute and clarinet.

Twister

Twister has been writing some originals so they can start recording soon. They recently got a new bass player, **Jeff** through October they'll be at **Keaton's**, **Tequila Mockingbird** and the **Sheraton Rio Rico**.

Neck Romance

A new band should be hitting the clubs in mid-October. **Neck Romance** is a four-piece southern rock band. Right now, they are doing cover tunes and they are working on originals for a demo tape. Two members of band came from **Desert Fire**, who broke up last month.

Tucson comedy scene: Take my jokes, please! Karmel's melts.

By P.L. Wylie
October 1985 - Entertainment Magazine. Page 22

Marc Levinson of the former **Comedy Zone** and his partner **Howard Stern** are planning on reopening the Comedy Zone, which was discontinued recently due to the closing of **Karmel's**. Levison says the new Comedy Zone "will be bigger and better, and at a more convenient location." Their format will not change and the same high quality type of acts will appear. Levison says the press will be notified two weeks before the opening.

October 18th &19th (1985) begins six weeks of comedy at **Nino's** presented by the **Southwest Comedy Jam**, a group of local comics who will appear at 9:30PM and 10:30PM. It sounds like it will be a welcome sight to Tucson comedy. **Cheers**, 7000 E. Tanque Verde Road, recently had a comic's night on Sunday, and might have others in the future. Best to check with them on their schedule before trotting over there.

On Tuesday, September 17th, **Tequila Mockingbird's** Comedy Night was the scene of a packed house, with many well-known local comics appearing. Among them were **Joe Ryan**, **Faith** (the lone female comic appearing in Tucson), **Adam Graham**, **Gary Hood**, The **Kruiser Experience**, **A.Q.**, **Genesis, Cory and Dave** (his puppet), and others. The Bird seems to be filling the need Tucsonans have for comedy. Any comic interested in appearing on stage there, call before 9:00PM Tuesday nights.

Howard "The Magi" Morgan has a production company called **Magi Productions**. This group is presenting a ten-week course on mind dynamics and hypnotherapy, beginning October 8th with Morgan as the instructor.

We all know Halloween is sneaking up on us when we check out the next production of the **Gaslight Theatre**. Through November 19th, Gaslight is presenting "The Bride of Frankenstein, or the Girl of My Screams!" Featured in the cast are: **Armen Dirtadian** (*EM* September 1985 interview), **Stewart Gregory**, **Tim Gilbert**, **Tim Tully**, **Dan Gunther**, **Nancy LaViola**, **Jane Merrifield** and **Susan Wedekind**. The play was written by **Peter Van Slyke**.

Career Threads (owned by Letty Zucker, namesake of the 1950's Letty Shop) advertisement October 1985, *Entertainment Magazine*.

November 1985: Comedy, clubs, variety and spice

By P.L. Wylie
November 1985 - Entertainment Magazine. Page 11

The newly reopened **Comedy Zone** is now located at **Terry & Zeke's Friendly Tavern** on East Speedway. **Terry Glassman**, says they are trying a new concept. Tucson presently doesn't have a combined comedy and music show. The comedians will appear on Friday and Saturday nights at 7:00PM and 8:30PM. The audience for the same cover can then stay to hear the music show beginning at 10:00PM to 1:00AM without having to pay an additional cover charge. They want to promote a club atmosphere like the big cities have.

Promoter **Marc Levinson** and **Howard Stern** will have a headline guest comic (from out of town), a special guest comic and a host comic. An offshoot of the recently formed **Tucson Comics Association** is a group called **Southwest Comedy Jam**. They appear on Friday and Saturday nights at **Nino's**.

Don't forget the ever-popular **Tequila Mockingbird** continues their policy of open mike for comedians on Tuesday nights beginning at 9:00PM. If you want to appear, call before 9:00PM. **Mike Suarez**, manager of the Bird says, "Remember, the Bird is the originator of comedy shows in Tucson, and we have stuck by them. We are continuing to support the comics."

Local funnyman **Gary Hood** has been "hired" by **KRQQ** to work with **Scotty Johnson** on the 6:00PM to 10:00AM show as "guest character" and to tape special comedy segments, including "the man on the street, the weatherman, entertainment editor, traffic reporter, etc." (all take offs). Tune in. At **Voila**, a contest called "comic of the month" is scheduled for November 9th. The winner gets to appear on Show Time.

No lack of blues

By S. Castillo Samoy
November 1985 - Entertainment Magazine. Page 15

KXCI, Tucson's "true" community radio station, started its Fall Membership Drive last month. The jazz on is programming is definitely worth your tour contribution.

The **University of Arizona** celebrated its Centennial in a special way. Dizzy Gillespie filled the **Tucson Community Center** Music Hall last month with his marked tooting. The first time I heard his musicianship was on Chaka Khan's "Night In Tunisia." It's a satisfying feeling to know oven the younger generation has channels to Gillespie's sound

Keeping up with Tucson bands

By Angie Lumia
November 1985 - Entertainment Magazine. Page 16

Affirmative

The **Affirmative** will be cutting a single this month. They will also be playing three dates this month, one in Phoenix with The White Animals from Nashville. Starting this month, the Affirmative will be welcoming drummer **Jim Miller** to the group.

Bluewave

October was a good month for **Bluewave**. Besides being one of the bands in the **Tucson Blues Society**'s Blues Festival, they also opened up for Otis Rush, a blues guitarist who has toured nationwide. They also opened for **Man Dingo Groit Society,** a blues group. This month they will be performing at **Splinter Brothers Warehouse**, The **Oasis**, **Gentle Ben's** and The **Chicago Bar**.

Chance Romance

Chance Romance has been busily playing club dates. Because of these club dates, they've been hired to do a lot of casual dates, for instance, parties at the **Sheraton El Conquistador**. Chance does an Elvis show for **Billy Templeton**, which is a Las Vegas type show. They have two of these shows lined up for November. Chance has become the house band for the **Harp and Shamrock**. Their music is a variety of everything.

HMS

Because of lack of funds, the new **HMS** video has been stalled. The film should be processed by the end of this month. Their second audiocassette, which was to be released in October, has been held up because the cover hasn't been finished yet. It should be out by the end of this month. **Friendly Warning** keyboardist, **Phil Stevens**, may join HMS for a guest appearance at the Gentle Ben's show on the 15th and 16th.

Eighty Go Ninety

Eighty Go Ninety will be performing at The Oasis every weekend in November. Their music is selected hits from the '60s and some originals. All the music is upbeat dance music. Band member **Keith Miracle** does a solo act on Fridays at The Oasis.

Eighty Go Ninety performing in February 1982 at the Pima County Fairgrounds concert event for the *Tucson Teen* newspaper. Photo by Bob Jasinowski. *Tucson Teen* archives.

Boogie Man Blues Band

The two month old, straight-ahead blues band, **Boogie Man Blues Band**, will be performing at the **Chicago Bar** on November 22nd and 23rd and at Café Olé through the month.

Twister

Twister will be playing some private weddings this month. On the 6th they will be performing at **Gentle Ben's**, on the 14th through 16th they will be at **Keaton's** in the Foothills Mall. Twister will also perform at the **Sheraton Rio Rico** on November 22nd and 23rd.

Blues All Stars

The **Blues All Stars** will soon be going under a new name. Under the new name they will be opening for **Blue Lizard** on the 8th and 9th at **Nino's**. Blues all Stars can be seen through November weekly at **Terry & Zeke's** on Mondays and Tuesdays.

Nue Venue: New Dance Club near the UA

Plans are being developed for a University-area non-alcohol dance club, called **Nue Venue**, on the weekends as an alternative to "nothing else to do." The dance club, located at the **Tucson YWCA**'s gymnasium hall, will showcase Tucson's upcoming and established local rock, jazz and country bands. Regional bands will be booked when available. The best thing about it is that all proceeds will go to two non-profit organizations and is sponsored by the Tucson YWCA and the *Entertainment Magazine*. Listen to your favorite station to find out more details.

Ronnie Mack: November Country Licks

By Ronnie Mack
November 1985 - Entertainment Magazine. Page 17

I would like to thank everyone for their kind words on my first column for *EM*, It's great encouragement. I pray that all future columns are as well received.

The **Southern Arizona Entertainment Association** (SAEA) is holding a Benefit Concert at the **Spanish Trail Motel** on S. Fourth Avenue and I-10 on Sunday, November 17th from noon to midnight. Some of Tucson's finest pickers will be spotlighted. The proceeds will go to the American Cancer Society/Camp Sunrise. Stop out there for some real fine listenin' and dancin'. There will be lots of prizes and a fun auction.

As you move about town, on the North West side, you have a veritable array of country nightspots to choose from. This month, I'll take you through a few of them.

Beginning at Grant and Stone with **Tovi's Hoof & Horn** you'll hear great vocals by **Dan Woodberry** and **Westbound**. My old friend **John Jenson** is on lead guitar– formerly with **Rock West** and **Longshot**.

North of Grant on 1st Avenue, just past Ft. Lowell Rd., you discover **Boon Docks**. They have pool, darts, dancing, big screen TV, a nice dance floor and always good music to dance to. On Sundays, you'll have fun at their Jam Session with the **All Bob Band** and **Bill Murray**.

Further west and north at Roger and Romero, you find the **Bull Pen Lounge** with live music since 1962. Now appearing are **Frank and the Hurricanes**. **Frank Manandt** is half of the famous **Frank & Woody Show**, who used to appear at the **Old Buckskin Bar** on Oracle. Stop over Wednesday through Sunday nights and catch one of Tucson's really hot spots.

Just around the corner from the Bull Pen is the **Swing Inn Lounge** where **Wayne Darnell and His Slick Band** are performing Thursday through Sunday. Darnell won the talent contest in Willcox and performed at Willcox Rodeo Dance with **Rex Allen Jr.** and his band.

The **Sportsman** is just south of the bridge on N. La Cholla with plenty of parking. Now appearing there are **Connie and the Bandits** Fridays, Saturdays and Sundays, from 9:00 PM to 1:00 AM.

North of Wetmore on Flowing Wells, you'll find the **Bushwacker Steak House** where **Dusty Rhodes**. They had been out in Catalina at the **Lariat Lounge** are now back in town. Stop over there, and "say hi," to **Jim Tuccio** on the bass.

Moving along Oracle you'll find fine dining and great music by my old friend **Paul Evans** and his band. Some of you may remember Paul from the **Round Up** on Benson Hwy. Or, maybe you remember him from the **Maverick**.

The **Sheraton El Conquistador** on North Oracle features country and western music, gun fights, bar-b-ques, hay rides and all sorts of things for people to enjoy. The music is by **Silver Sage** with **Billy Buel** doing it up hot on lead guitar Thursdays, Fridays and Saturday nights in the **Last Territory**.

The last, but far from the least, nightspot on North Oracle is all the way out in Catalina, the **Lariat Lounge** that offers a great time. Live music is by **Leanne McCabe Band**. The **All Bob Band** will appear November on Fridays, Saturdays and Sundays.

I'd like to stress Sunday Jam Sessions once again. Musicians working the jams would sure appreciate more involvement. If you play or sing, come out on Sunday to any one of the Jams. Ask the person in charge of the Jam. This is great for aspiring musicians to be heard. **Dan**, with **Westbound** over at **Tovi's Hoof & Horn** , runs a real fine Jam Sunday from 8:00 PM to 12:00 AM.

Be sure to catch the **Rincon Optimist Blue Grass Festival** featuring **Hot Rize**, **Red Knuckles** and **The Trailblazers** on Friday-Sunday, November 1-3rd at **Rillito Race Track**. Some of Tucson's finest bluegrass pickers will perform including **Gail Gowan**'s **Desert Riders** and **George Jones** with the **Salt River Ramblers**. Also **Titan Valley Warheads**, who appear at **Al Smith's Pub** on Wednesday nights.

Next month, I will take you on a tour of the centrally located and east side clubs for some country style listenin' and dancin.' In answer to those glaring questions you can find me, and the **Sun Downers**, at the **Silver Room**, 673 N. Plumer Avenue.

December 1985: A Grab Bag of Comics

By P.L. Wylie
December 1985 - Entertainment Magazine. Page 7

Tucson clubs continue with a potpourri of comedy. **Tequila Mockingbird** in **El Con Mall** (the granddaddy of comedy nights) has an open mike for aspiring or professional comics on Tuesday nights beginning at 9:00PM. Some folks make this a "regular" for their fun time during the early part of the week.

Over at **Terry & Zeke's**, on East Speedway, there are two comedy shows nightly on Friday and Saturday nights at 7:00PM and 8:30PM. Featured are out of town comics who "make the circuit" with a local host and headliner. For the price of admission to the **Comedy Zone** you can stay and dance to the current blues band, beginning at 10:00PM. Call for reservation, especially for the later show.

A local well-known singer/actor is taking a turn at directing. **Armen Dirtadian** is directing the play "Oliver" at **Amphitheatre High School**, December 5th-8th at 8:00PM.

The **Gaslight Theatre's** Christmas production of "Just a Little Bit of Magic" plays through January 4th. This is a musical fantasy about a little boy in a toy store. Show times until December 1st are Wednesday and Thursday at 8:00PM, Friday and Saturday at 7:00PM and 9:30PM, and again on Sunday at 7:00PM. Extra shows will be added the following weeks for the holidays.

Country Cub hopping with Ronnie Mack

By Ronnie Mack
December 1985 - Entertainment Magazine. Page 12

Season's Greetings! Time is once again upon us, and I hope this year none of my friends end up in accidents. Let's all remember to slow down and not to drink and drive. Enjoy the "Christmas Spirit" without overdoing it– let your friends drive you home if you had too much to drink.

Come along with me, beginning on the north central part of Tucson. I'll take you to where there are good times to be had by anyone who likes dancing, good music and great company!

We'll begin our night out at The **Ft. Lowell Depot** at 3501 E. Ft. Lowell. An old friend of mine, who has been performing in and around town for a long time, Mr. **Leo Domingus & the Brakemen** appears Tuesdays thru Saturdays. The Depot's team won the 5th Annual Greased Pig Contest at **Rillito Race Track** in October. The gang sure knows how to have fun!

Leaving the Depot, we can stop by one of Tucson's clubs that doesn't look country from the decor, but the music sure is– The **Plush Horse Pub** at 4400 E. Broadway. Most bandleaders are usually the lead singer, but the **Dalton Gang** has a drummer in the driver's seat, Mr. **Stan Washmon**. They feature great vocals by **Ray Butler** and **Johnny Walton**, with some great hot licks by lead guitarist **Gary Lee** playing Thursdays through Saturdays, 9:00PM to 1:00AM.

Next, we'll go to the **Wooden Nickel Tavern** at 1908 S. Country Club. There you'll see another fine group, **Gary Rust's** band with **Sabra** on bass, **Wade** lead guitar, and **Deacon** on drums. They play every other Friday and

Saturday. Next on our tour is the **Maverick**, on 22nd St. and Swan, to see **Johnny Mann & the Country Kings**. They perform Tuesdays through Saturdays with Rust's band on Sunday and Monday nights.

The **Post Time Pub**, 2545 S. Craycroft, has had more facelifts than Roy Rogers. I have performed there for ten different owners myself. Still, they continue to provide us with fine entertainment. Now appearing are The **Jack's**. You can hear them Wednesdays, Fridays and Saturdays, 8:30PM to 1:00AM. Don't forget the Jam Session on Sundays, 4:00PM to 8:00PM. Just north of the Post Time Pub is the **Driftwood** at 2001 S. Craycroft. A new band, The **Silver Rose** plays Fridays and Saturdays 9:00PM to 1:00AM. Stop in and say hi to "**Mamma and Papa K.**"

From there, we go to the **New Outlaw** at 5822 E. Speedway. It also has undergone some facelifts. It now provides us with Tucson's hottest in country rock, The **Saddle City Band**, Wednesday through Saturday, 9:00PM to 1:00AM. Band member **Duncan Stitt** composes some really fine material. There is Rock Monday with **George Hawke & the Cary Grants,** 9:00PM to 1:00AM.

Going from East Speedway, let's head up to the Tanque Verde Strip to 6511 E. Tanque Verde for **Sneaky Pete's Steak House**. Now appearing Wednesday through Saturday is the **Desert Express Band** featuring the **Dick Wannabo** family. They play good, easy listening country music that is a pleasure to hear. **Dave King** plays Sunday and Monday from 6:00PM to 10:00PM.

By this time of the night, we are at the most eastern of the country spots, **Chandelle's Restaurant & Lounge**, 7810 E. Broadway. It's a late hour on my little tour and we have already visited eight clubs. But, if you're not tired yet, we don't have to stop having fun, only cocktails. Remember, no liquor served after 1:00AM.

Our last stop is Tucson's only after hours club, Chandelle's, **Borderline** performs a wide variety of music, featuring my old friends **Larry Allen & Charley Yates**, with some real fine fiddle, banjo and sax by **Tim O'Conner**. They play Wednesday thru Sunday from 8:30PM to 12:30AM, and Friday and Saturday until 3:00AM. We can eat our breakfast while enjoying the music and then call it a night. Also, on Monday and Tuesday, **Stars & Bars** play 8:00PM to 12:30AM.

Once more, spend your holidays safe and happy!! I'll be spending mine playing music at the **Swing Inn Lounge**, 1618 W. Wetmore. So, until next year, when I'll be taking you out for a night on the south side of town, take care and enjoy all that good entertainment out there. And remember, support local music.

Tucson bands wrap up the holidays

By Neil Costin
December 1985 - Entertainment Magazine. Page 18

The Speedways

The **Speedways** will have a special show December 13th (1985). On this superstitious, bad luck day, The Speedways will be doing four sets of dead rock stars; Janis, Kimi, the Doors, etc. The show is called "Dead Rock Star Set." This will also be repeated on the 14th at the **Chicago Bar** and on the 31st when they headline at the **Showtime Lounge** with **Bluewave** opening the show. There will be a $5 cover charge at this New Year's Eve show and the band is expecting a full house. The **Speedways** will also be playing the **Showtime** from December 16-21st. After a two-month absence, **Vicki Borton** will be doing some of the singing. The band is looking forward to an exciting December, and also looking forward to the upcoming New Year working with all the clubs around town.

HMS: Tucson Collection

One of Tucson's finest players of original music, **HMS**, has just released their second cassette of tunes. Called "Untitled Wish," the tape is engineered by **Steve English**. It has six original compositions by the band that has been included in their sets for the past few months. The trio guitarist/vocalist **John Venet**, drummer/vocalist **John Booth** and bassist/vocalist **Mark Mellinger** have one of the tightest sounds to be heard in local clubs over the last year. Their new tape is available only at gigs and **Al Bums**, this band has the sound of the 1960s written all over it, and should be heard by all.

Nadine & the new band members

Nadine & the MoPhonics recently got a new drummer, **Eric Kritzer** and a new bass player **Jim Monahan**. Nadine doesn't have any dates set until the end of January. The band is writing and learning a lot of new material.

Audience at the Bird

Audience has been together since last summer. The momentum has really picked up since they got their new drummer. Audience plays all original rock. They are a very versatile group. They played at **Tequila Mockingbird** on December 4th through the 6th. Opening the show was The **Distant**, formerly **Buddy System**.

FRIDAYS

Affirmative/Assorted Images-*Global Village* (12/6)
Fiction-*Global Village* (12/13)
Bottom Line-*Global Village* (12/20)
TBA-*Global Village* (12/27)
Bourbon Street-*Doubletree Lounge* (12/6)
Brian Bromberg-*Doubletree Lounge* (12/13, 20, 27)
Neon Prophet-*Brooklyns* (12/6)
Live Reggae, TBA-*Brooklyns* (12/13)
Blue Wave-*Brooklyns* (12/20)
The Meditations-*Brooklyns* (12/27)
Audience/The Distant-*Tequila Mockingbird* (12/6)
Roc Lochner-*Tequila Mockingbird* (12/13)
Mobile Cubes-*Tequila Mockingbird* (12/20)
Last Flite-*Tequila Mockingbird* (12/27)
The Works- *Chicago Bar* (12/6)
The Speedways-*Chicago Bar* (12/13)
Boogie Man Blues Band-*Chicago Bar* (12/20)
Blue Wave-*Chicago Bar* (12/27)
David Spade/Ben Tyler-*Terry & Zekes Comedy Zone* (12/6)
Gary Hood/Marc Levinson-*Terry & Zekes Comedy Zone* (12/6)
Stan Howard/Danny Boskowitz/Marc Levinson-*Terry & Zekes Comedy Zone* (12/13)
Joe Corcoran/Mark Cordy/Dean Rhodes-*Terry & Zekes Comedy Zone* (12/20)
Scott Carter/Gary Hood/Jay Hewlett-*Terry & Zekes Comedy Zone* (12/27)
Ronnie Mack & the Sundowners-*Swing Inn* (12/6, 13, 20, 27)
Dusty Rhodes-*Bushwacker* (12/6, 13, 20, 27)

SATURDAYS

Bourbon Street-*Doubletree Lounge* (12/7)
Brian Bromberg-*Doubletree Lounge* (12/14, 21, 28)
Barbara Bird & Da Fellas-*Brooklyns* (12/7)
Naked Prey-*Brooklyns* (12/14)
Brain Damage-*Brooklyns* (12/21)
TBA-*Brooklyns* (12/28)
Audience/The Distant-*Tequila Mockingbird* (12/7)
Roc Lochner-*Tequila Mockingbird* (12/14)
Mobile Cubes-*Tequila Mockingbird* (12/21)
Last Flight-*Tequila Mockingbird* (12/28)
The Works-*Chicago Bar* (12/7)
The Speedways-*Chicago Bar* (12/14)
Boogie Man Blues Band-*Chicago Bar* (12/21)
Blue Wave-*Chicago Bar* (12/28)
David Spade/Ben Tyler-*Terry & Zekes Comedy Zone* (12/7)
Gary Hood/Marc Levinson-*Terry & Zekes Comedy Zone* (12/7)
Stan Howard/Donny Boskowitz/Marc Levinson-*Terry & Zekes Comedy Zone* (12/14)
Joe Corcoran/Marc Cordey/Dean Rhodes-*Terry & Zekes Comedy Zone* (12/21)
Scott Carter/Gary Hood/Jay Hewlett-*Terry & Zekes Comedy Zone* (12/28)
Ronnie Mack & The Sundowners-*Swing Inn* (12/7, 14, 21, 28)
Dusty Rhodes-*Bushwacker* (12/7, 14, 21, 28)

SUNDAYS

Brian Bromberg-*Doubletree Lounge* (12/15, 22, 29)
Male Dancers/Funk & Soul-*Brooklyns* (12/8, 15, 22, 29)
Split Decision-*Terry & Zekes* (12/8, 15, 22, 29)
Ronnie Mack & The Sundowners-*Swing Inn* (12/8, 15, 22, 29)
Dusty Rhodes-*Bushwacker* (12/8, 15, 22, 29)

MONDAYS

Brian Bromberg- *Doubletree Lounge* (12/16, 23, 30)
Blues All-Stars-*Terry & Zekes* (12/9, 16, 23, 30)

TUESDAYS

Brian Bromberg-*Doubletree Lounge* (12/10, 17, 24, 31)
Second Hand Newz-*Brooklyns* (12/10, 17)
Funk Soul, w/Sir Reginald-*Brooklyns* (12/24, 31)
Funk/Soul, w/Mista "T"-*Brooklyns* (12/31)
Comedy Nite-*Tequila Mockingbird* (12/10, 17)
Christmas Eve, closed for Comedy-*Tequila Mockingbird* (12/24)
Last Flight/N.Y. Eve Party(no comedy)-*Tequila Mockingbird* (12/31)

WEDNESDAYS

Brian Bromberg-*Doubletree Lounge* (12/11, 18, 25)
Male Dancers/Funk & Soul-*Brooklyns* (12/11, 18, 25)
Montreal-*Tequila Mockingbird* (12/11, 18)

THURSDAYS

Brian Bromberg-*Doubletree Lounge* (12/12, 19, 26)
Radio Free America-*Brooklyns* (12/12)
The Affirmative-*Brooklyns* (12/19)
Second Hand Newz-*Brooklyns* (12/26)
Roc Lochner-*Tequila Mockingbird* (12/12)
Mobile Cubes-*Tequila Mockingbird* (12/19)
Last Flite-*Tequila Mockingbird* (12/26)
Zeke Taylor-*Terry & Zekes* (12/12)
Statesboro Blues Band-*Terry & Zekes* (12/12)
Dusty Rhodes-*Bushwacker* (12/12, 19, 26)

Arizona LIVE!

15

Arizona LIVE! listings are published, as a service, by your advertisers. Schedules are subject to change. Call before venturing out. Happy Holidays!

Talisman
at the Lookout Lounge
Westward Look Resort
Tuesdays through Saturdays

Brian Bromberg
at the Doubletree Lounge
Tuesdays through Saturdays

COMEDY

Comedy Zone/Terry & Zeke's
4376 E. Speedway/325-3555

Tequila Mockingbird
3601 E. Broadway/881-5582

COUNTRY

Bushwacker
4635 N. Flowing Wells/888-7959

Swing Inn Lounge
1618 W. Wetmore/293-9813

JAZZ/BLUES

Terry & Zeke's Friendly Tavern
4376 E. Speedway/325-3555

VARIETY

Brooklyn's
2437 N. Stone/791-7542

Chicago Bar
5954 E. Speedway/748-8169

Doubletree Inn
445 S. Alvernon/881-4200

Global Village
304 E. University Blvd./623-3733

"Arizona Live" nightclub calendar, *Entertainment Magazine*, December 1985, page 15.

Affirmative was a show stopper; TFD closes down Splinter Bros.

December 1985 - Entertainment Magazine. Page 16

Just as **Affirmative** finished playing an opening set at the **White Animals**/Affirmative concert November 22nd (1985) at **Splinter Brothers Warehouse** the show was suddenly stopped. It wasn't because the band was playing bad music. The music was smoking.

The **Tucson Fire Department** (TFD) closed Splinter Brothers and ordered all patrons to immediately evacuate because the 13-year old building didn't meet current fire code standards. At 10:00PM, about a half dozen members of the TFD filtered into the crowd and ordered the building to be evacuated during the show after citing a number of fire code violations.

At about the same time, **Brooklyn's Night Club** was being checked by TFD. When a TFD officer overhead someone at Splinter Brother's determinedly say "We're going on," he called for police back up to avoid any incident. The 100 people were ushered to the exits as TFD and **Tucson Police Department** made sure the show wasn't going to go on. Disgruntled patrons questions the ethics of shutting the building town in the middle of the performance. It was an incident that could have been avoided.

The Bottom Line at Global Village

Andy Meshel, David McMahon, Kevin Cunneely, David Every and Kevin Free are the diversified musical talents that make up the fresh new group The **Bottom Line**. The band will be performing for the new under 21 night club called **Global Village** (formerly called **Nue Venue**) at the **Tucson YWCA** building, on December 20th (1985).

Originals songs of varying tastes will be debuted as well as compositions by other artists. Some of these "covers" include selections from the Police, U2, Oingo Boingo and the Talking Heads. The members of The Bottom Line draw on many different musical backgrounds to compose their originals. Bottom Line's sets are representative of danceable cuts that can still be considered music. In late December, The Bottom Line will be recording an album at **Westwood Recording Studio**. There will be a debut party for the recordings on New Years Eve.

The Press are pressing on

By Angie Lumia
December 1985 - Entertainment Magazine

The **Press** has a very confident outlook for their music. As founding member, guitarist, composer and vocalist **David Moskowitz** put it, "quality music, professional musicians, enthusiasm, vivaciousness, friendliness with an open aesthetic appearance."

The band members have been working with music for a long time. Some of them are professional performers as well. **Robin Wall** is the vocalist, keyboardist and composer. **Dave Cannal** plays bass, sings and composes. **Shawn Burch** is the bands percussionist. He has been playing since he was six years old. **Bonnie Essig** is vocals, keyboards, and composer.

Fiction's new video

One of Tucson's youngest bands has been making headway on the local music scene. **Fiction**, a two-man synthesizer group, has performed at **Tequila Mockingbird**, **Brooklyn's**, **Nino's**, and the **UA Cellar**. The band has also performed for the Jerry Lewis Muscular Dystrophy Telethon.

Fiction's first video, "The Insanity Song," was broadcast on the final edition of **KVOA**-TV's Midnight Music Videos.

The group is currently working on a second video and plans to begin production on a half-hour special for **Tucson Community Cable Corporation** public access channel in the future.

Band members **Mike Fisher** and **Keith Arem**, juniors at **University High School**, will be recording their first demo tape in the coming months. The all keyboard group will appear at **Global Village** (formerly NueVenue) at E. University Blvd. and 5th Avenue in the **Tucson YWCA** building on December 13th.

Fiction (left) Keith Arem, Mike Fisher. 1986. *Entertainment Magazine* archives.

\

It's Plan B for Blues All Stars

Plan B is the new name that the **Blues All Stars** chose for their title. They will no longer be playing under their former name. Plan B is holding off on booking until their new set of originals are complete.

Assorted Images: The Images have plans

By Brian Atkinson
December 1985 - Entertainment Magazine

This month's profile is on Tucson's newest bands– **Assorted Images**. **Sergio Bustamante**, **Joel Pust** and **Karl Deemer** began Assorted Images one year ago. Sergio said, "that ever since seventh grade, Joel and I had thought about forming a band, but we didn't seriously consider it until we started playing. That's when we found Karl."

Assorted Images (left to right) Joel Pust, Karl Deember and Sergio Bustamonte. December 1985 edition, *Entertainment Magazine*.

The group plays "modern rock almost techno-rock," explains Deemer. "We listen to a lot of British groups and get influenced by them.

Assorted Images seems to be well received by the public. They have opened for **Friendly Warning** at **Nino's** and have also played at various parties and social events.

Deemer believes "our style is completely different from anything in Tucson."

Bustamante agrees. "Most other local bands are rougher than we are. We tend to worry about our melodies. Joel will work on the melody, Karl will play it on the keyboards, and I'll do the vocals."

Both Karl and Sergio agree that their age does pose a major setback. "It's hard to get other people to accept us because of our age. They don't seem to respect us as musicians."

Despite their ages, Assorted Images plan on making a name for themselves locally. With their drive and talent they will surely make it. Assorted Images will be performing at the new **Global Village** on December 6, 1985.

TWIT is serious about TV

By Casey
December 1985 – Magazine. Page 16

Barrio Historico is dark. Down by **Jerry's Lee Ho Market**, some neighbors are talking. Mariachi music spills lightly from a nearby home as a door opens to greet a guest. The muted shrill of a telephone rings from inside the darkened **TWIT (Tucson Western International Telethon)** cable television program headquarters. As the minutes pass, the phone continues to ring.

A tall, thin figure materializes from the light near Cushing Street and strides purposefully towards TWIT headquarters. The light from a passing car frames **Dave Bukunus'** six-feet two-inch frame as he bends over to unlock the door and then points around the room. "We've been rearranging." He walks into the kitchen of TWIT's combined living room and working headquarters. "Sort of a television half-way house," laughs Dave.

Returning from the kitchen with a cup of coffee, Dave settles into an easy chair. "Rearranging the traffic flows and patterns. It's good for changing creative perspective."

Creative perspective. Constantly shifting perspectives and people that contribute to the monumental task of three hours of weekly television programming known as TWIT.

As other TWIT founders move on– Dave finds himself emerging as "the" TWIT– an attention-loving bundle of ultra high energy whose perspective is divided between organizing television production and personally fulfilling spontaneous bursts of creative artistic license.

Bukunus has a perspective that has been intertwined with television through the years. "I got into the field through the performing arts. I joined the theatre group in high school my sophomore year. My first year was spent on sets and lighting. After that I was acting in school plays."

Dave paused for a sip of coffee before continuing. "As an undergraduate at Rutgers I got involved in the Division of Instructional Television. That was in '68 or '69. Joe Durrand was the head of that. He was former director of Howdy Doody show, a living legend from the Golden Age of Television. After I graduated, I did a live news show in California. Then, I did a cable show in Texas. We'd do things like pick up trash in the streets and give it to people. It was a crazy show."

Among other things the 35 year-old producer did was a stint as a stand up comic in San Francisco. He also spent seven years doing marketing surveys for a cable company. Describing himself as a video addict, Dave does admit to sneaking off for an occasional game of tennis or a movie. And, sometimes, he sits down to read a book.

The phone shrills. "Hi, Rosemary. No, there wasn't any equipment available. I'm going to work on it in the morning ...

The small conference room in the **Tucson Community Cable Corporation's** (**TCCC's**) administration building is almost empty. Dave Bukunus has been brainstorming with other TCCC volunteers in an attempt to figure out how to accommodate the growing swell of volunteers attracted to public access video production.

The others have left. Dave brushes his brown hair with a wave of his hand, then speaks. "Public access is coming together to focus television on something in the community. The philosophy is that everyone is created equal in their access to television production. Philosophically, I agree. As a producer, though, I find it necessary to be aggressive and demanding in fighting for TWIT's share of production equipment and facilities."

Jan Lesher, TCCC Director, recently told me that Tucson has seen about 800 hours of public access cablecasting since the TCCC's kick off in July (1985). TWIT has provided about 120 of those hours.

He pauses a moment, changes direction. "Public access is such a wonderful thing. Where else do you go to get television experience? It's a place to learn, experiment, and have fun while producing television programs. Public access is the great proving ground– the summer stock of television."

At TCCC studios on 10 W. Congress, the band is being set up outside. Inside, three sets go up against three different walls. The technical crew is in the booth, moving towards its Friday night brush with fame.

Dave is all over, trying to line up the talent as they arrive. He finds a moment to breath and reflects on TWIT's beginnings.

"When TCCC came into being a group of us pulled together with the thought that we are the common people. We can take over television. We can do it. The TWIT takeover of the TCCC studios occurred on a Friday night late last July.

Problems with the microphones whisked Dave away. A teenage cameraperson liberated a studio camera from its tripod so he could flex his creative muscle by getting shots from the floor.

Suddenly, Dave was talking to a couple of young fellows who had contacted him several days before about doing some impromptu spots. After they worked out the final details, the two left the studio for the street. Dave Bukunus blessed their backs with a pontifical smile of gratitude for a new infusion of creativity.

The word filtered through the crew– "fifteen minutes until nine o'clock." The pace in the studio quickened as Dave turned to me. "There's so much to television production. Scheduling people, talking to people …"

He builds up energetic steam as he continues, "Bringing an idea in, getting the graphics. Where's the music? Where's the camera people? How does this work? Do we have enough time to do that?" He pauses for a breath of air.

"Where'd my costume go? Where's my make-up? Who is going to do make-up? Is the guest on time? Where's the rest of the crew? Where's the script for that? Did it get typed? Who picked up the Xerox copies? Where are the costumes? Is the lighting okay? Are the camera white balanced? Have the microphones been checked..."

Finally, Dave Bukunus is at stage center ... "Live from Tucson, it's the **Tucson Western International Telethon**..."

TWIT logo, December 1985, The *Magazine*. Page 16.

Kruiser Experience: Kruising for a bruising

By P.L. Wylie
December 1985 - Entertainment Magazine. Page 6-7

"What I am is basically a ham. I have never been shy in my life. I have baby pictures of me that show an eight-month old infant mugging for the camera," states **Stephen Krzyzanowski**, a local comic professionally known as "The **Kruiser Experience**."

Krzyzanowski is your oddity in Tucson, a native. He spent his formative years in Show Low, Arizona, went on to San Diego, New York and Phoenix and then returned to the city of his birth. Besides appearing at local clubs as a comic, he has a real estate company called **Forest Properties, Inc.,** where he works days. His sales career alternates him between Tucson and Show Low.

Kruiser photo by Robert Schotland.
Entertainment Magazine, December 1985, page 6

Kruiser was the recent winner of the now defunct Karmel's **Comedy Zone** contest for all-around best comic, which attracted an audience of between 300 and 400 people.

"At first I just went along with the contest as something to do, and then I really got into it," Kruiser said. "The whole day before the contest I thought I was going to explode. The night of the contest I stayed outside while the other acts were on because I didn't want to hear their laughs."

"There were several comics appearing that I had never seen before so I didn't know how good they were going to be. Every 15 minutes or so I would run in and ask my friends how I was holding up. I knew I was in the running, but I was really pleasantly surprised when I won. But I don't want to sound too humble here, or my friends will know this interview is a crock." The prize Kruiser won was a guaranteed six-minute spot at the famous Comedy Store in Los Angeles. The details of the payment of expenses by the promoters of the contest still have to be worked out.

Kruiser also recently appeared in Phoenix, opening for **Street Pajama** at their special promo party. Previous to that, he branched out and appeared at the **Gaslight Theatre** with Fish Karma (a comic from L.A.) as an opening act for **Ace Baker**.

The comedy career of Kruiser started two years ago when he paired up with an old high school chum, **Rob Ferguson** (son of **Jim Ferguson** of local TV fame). They started at the then **Comedy Boat**, and appeared at **Tequila Mockingbird** and **Characters**. When Ferguson moved, Kruiser decided to go it alone. He writes his own material, and says, "the more you work, the better you get. When you are not appearing regularly on stage, you begin to lose steam. When you are working four nights a week, everyday things begin to look funny."

One part of Kruiser's act that is highly successful is his dealings with hecklers. When questioned where he acts his lines, he said that three or four are stock comic lines but the rest are his own. "I like to deal with real hecklers, but not real drunks, because they probably don't even remember they were at the show" states Kruiser: "I have only had one person get upset with me over this, and it was at something I said to someone else. Most people love it when you put down a heckler. Also, I think most hecklers want to be part of the act."

"I always get nervous before going on. If I don't, then I begin to worry. I do not have a laid back type of act. The only thing that really throws me off from an audience is dead silence. But, I have learned tricks to overcome this. In my estimation comedy is just as much an art form as playing a guitar or singing someone else's songs. In fact it is harder to do. I don't think in the past in Tucson that comics were afforded much, much respect, but that is certainly changing now. The **Tucson Comics Association** is going to see that that change continues. And financially, we are not working for just 'exposure' any more. We might be inexpensive, but we are not free. Comics are not going to get rich in Tucson or make enough money to buy a Porsche, but we want to be adequately compensated. I think people in Tucson realize now that we are legitimate entertainers. I do credit the producers and performers at the previous **Comedy Zone** with helping to upgrade people's perception of us in Tucson. Also, **Tequila Mockingbird** (El Con) has stuck with the comics for better or worse through the years by having a weekly showcase for them. Now, we can go to the other club owners with straight faces and tell them what we have done professionally. This helps us greatly with our bargaining position. We were treated so well in our recent dealings with a club that I thought I was dreaming," relates Kruiser.

Kruiser is the acting head of the recently formed **Tucson Comics Association**. He says the members also have a chance to join the national professional organization if they desire. The TCA was newly formed when the Comedy Zone folded, and many of the members, consequently, were not working.

"When that happened, the Association wasn't foremost on our minds. But now that there are two clubs other than **Tequila Mockingbird** (**Terry & Zeke's** and **Nino's**) where comics can work in Tucson, I think we will go forward with the Association. It is so much easier when we all are speaking as one professional voice, which is what we are proposing the Tucson Comic's Association to be."

When questioned about where his sympathies lie in the rumored local "comic's war" Kruiser replies: "I don't think there is one. I think it is friendly competitive now- maybe three years ago was an adversary attitude among the comics, but it has changed. I personally like something of every comic's act that I have seen in Tucson, and I especially admire **Gary Hood**'s work."

Kruiser says he is on the fence about way to go, career-wise. "I really can't see myself now playing the starving artist bit in Los Angeles. I do get a real high from going on, and I can't sleep after a good show. It is a let down to go back to my daytime job. But, the checks help a lot. Actually I love both of my jobs and I have the best of both worlds. I was brought up in Show Low, and I sell resort vacation property there. I know that area. I used to hunt on some of that property and it is fantastic now for me to show it to people. Maybe eventually if I make enough money, I will produce my own comedy show. Or be an executive producer, because all they have to do is sign checks."

Kruiser has a sister in Tucson who goes to **Pima Community College**. "She picked up all the student ability that I somehow lost," he says. Actually, he went to Pima for one year and to the **University of Arizona** for one year. "Someday, I will have a degree. I am studying psychology now and I have this dream. Wouldn't it be pretty intimidating to walk into my real estate office and see a degree in psychology hanging there? People would probably just ask– where do we sign?"

"In the past year in Tucson we have gotten a lot of regular comics working, and I would like them to get their friends involved. We are getting a lot of people active who have real talent, and I can only see it getting better now. I think there is a bigger market in Tucson for comedy than we have proved so far – just ask people to come out and enjoy the shows. That's what you do. It is not a terrible experience. You just sit around and laugh."

Garry Shandling: keeping Johnny's seat warm

By P.L. Wylie
January 1986 - Entertainment Magazine. Page 5

"**D**o your work and put on blinders to every thing else, because it only messes you up. Just do your work well and the rest takes care of itself. My philosophy is that I was never concerned with my career– just my work."

So states **Garry Shandling**, nationally known stand up comic originally from Tucson, in a recent interview. Shandling's parents moved here from Chicago when he was 10 years old.

He is a 1969 graduate of **Palo Verde High School** and **University of Arizona** in 1972. He majored in engineering and business and creative writing in graduate school. His mother still lives in Tucson and has a business on the east side. Shandling says he tries to get back to Tucson for visits a couple of times a year. He says he misses the Tucson heat.

"I like to float in the pool and get my body as hot as possible." Shandling confesses.

Shandling was always interested in comedy. In Tucson in 1967 there was no way to explore that possibility without any comedy nightclubs in the city. "I never met anyone while I was growing up that was interested in any phase of comedy. Had there been any clubs, there was a chance I would have started earlier in standup comedy. There was no outlet for me as a comedian, and I really thought I was crazy to even consider becoming a comic."

"I took engineering at the University of Arizona for three years because I was interested in electronics," says Shandling. But after three years of it, one day, just like in a movie, I walked out of one of my engineering labs to get a drink of water and never walked back in. I had to get away." Shandling then dropped out of engineering school and transferred to a business college to get his degree. "After engineering courses, business college was easy for me," Shandling says. "So, I started to write comedy material in some of my classes. I had taken 21 units of math and physics in engineering college. To me, the accounting courses were incredibly easy. When they were lecturing on how to add up debits and credits, I sat in the back row and wrote comedy monologues."

"George Carlin was appearing at a club in Phoenix at that time, so I took some of my routines to him," Shandling continues. "He writes his own material, but he read mine and said they were really very good. He encouraged me to move to Los Angeles."

After his graduation from the University of Arizona, Shandling moved to Los Angeles in 1972. "It took me a couple of years to figure out what was going on, and then I sold one of my scripts to the "Sanford and Son" TV show. After that, I was on my way to a comedy script writing career."

"After three years of writing for TV it was like I was in engineering school again. I couldn't continue. I had a sense of deja-vu. I couldn't go on. So, I just quit. I was making very good money. But, it wasn't what I wanted. I called my agent and told him to get me out."

After that, Shandling started to work in "real dives" doing his stand up routines. He worked in discos on comedy nights and entered numerous talent contests.

"Comedy was always my underlying love," states Shandling, "I didn't start doing it seriously until I was 27 years old, which is late to start nowadays. It has always been natural for me. It would have been more evident if I could have explored it more fully earlier. That is why I think it is great now there are comedy clubs available."

It took Shandling a few years to get a spot at The Comedy Store in Los Angeles. While appearing there in 1975, his agent brought in a talent scout from "The Tonight Show" to catch his act. The scout thought Shandling was good and booked him on "The Tonight Show" two weeks later. "It was great. I hosted the 'Tonight Show' and that is funny from something that has happened to me– especially my experiences as a single man in the '80s. So, I use it and then I also ad lib on stage."

When questioned if he exaggerates his "single life" problems in his act, Shandling admits he does. "However many of the things have happened. For instance, I went on a date– the latest in November, 1985 – and I have hosted several time since then," recalls Shandling.

When questioned if his appearances as a host and comedian on "The Tonight Show" make him nervous, he replied, "I get a little nervous, but it is a comfortable place for me. Being spontaneous makes me less nervous than if I have to follow a script. It is usually the other way around. I write my own material. And the writing is the hardest part of this business."

Shandling says he never has "gone blank" on stage. If he is off for several months he sometimes forgets a routine. "But then I just do another one. So, nobody really knows."

He gets his ideas for comedy material in several ways. "I tend to say funny things in my life and then when I realize it is funny I put it in my act. Sometimes, I get an idea with a girl from the Miss Universe contest, and she wore her crown on the date. Everyone wondered if she had been eating too much margarine."

The "Garry Shandling's 25th Anniversary Special" was on Showtime on January 8th. The guests on the special included Donny Osmond, Señor Wences, Roy Firestone and Johnny Carson. "This was a takeoff on other 25th Anniversary Specials, as obviously I haven't been on TV for 25 years. We took clips from some of my previous shows and made them look old, and then flash back. I also mention Tucson in this special. I think it was a good one- and hoped that everyone watched."

Shandling will have a situation comedy television series that will begin production in early 1986. He is writing the script for it himself. "It will be like the old Jack Benny Show. It will feature Garry Shandling playing himself, not some character. I will get to talk to the camera. I think it will be funny," he says.

There are offers of movie work and Shandling is going to decide if that is what he wants to do. "I don't have any desire to be in anything but a comedy at this point, however."

On New Years Eve, Shandling appeared at Atlantic City with Joan Rivers. When asked about Rivers, Shandling says she is basically the same offstage as on. "We laugh a lot together," he states.

Regarding Johnny Carson, he says, "I am grateful to him for having me on "The Tonight Show." I have enormous respect for him, as do all comedians. He is very funny and very quick. He seems to like my work, and that is a real compliment."

Shandling says he will appear in Tucson sometime in the future as a comedian. "I still think of Tucson as home," he states.

He now lives in a new home at Oaks, California and likes to find solitude when he can in the nearby mountains of Big Bear. He is fastidious in making sure he is in good shape by running daily working out at a gym. He loves animals and has a 12-year old sheepdog. He is an only child. His brother died from cystic fibrosis when Shandling was ten years old. His father passed away last March.

This reporter was impressed Shandling's low-key style, and modesty. He told of an incident when somebody came up to him in a restaurant said he was a big fan of his. "I don't picture anyone being a big fan of mine," said Shandling.

Garry Shandling (first photo) press photograph, cover photo *Entertainment Magazine*, January 1986.
"It's Garry Shandling," (second photo) promotional photo, Fox Broadcasting Co., 1985.

Entertaining Tucson Across the Decades: Volume II: 1986-early 2000s

The second volume of "Entertaining Tucson Across the Decades" continues the stories and photographs of Tucson's nightlife scene from 1986 through the early 2000s. These are just some of the entertainers featured in Volume II:

911
Aftermath
Affirmative
Alias
Ed Alexander
American Pie
American Radio Theater
Anti-M
Robert Apel
Arthur/Brand Band
Ash Alley
Ashes and Dust
Assorted Images
Atrophy
Audience
Ada Redd Austin
Autocatz
Backstreet Boogie
Bad Habit
Mary Baker
Believer
Bergoetz, Brian
Bernhart, Robert
Betty & the Bebops
Betty Stress
Big Bug
Bill Shears Band
Barbara Bird & Das Fellas
Black Sun Ensemble
Blitz Creek
Bluegrass Blues Festival
Bluelight Blues Band
Blue Lizards
Boogie Animals
Boogieman Blues
Charles Bowden
Brain Damage Orchestra
Broken Romeo
Buddy System

The Bullies
The Cadillac's
The Cattle
The Chambers
Chance Romance
Chuck Wagon & the Wheels
Coupe de Ville
Crazy Heart
Crosswind
Cryptics
John Denman
D.N.A.
Dennis Mitchell and the Wilsons
Desertfire
Desert Reign
Dillenger
Armen Dirtadian
Distant
Domino Theory
Dover Trench
Elektric
Fall from Grace
Fanatiks
Fastbreak
Fireheart
Liz Fletcher
Four-in-Force
George French
Vince Frighetti
Funky Bonz
Timothy Gasson
Genesis
Giant Sand
Giant Sandworms
Gerry Glombecki
Michael Gulezian
Mickey Greco
Gunga Din

Hackensack
Haus
Helen Hammer
Highbeam Blues Band
Sharon Hodges
The Host
Hot Pursuit
George Howard
Insane Jane
Scotty Johnson
Ken Lofton
Las Cruces
Last Round Up Band
Craig Lavelle
LifeForce
Liz Fletcher
LRQ
McRea, Bill
Mad Dog
Bobby Mahon
Marshmallow Overcoat
Metal Aftermath
Mobile Cubes
Mollys and McGuire
Molly Who
Miguel Monroy
Daniel Moore
Ted Moreno
Joe Myers
Nadine & the MoPhonics
Naked Prey
The Naturals
Necromancer
Nemesis
Ross Nickerson
Neon Prophet
Ockham's Razor
One Blood
Only's
Passionflies

Al Perry
Plastic Museum
Pollo Elastico
Cass Preston
Pulse
Rain Convention
Larry Redhouse Quartet (LRQ)
Don Reeve
Reggae, Tucson Style
Revivers
RFA
Riff Raff
Roadhouse Hounds
Roadies
Rockefeller
Hector Rodriguez
Linda Ronstadt
Peggy Rose & Company
Rowdies
Audrey St. Clair
Sand Rubies
LeeAnne Savage
Garry Shandling
Sharp Rain
Billy Shears Band
Shooters
Short Circuit
Short Stories
Sidewinders
Sippin' Whiskey Band
John Sirkis
J.C. Skinner
Sam Smiley
Speedways
Kidd Squidd
Cynthia Stacey
Statesboro Blues Band
Daniel Steenken
Duncan Stitt

Dan Starr
Stone Giant
Street Pajama
Street Gypsy
Sugar And Spice
Summit Studios
Ave Sunderman
Surge
Swing Shift
Tailormade
T.J. Canyon Band
Vicki Tapp
Bobby Taylor & Real Deal
Sam Taylor
Terry Dee
Thin Men
Titan Valley
Top Dogs
Tucson Mardi Gras at Rillito Downs
Tucson Rodeo
Tumors
Twister
U and the Risk
Uncle Bob
Up With People
Vince Frighetti
Virgin Vinyl
Visitors
White Rabbit
Chuck Williams
Paul Young
Xavier Marquez
911
XL
X-Rays
Zebbhi Niyah
And dozens more to be added…

Copies of "Entertaining Tucson Across the Decades, Volume II: 1986-early 2000s" is available for sale on Amazon.com and other outlets in both print and digital formats.

For more information and extra features, visit the "Entertaining Tucson Across the Decades" web site: http://emol.org/entertaintucson/

Post-logue

Technology sure has advanced since these articles were first published between 1974 and 1985. At the time, there were no personal computers, no Internet and no cell phones. Cable television was just on the horizon. Newly introduced phototypesetting in the 1970s brought some electronic advances to the publishing industry and reduced the cost to produce a newspaper. Personal desktop publishing was on another horizon– a decade later.

The original articles published in this compilation were first typed on either a manual or electric typewriter. They were edited – usually with a red pen– and often retyped again to provide a "clean" copy to be sent to a typesetter. At the time, typesetting was done through a local printing company. They could afford the expensive equipment needed to produce the stream of printed text. The typeset copy was provided in long rolls of photosensitive paper that had to be cut with an X-Acto blade and pasted onto large layout sheets with hot wax. Then, the "camera ready" sheets are taken to the printer where they are finally printed.

The entire layout had to be manually produced– the original "cut and paste." That grueling job was painstakingly slow and often lead to crooked blocks of copy and borders. But, it was still an advancement of the early printing days when every single letter had to be placed by hand.

In early 1980, the *Youth Awareness Press* (*YAP*) newspaper received a grant to purchase its own phototypesetter (about the size of a desk) to reduce outside typesetting costs and provide students with typesetting skills. While it saved hundreds of dollar each edition, the chemicals and photography paper needed to stock and operate the phototypesetter were expensive. It was also a messy process.

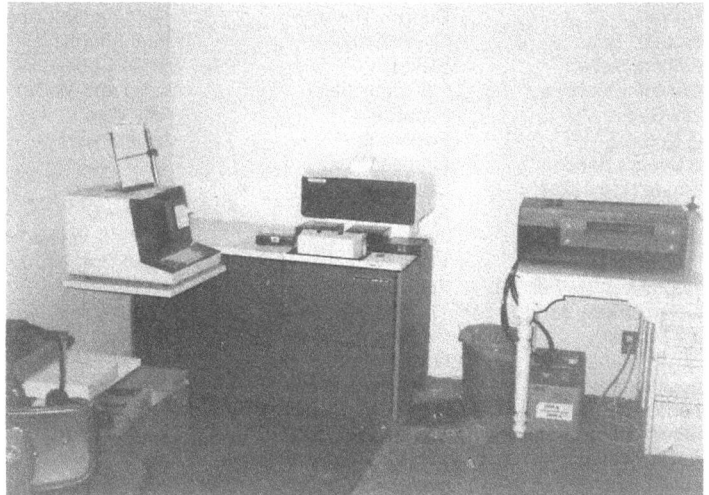

A Macintosh SE (above), with an 8" wide black and white screen, was finally acquired in 1988. This was long after the articles in this first volume were originally published. Using Microsoft Word for Macintosh, Aldus PageMaker desktop publishing software and an Apple LaserWriter Plus printer– desktop publishing was born.

Above: One of the first typesetting computers— an early 1980s AM Verityper Compset 510 model with a video display terminal, dual floppy disc drive and a photo-chemical developing unit.

Left photo: A 1988 Macintosh SE (left) and Royal manual typewriter, circa 1920s. Both were used to prepare the original newspapers.

It was much easier to produce this book. The *YAP, Tucson Teen*, *Entertainment Magazine* and *Newsreal* archives contain the original newspaper editions and hundreds of files on local bands, entertainers and people who were active during the years featured in this book.

These articles were scanned from the original, yellowing, newspaper pages or the surviving layout sheets (also called "flats"). The scanned images were converted to text (using Read IrisPro 12). The photos were scanned from the original photographs, when available, to provide the highest quality. When the original was not available, the newspaper copy was reproduced. The text was pasted into a Microsoft Word document using an iMac (OSX 10.6.8). After the final proof was converted to a PDF, it was uploaded to CreateSpace.com to be printed on-demand.

Robert Zucker, founder of several local tabloids on a typical deadline night with the layout sheets spread out across the tables and rolls of border tape hang from the board. *Youth Alternatives* archives, 1979. Tucson YWCA basement offices.

The original newspapers are available at the University of Arizona Library Special Collections in Tucson, Arizona and on microfilm in libraries across the country. These new printed volumes makes it possible for people to once again enjoy– and learn about– Tucson's nightlife in the late 20th Century.

There is a common theme in the local scene that seems to stretch across the decades– the constant struggle among musicians trying to get a break against the whims of nightclub owners and fickle fans. A fluid base of followers kept some bands alive, but many musicians couldn't generate the turnout needed to sustain fledging venues. Dreams of better gigs would sidetrack star-struck entertainers who would often return to Tucson and become content as local celebrities. The sudden closures of local businesses which propelled the entertainment scene often left musicians, creditors and the media taking the financial hit. Yet, dedicated entertainers entertained on.

Publishing these newspapers over the decades, and producing some local events, has been such a rewarding career. I am so fortunate to have been a part of it– and glad that I was able to preserve it and now share it, once again.

By Robert Zucker
April 2014

Tucson City Map

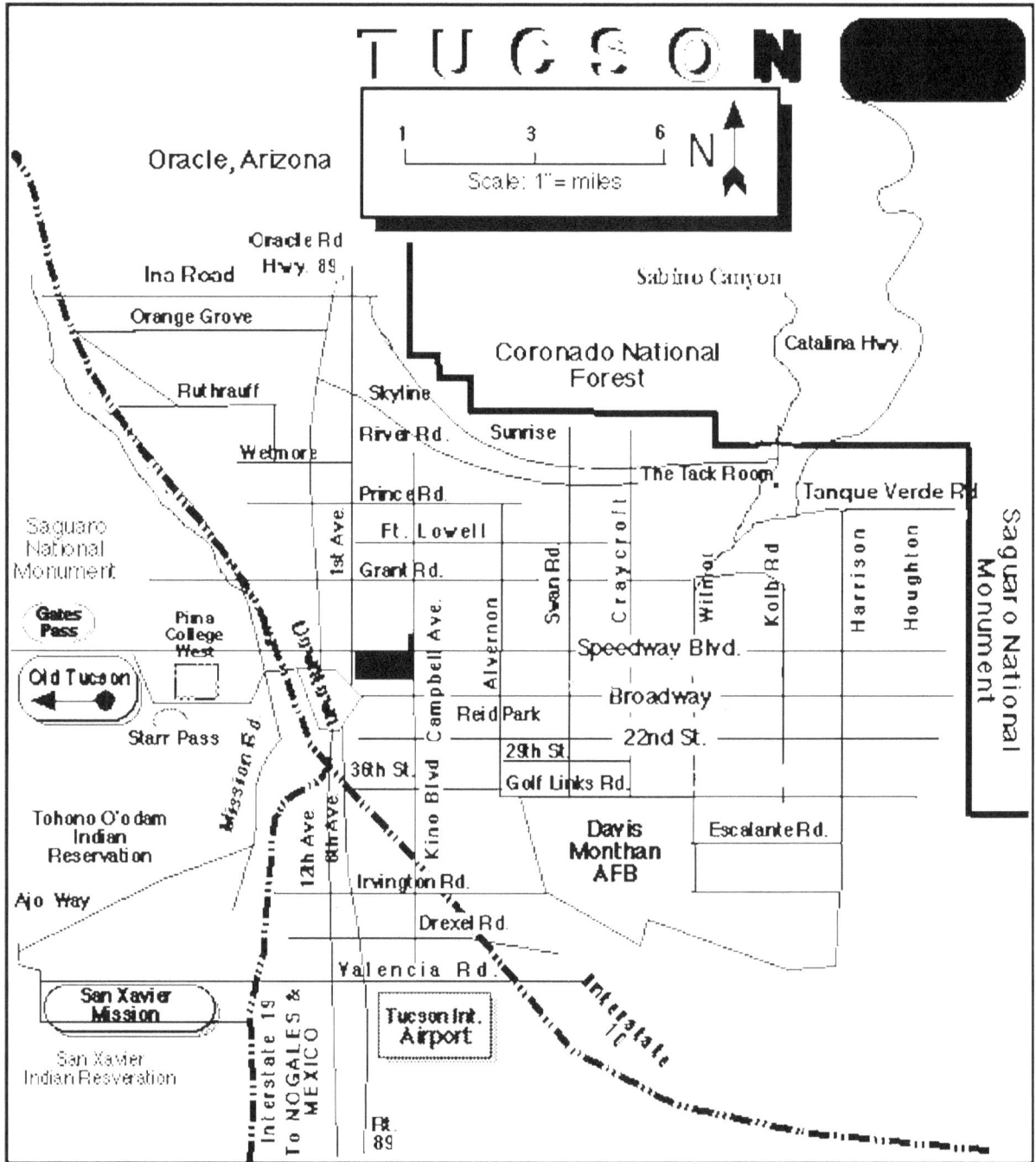

T U C S O N

Oracle, Arizona

| 1 | 3 | 6 |

Scale: 1" = miles

N

Oracle Rd
Hwy. 89

Ina Road

Sabino Canyon

Catalina Hwy.

Orange Grove

Coronado National
Forest

Ruthrauff

Skyline

River Rd.   Sunrise

Wetmore

The Tack Room

Prince Rd.

Tanque Verde Rd

Saguaro
National
Monument

1st Ave.

Ft. Lowell

Grant Rd.

Craycroft

Wilmot

Kolb Rd

Harrison

Houghton

Saguaro National Monument

Gates
Pass

Pima
College
West

Swan Rd.

Alvernon

Campbell Ave.

Speedway Blvd.

Old Tucson

Broadway

Starr Pass

Reid Park

22nd St.

Mission Rd

29th St.

36th St.

Kino Blvd

Golf Links Rd.

Tohono O'odam
Indian
Reservation

12th Ave

8th Ave

Davis
Monthan
AFB

Escalante Rd.

Ajo Way

Irvington Rd.

Drexel Rd.

San Xavier
Mission

Interstate 19
To NOGALES &
MEXICO

Valencia Rd.

Interstate 10

Tucson Int.
Airport

San Xavier
Indian Resveration

Rt.
89

The black rectangle in the middle of the page is the University of Arizona campus.

Tucson map, 1992.

Publishing Title Holdings

Copies of the newspapers used in this compilation are available, in print and on microfilm, at the University of Arizona Library Special Collections, Tucson, Arizona. Some early editions are available on microfilm nationwide in public libraries.

Title/Record	Catalog	Editions	Publishers
1. *Youth Alternatives* 1978	HQ799.73.T9 M3 No OCLC, ISSN record	No. 1 (Sum. 1978); no. 2 (Fall 1978) Desc: 1 v: ill ; 44 cm.	Tucson YWCA, PCJJC, 1978 Loc: UA Special Collections (Oversized)
2. *Youth Awareness Press*	HQ799.73.T9 M3 OCLC 4479925 (period)	Autumn 1978-Winter 1980-81 Desc: 3 v.: ill ; 28-44 cm.	YWCA, Youth Services (1978-1980) Issue 3 (winter 1978-79)
3. *Youth Awareness Press* 1963-1984 1979-	Micro-film 3501 PN4888.U5 U49 Underground Newspaper Collection; Underground Press Syndicate, UPS. [48] OCLC 7983175 Microfilm: Roll 4: V. 2, no 4, v. 3, no 1-3 (1980) reel 343		
4. *Tucson Teen*	HQ799.73.T9 M31 ISSN: 1044-954X OCLC: 7868864	Summer 1981-Mar. 1982; May 1987 Desc: 2 v. : ill ; 43 cm	Southwest Alternatives, 1981, 82, 87
5. *Tucson Teen*	OCLC: 10857773	Microfilm (Underground Newspaper Collection; UPS) SAI, Inc., 1981-1982	
6. *Tucson Teen Magazine*	HQ799.73.T9 M32 OCLC: 11377638	1984 IN LIBRARY Southwest Alternatives Institute, Inc., 1982-1983 27-44 cm	
7. *Magazine* 1985 8. *Magazine*	HQ799.73.T9 M32 ISSN: 0742-9568 OCLC: 10857843	v5 1984, v6 1985, v7 1986, v8 1987 Southwest Alternatives,1982-1985 Issued: Vol. 5, no. 3 (Aug-Sept 1982)-v. 8, no. 4 (March 1985) Microfilm 3501 v5, n 3 (9/82) (Underground Newspaper Collection, UPS)	
9. *Tucson Entertainment*	HQ799.73.T9 M32 OCLC: 137357054	May-Nov. 1987. 37 cm	SW Alternatives Institute, 1987
10. *Entertainment Magazine*	HQ799.73.T9 M32 ISSN: 0883-1890 OCLC: 12210770	Apr 1985- v8 1987; v9 1988; v10 1989; v11 1990	SW Alternatives Institute, Inc., 1985-
11. *Entertainment & Dining Guide Magazine*	HQ799.73.T9 M32	Feb-March 1992, May-June 1992; -Sept. 1992 35 cm (no WorldCat; OCLC record; UA SC only) Community Media Services thru SAI	
Robert E. Zucker	OCLC: 4779622841	Publisher, educator: Instructor, Journalism UA, 1985-2005. Publisher, SAI, Inc,	

Trademarks
Entertainment Magazine	ID: 28573	State of Arizona. Robert Edward Zucker 109240; SAI 109241	4/1/1985
Tucson Teen	ID: 28574	State of Arizona. Robert Edward Zucker 109242; SAI 109243	6/1/1981

Internet Resources (WorldCat):
A. *Teen on-line*	ISSN: 1088-0984 OCLC: 34523047	eJournal/eMagazine April 1996
B. *Entertainment magazine On-Line: EMOL*	ISSN: 1087-8971 OCLC: 34522805	eJournal/eMagazine print out vol. 2, No. 3 March 11, 1996;
C. *EMOL: Entertainment Magazine On Line*	OCLC: 44311457	eJournal/eMagazine publisher Entertainment Magazine
D. Phoenix, Arizona	OCLC: 44301267	ebook Entertainment Magazine Online (EMOL)
E. Tucson, Arizona's VirtualMall	OCLC: 44291397	ebook Entertainment Magazine Online (EMOL)

Newsreal editions and microfilm at the University of Arizona Library Special Collections

Mountain Newsreal	1974-1979	OCLC: 3520327 Microfilm, Underground Newspaper Collection	
Mountain Newsreal	1976	Call: L9791 T891 M928 OCLC 7237673 Tucson, Arizona	
Newsreal	1981-	ISSN: 0730-224X OCLC: 7968988 Tucson, AZ. Jon Rosen. UA Library Special Coll.	
Tucson Mountain Newsreal	1981-	OCLC: 53216492 Microfilm, Underground Newspaper Collection	

---

[48] Underground Newspaper Collection: 1960s Counterculture. Underground Press Syndicate. Wooster, Ohio; Bell & Howell. Microfilm copies available at most public libraries. Z6944.U5U53X. http://libguides.jsu.edu/undergroundnewspapercollection

Publishers

Robert Zucker, *Entertainment Magazine*

Tucson native **Robert Edward Zucker**, born in the mid-1950s, has been publishing for nearly four decades. He launched several Tucson, Arizona tabloid newspapers and authored dozens of manuscripts that are now being printed and digitized.

While publishing over monthly 200 newspaper editions, between 1978 and 1994, Robert also organized numerous local entertainment events, concerts, movie screenings and community projects. Originally hired by the Tucson YWCA in 1977, Robert developed *Youth Alternatives* (1978-1979), the first newspaper for Tucson teenagers and continued the publication as *Youth Awareness Press* (1979-1981). The newspaper was later titled as the *Tucson Teen* (1981-1990) after the original funding sources ended for the non-profit project. The *Magazine* (1982-1985) and the *Entertainment Magazine* (1985-1994) newspapers published for an older audience with a focus on local entertainment and national celebrities.

In January 1995, the Internet version of the *Entertainment Magazine On Line* (EMOL.org) was launched as one of the first Arizona publications to have a web presence. Robert spent a dozen years teaching desktop publishing and web publishing at the University of Arizona Department of Journalism (now School of Journalism) and launched the UA Journalism Department web site (1995). He spent eight years at Pima Community College as an instructor and adviser for the *Aztec Press*, the college newspaper. At Pima, he also developed an Internet journalism lab and the online version of the *Aztec Press* (1998).

Official Websites: http://emol.org/ and http://Robert-Zucker.com

Jon Rosen, *Newsreal*

Jonathan L is an American radio presenter, programmer, and entertainment media publisher who has lived in Berlin, Germany for the past four years. He published the *Newsreal*, an alternative Tucson, Arizona monthly music publication from the 1970s until October 1985. His radio career began in Tucson in 1982 at **KLPX-FM** with a show "**Virgin Vinyl**" which predates Alternative radio. He left Tucson in 1986 to start up Alternative radio station KEYX-FM.

Jonathan L organized his first large music festival for alternative station KUKQ in Phoenix, Arizona in 1989, years before the launch of festivals like Lollapalooza and the KROQ Weenie Roasts. For this reason, he is often called the "father of all radio festivals." In 2005, he returned form Los Angeles to create "Lopsided World Of L" which ran on Saturday mornings and Sunday evenings on KUPD-FM until he moved to Germany in 2010. The "Lopsided World of L" is produced and presented internationally every week by Jonathan L from his flat in Berlin, Germany. Now in it's 9th year, the "Lopsided World of L" is broadcast across the planet from Los Angeles, Phoenix, Berlin, Athens, Greece, Gothenburg, Sweden, and Brasov, Romania.

Official Website: http://www.jlradio.com

Contributing Writers/Artists/Photographers

For this volume, the following people and companies had contributed their own time and work to be published in the original publications– *Entertainment Magazine, Newsreal, The Magazine, Tucson Teen, Youth Awareness Press* and *Youth Alternatives* from 1974-1985.

Writers

Roxanna Alday
Ed Alexander
Tina Alvarez
Cindy Aquillo
Brian Atkinson
Bryn Bailer
Hilary Bass
Elizabeth Bellamy
Connie Breeze
Casey
Constance Commonplace
Neil Costin
Curtis Dutiel
John Engle
Caylah Eddleblute
Fonda
Timothy Gassen
Anne Griffin
Michael Hamilton
Lori Hornback
Bennie Jasinowski
Lee Joseph
Ilaina Krauss
Jonathan L
Tracy Landers
Jeff Latawiec
Angie Lumia
Ronnie Mack
Sharon S. Magee
Byron McClure
Mainstream Blues Society
Kata Mapes
Tim Martin

JoAnn Mesa
Donna Morgan
David Moskowitz
Mark Newland
Nick Nicholas
Steven M. Rabinowitz
Aaron Rey
Diana Rey
Jodi Rigberg
Veronica Rivera
Laurie Robinson
Peggy Rose
H. "Slitboy" Salmon
S. Castillo Samoy
Peri Savery
Joel Schenkenberg
Brian Schottlaender
Mary Simon
Dan Starr
Michelle M. Sundin
Carol Tepper
John Thompson
Neal Ullestad
Katherine Van Holzer
Richard Whitmer
P.L. Wylie
Charley Yates
Lydia L. Young
Robert E. Zucker

Artists/Photographers

Manuel Abril
Simon Alev
George Alford
Art Attack Records
Asylum Records
Hilary Bass
Jacqueline Blancato
Seymour Butz
Cabaret Attractions & Talent
Jeff Carter
David Bean Photography
Déjà vu Photography
Bill Doyle
EMC Entertainment
Fonda
Bill Greener
Marc Hauser
Dave and Kay Fintel
Tim Fuller
Galvin Larson
Connie Leinbach
Leora McCabe
Byron McClure
John Noyce
Olan Mills Studios
Stephanie Samoy
Bruce Schockett
Robert Schotland
Jeff W. Smith
Balfour Walker
Lydia L. Young
Bertram J. Zucker
Robert E. Zucker

Illustrations/Credits

Photographs and graphics used in this book were either previously published or stored in the archives of the participating newspapers. Credits are provided with the accompanying images and articles, as available. The original newspapers are available at locations listed in the Title Holding page. Digital copies are in preparation.

When articles, graphics, photograph credit is unknown, the source is noted from any of the following:

> *Entertainment Magazine* archives
> EMOL.org archives
> *Newsreal* archives
> *Tucson Teen* archives
> *Youth Alternatives* archives
> *Youth Awareness Press* archives

Front Cover photo

Compilation of the following archived photos: (right to left, top row) Logos of *Entertainment Magazine* and *Newsreal* newspapers. Next row: Sam Taylor, The Pills, Dean Armstrong, LeAnne McCabe and band, David Moskowitz of Sidewinders, Sons of the Pioneers, Ed Alexander, Margie Wrye, Linda Ronstadt, Al Perry, Statesboro Blues Band, The Molly's, Merle Harmon of Street Pajama and Robert Zucker.

Photo Captions

Index

Nearly two thousand entertainers, bands & venues

From BZB Publishing, Inc.

Available now in print:
"Entertaining Tucson Across the Decades, Vol. I: 1950s-1985," by Robert E. Zucker
"Traveling Show," by Robert E. Zucker
"Searching for Arizona's Buried Treasures," by Ron Quinn
"Mysterious Disappearances and Other Strange Tales," by Ron Quinn

Other titles in preparation:
"Entertaining Tucson Across the Decades, Vol. II: 1986-early 2000s," by Robert E. Zucker
"Mysteries in the Santa Catalina Mountains: Legends & History," by Robert E. Zucker
"From Print to Pixels," by Robert E. Zucker
"Twilight of Consciousness," by Robert E. Zucker
"Ballads of the Santa Catalinas," by Gary Holdcroft (CD)
"The Miner's Story," conversation with William "Flint" Carter (CD)

Titles can be purchased at Amazon.com, at web sites below, and other retail outlets.

For more information, purchase titles directly, or to contact publisher:
BZB Publishing, Inc.
P.O. Box 91317
Tucson, Arizona 85752-1317 USA
520-623-3733

Email: publisher@emol.org

"Entertaining Tucson Across the Decades": http://emol.org/entertaintucson/
Entertainment Magazine: http://emol.org/
Robert Zucker: http://robert-zucker.com